3 vols. £3-95

The life of Bertrand Russell, probably the greatest of modern philosophers, extended over nearly a century. A great thinker in his own right—philosopher, mathematician, scientist, educationist, politician—and a writer of incomparable lucidity and style, renowned for his advanced views on many controversial questions, Earl Russell's thought and character have left a profound mark on the generations. Views for which he was once an outcast are now commonly held by a broad segment of the people, and his work was publicly crowned by the award of an O.M. and a Nobel Prize.

In ninety-seven years of multi-faceted activity, the range of Russell's friendship was vast; simply to read this first volume is to enjoy a portrait in breadth of a fascinating epoch of English social and intellectual life.

This is the first of three volumes, an uninhibited story of the life of an extraordinary man. On first publication it was widely acclaimed as a work of genius.

THE AUTOBIOGRAPHY OF BERTRAND RUSSELL

VOLUME I

THE
AUTOBIOGRAPHY
OF
BERTRAND
RUSSELL

1872 — 1914
(VOLUME I)

LONDON
GEORGE ALLEN AND UNWIN LTD
RUSKIN HOUSE   MUSEUM STREET

FIRST PUBLISHED IN 1967
SECOND IMPRESSION 1967
THIRD IMPRESSION 1967
FOURTH IMPRESSION 1971
THIS EDITION 1971

© *George Allen and Unwin Ltd., 1967, 1971*

ISBN 0 04 921003 3 *Cased*
0 04 921012 2 *Paper*

PRINTED IN GREAT BRITAIN
BY OFFSET LITHOGRAPHY
BY BILLING & SONS LIMITED
GUILDFORD AND LONDON

To Edith

Through the long years
    I sought peace.
I found ecstasy, I found anguish,
    I found madness,
I found loneliness.
I found the solitary pain
    that gnaws the heart,
But peace I did not find.

Now, old & near my end,
    I have known you,
And, knowing you,
I have found both ecstasy & peace,
    I know rest.
After so many lonely years,
I know what life & love may be.
Now, if I sleep,
I shall sleep fulfilled.

CONTENTS

PROLOGUE

WHAT I HAVE LIVED FOR

THREE PASSIONS, simple but overwhelmingly strong, have governed my life: the longing for love, the search for knowledge, and unbearable pity for the suffering of mankind. These passions, like great winds, have blown me hither and thither, in a wayward course, over a deep ocean of anguish, reaching to the very verge of despair.

I have sought love, first, because it brings ecstasy—ecstasy so great that I would often have sacrificed all the rest of life for a few hours of this joy. I have sought it, next, because it relieves loneliness—that terrible loneliness in which one shivering consciousness looks over the rim of the world into the cold unfathomable lifeless abyss. I have sought it, finally, because in the union of love I have seen, in a mystic miniature, the prefiguring vision of the heaven that saints and poets have imagined. This is what I sought, and though it might seem too good for human life, this is what—at last—I have found.

With equal passion I have sought knowledge. I have wished to understand the hearts of men. I have wished to know why the stars shine. And I have tried to apprehend the Pythagorean power by which number holds sway above the flux. A little of this, but not much, I have achieved.

Love and knowledge, so far as they were possible, led upward toward the heavens. But always pity brought me back to earth. Echoes of cries of pain reverberate in my heart. Children in famine, victims tortured by oppressors, helpless old people a hated burden to their sons, and the whole world of loneliness, poverty, and pain make a mockery of what human life should be. I long to alleviate the evil, but I cannot, and I too suffer.

This has been my life. I have found it worth living, and would gladly live it again if the chance were offered me.

CHAPTER I

CHILDHOOD

MY FIRST VIVID RECOLLECTION is my arrival at Pembroke Lodge in February 1876. To be accurate, I do not remember the actual arrival at the house, though I remember the big glass roof of the London terminus, presumably Paddington, at which I arrived on my way, and which I thought inconceivably beautiful. What I remember of my first day at Pembroke Lodge is tea in the servants' hall. It was a large, bare room with a long massive table with chairs and a high stool. All the servants had their tea in this room except the house-keeper, the cook, the lady's maid, and the butler, who formed an aristocracy in the house-keeper's room. I was placed upon the high stool for tea, and what I remember most vividly is wondering why the servants took so much interest in me. I did not, at that time, know that I had already been the subject of serious deliberation by the Lord Chancellor, various eminent Queen's Counsel, and other notable persons, nor was it until I was grown-up that I learned to know of the strange events which had preceded my coming to Pembroke Lodge.

My father, Lord Amberley, had recently died after a long period of gradually increasing debility. My mother and my sister had died of diphtheria about a year and a half sooner. My mother, as I came to know her later from her diary and her letters, was vigorous, lively, witty, serious, original, and fearless. Judging by her pictures she must also have been beautiful. My father was philosophical, studious, un-worldly, morose, and priggish. Both were ardent theorists of reform and prepared to put into practice whatever theory they believed in. My father was a disciple and friend of John Stuart Mill, from whom both learned to believe in birth-control and votes for women. My father lost his seat in Parliament through advocacy of birth-control. My mother sometimes got into hot water for her radical opinions. At a garden-party given by the parents of Queen Mary, the Duchess of Cambridge remarked in a loud voice: 'Yes, I know who you are, you are the daughter-in-law. But now I hear you only like dirty Radicals and dirty Americans. All London is full of it; all the clubs are talking of it. I must look at your petticoats to see if they are dirty.'

15

The following letter from the British Consul in Florence speaks for itself:

Sept. 22, 1870

Dear Lady Amberley

I am *not* an admirer of M. Mazzini, but have an utter detestation and abhorrence of his character and principles. The public position which I hold, moreover, precludes me from being the channel for his correspondence. Not however wishing to disoblige you in this instance, I have taken the only course which was open to me with the view to his receiving your letter, viz. to put it in the Post to the care of the Procuratore del Re, Gaeta.

I remain,
Yours very faithfully,
A. Paget

Mazzini gave my mother his watch-case, which is now in my possession.

My mother used to address meetings in favour of votes for women, and I found one passage in her diary where she speaks of the Potter Sisterhood, which included Mrs Sidney Webb and Lady Courtenay, as social butterflies. Having in later years come to know Mrs Sidney Webb well, I conceived a considerable respect for my mother's seriousness when I remembered that to her Mrs Webb seemed frivolous. From my mother's letters, however, for example to Henry Crompton, the Positivist, I find that she was on occasion sprightly and coquettish, so that perhaps the face she turned to the world was less alarming than that which she presented to her diary.

My father was a free-thinker, and wrote a large book, posthumously published, called *An Analysis of Religious Belief*. He had a large library containing the Fathers, works on Buddhism, accounts of Confucianism, and so on. He spent a great deal of time in the country in the preparation of his book. He and my mother, however, in the earlier years of their marriage, spent some months of each year in London, where they had a house in Dean's Yard. My mother and her sister, Mrs George Howard (afterwards Lady Carlisle), had rival *salons*. At Mrs Howard's *salon* were to be seen all the Pre-Raphaelite painters, and at my mother's all the British philosophers from Mill downwards.

In 1867 my parents went to America, where they made friends with all the Radicals of Boston. They could not foresee that the men and women whose democratic ardour they applauded and whose triumphant opposition to slavery they admired were the grandfathers and grandmothers of those who murdered Sacco and Vanzetti. My parents married in 1864, when they were both only twenty-two. My brother, as he boasts in his autobiography, was born nine months and four days after the wedding. Shortly before I was born, they went to live in a very lonely house called Ravenscroft (now called Cleiddon Hall) in a wood just above the steep banks of the Wye. From the house, three days after I was born, my mother wrote a description of me to her mother: 'The baby weighed $8\frac{3}{4}$ lb. is 21 inches long and very fat and very ugly very like Frank everyone thinks, blue eyes far apart and not much chin. He is just like Frank was about nursing. I have lots of milk now, but if he does not get it at once or has wind or anything he gets into such a rage and screams and kicks and trembles till he is soothed off. . . . He lifts his head up and looks about in a very energetic way.'

They obtained for my brother a tutor, D. A. Spalding, of considerable scientific ability—so at least I judge from a reference to his work in William James's *Psychology*.[1] He was a Darwinian, and was engaged in studying the instincts of chickens, which, to facilitate his studies, were allowed to work havoc in every room in the house, including the drawing-room. He himself was in an advanced stage of consumption and died not very long after my father. Apparently upon grounds of pure theory, my father and mother decided that although he ought to remain childless on account of his tuberculosis, it was unfair to expect him to be celibate. My mother therefore, allowed him to live with her, though I know of no evidence that she derived any pleasure from doing so. This arrangement subsisted for a very short time, as it began after my birth and I was only two years old when my mother died. My father, however, kept on the tutor after my mother's death, and when my father died it was found that he had left the tutor and Cobden Sanderson, both atheists, to be guardians of his two sons, whom he wished to protect from the evils of a religious upbringing. My grandparents, however, discovered from his papers what had taken place in relation to my mother. This discovery caused them the utmost Victorian horror. They decided that if necessary they would put the law in motion to rescue innocent children from the clutches of intriguing infidels. The intriguing infidels consulted Sir Horace Davey (afterwards Lord Davey) who assured them that they would have no case, relying, apparently, upon the Shelley precedent. My brother and I were therefore made wards in Chancery, and Cobden Sanderson delivered me up to my grandparents on the day of which I have already spoken. No doubt this history contributed to the interest which the servants took in me.

Of my mother I remember nothing whatever, though I remember falling out of a pony carriage on an occasion when she must have been present. I know that this recollection is genuine, because I verified it at a much later time, after having kept it to myself for a number of years.

[1] See also J. B. S. Haldane, *British Journal of Animal Behaviour*, Vol. II, No. I, 1954.

Of my father I remember only two things: I remember his giving me a page of red print, the colour of which delighted me, and I remember once seeing him in his bath. My parents had themselves buried in the garden at Ravenscroft, but were dug up and transferred to the family vault at Chenies. A few days before his death my father wrote the following letter to his mother.

Ravenscroft,
Wednesday at night

My dear Mama

You will be glad to hear that I mean to see Radcliffe as soon as I am able—sorry to hear the cause. This is that I have a nasty attack of bronchitis which is likely to keep me in bed some time. Your pencil letter came to-day, and I was sorry to see that you too were knocked up. Exhausted as I am I may as well write, since I cannot sleep. It would be needless to say that this attack is not dangerous and I do not anticipate danger. But I have had too bitter experience of the rapidity with which illnesses may go to believe in absolute safety, or cry Peace when there is no peace. Both my lungs are inflamed and may grow worse. I beseech you not to telegraph or take any hasty action. We have a nice young Doctor in place of Audland, and for his own sake as just beginning to practise here, he will do all he can for me. I repeat that I expect to recover, but in case of a bad turn I wish to say that I look forward to dying as calmly and unmovedly as 'One who wraps the drapery of his couch About him and lies down to pleasant dreams'.

For myself, no anxiety nor even shrinking; but I do feel much pain for a few others whom I should leave, especially you. Writing in pain and weakness I can offer you only this most inadequate expression of my deep sense of your constant and immoveable love and goodness to me, even when I may appear not to have deserved it. It is a great matter of regret to me that I was sometimes compelled to appear harsh; I did not wish to show anything but affection. I have done very little of all I should like to have done, but I hope that little has not been of a bad kind. I should die with the sense that one great work of my life was accomplished. For my two darling boys I hope you would see them much, if possible, and that they might look on you as a mother. The burial you know would be here in my beloved wood and at the beautiful spot already prepared for me. I can hardly hope you would be there, but I wish it were possible to think of it.

Perhaps it is very selfish of me to give the pain of this letter; only I fear another day I might be too weak to write. If I can I shall let you know daily. I also have met with nothing but kindness and gentleness from my dear Papa all my life, for which I am deeply grateful. I do earnestly hope that at the end of his long and noble life he may be spared the pain of losing a son. I can only send my best love to Agatha and Rollo and poor Willy if possible.

Your loving son,
A.

Pembroke Lodge, where my grandfather and grandmother lived, is a rambling house of only two storeys in Richmond Park. It was in the gift of the Sovereign, and derives its name from the Lady Pembroke to whom George III was devoted in the days of his lunacy. The Queen had given it to my grandparents for their life-time in the 'forties, and they had lived there ever since. The famous Cabinet meeting described in Kinglake's *Invasion of the Crimea*, at which several Cabinet Ministers slept while the Crimean War was decided upon, took place at Pembroke Lodge. Kinglake, in later years, lived at Richmond, and I remember him well. I once asked Sir Spencer Walpole why Kinglake was so bitter against Napoleon III. Sir Spencer replied that they quarrelled about a woman. 'Will you tell me the story?' I naturally asked. 'No, sir,' he replied, 'I shall not tell you the story.' And shortly afterwards he died.

Pembroke Lodge had eleven acres of garden, mostly allowed to run wild. This garden played a very large part in my life up to the age of eighteen. To the west there was an enormous view extending from the Epsom Downs (which I believed to be the 'Ups and Downs') to Windsor Castle, with Hindhead and Leith Hill between. I grew accustomed to wide horizons and to an unimpeded view of the sunset. And I have never since been able to live happily without both. There were many fine trees, oaks, beeches, horse- and Spanish chestnuts, and lime trees, a very beautiful cedar tree, cryptomerias and deodaras presented by Indian princes. There were summer-houses, sweet briar hedges, thickets of laurel, and all kinds of secret places in which it was possible to hide from grown-up people so successfully that there was not the slightest fear of discovery. There were several flower-gardens with box-hedges. Throughout the years during which I lived at Pembroke Lodge, the garden was growing gradually more and more neglected. Big trees fell, shrubs grew over the paths, the grass on the lawns became long and rank, and the box-hedges grew almost into trees. The garden seemed to remember the days of its former splendour, when foreign ambassadors paced its lawns, and princes admired its trim beds of flowers. It lived in the past, and I lived in the past with it. I wove fantasies about my parents and my sister. I imagined the days of my grandfather's vigour. The grown-up conversation to which I listened was mostly of things that had happened long ago; how my grandfather had visited Napoleon in Elba, how my grandmother's great-uncle had defended Gibraltar during the American War of Independence, and how her grandfather had been cut by the County for saying that the world must have been created before 4004 BC because there is so much lava on the slopes of Etna. Sometimes the conversation descended to more recent times, and I should be told how Carlyle had called Herbert Spencer a 'perfect vacuum', or how Darwin had felt it a great honour to be visited by Mr Gladstone. My father and mother were dead, and I used to wonder what sort of people they had been. In solitude I used to wander about the garden, alternately collecting birds' eggs and meditating on the flight of time. If I may judge by my own recollections, the important and formative impressions of childhood rise to consciousness only in fugitive moments in the midst of childish occupations, and are never mentioned to adults. I think periods of browsing during which no occupation is imposed from without are important in youth because they give time for the formation of these apparently fugitive but really vital impressions.

My grandfather as I remember him was a man well past eighty, being wheeled round the garden in a bath chair, or sitting in his room reading Hansard. I was just six years old when he died. I remember that when on the day of his death I saw my brother (who was at school) drive up in a cab although it was in the middle of term, I shouted 'Hurrah!', and my nurse said: 'Hush! You must not say "Hurrah" today!' It may be inferred from this incident that my grandfather had no great importance to me.

My grandmother, on the contrary, who was twenty-three years younger than he was, was the most important person to me throughout my childhood. She was a Scotch Presbyterian, Liberal in politics and religion (she became a Unitarian at the age of seventy), but extremely strict in all matters of morality. When she married my grandfather she was young and very shy. My grandfather was a widower with two children and four step-children, and a few years after their marriage he became Prime Minister. For her this must have been a severe ordeal. She related how she went once as a girl to one of the famous breakfasts given by the poet Rogers, and how, after observing her shyness, he said: 'Have a little tongue. You need it, my dear!' It was obvious from her conversation that she never came anywhere near to knowing what it feels like to be in love. She told me once how relieved she was on her honeymoon when her mother joined her. On another occasion she lamented that so much poetry should be concerned with so trivial a subject as love. But she made my grandfather a devoted wife, and never, so far as I have been able to discover, failed to perform what her very exacting standards represented as her duty.

As a mother and a grandmother she was deeply, but not always wisely, solicitous. I do not think that she ever understood the claims of animal spirits and exuberant vitality. She demanded that everything should be viewed through a mist of Victorian sentiment. I remember trying to make her see that it was inconsistent to demand at one and the same time that everybody should be well housed, and yet that no new houses should be built because they were an eye-sore. To her each sentiment had its separate rights, and must not be asked to give place to another sentiment on account of anything so cold as mere logic. She was cultivated according to the standards of her time; she could speak French, German and Italian faultlessly, without the slightest trace of accent. She knew Shakespeare, Milton, and the eighteenth-century poets intimately. She could repeat the signs of the Zodiac and the names of the Nine Muses. She had a minute knowledge of English history according to the Whig tradition. French, German, and Italian classics were familiar to her. Of politics since 1830 she had a close personal knowledge. But everything that involved reasoning had been totally omitted from her education, and was absent from her mental life. She never could understand how locks on rivers worked, although I heard any number of people try to explain it to her. Her morality was that of a Victorian Puritan, and nothing would have persuaded her that a man who swore on occasion might nevertheless have some good qualities. To this, however, there were exceptions. She knew the Miss Berrys who were Horace Walpole's friends, and she told me once without any censure that 'they were old-fashioned, they used to swear a little'. Like many of her type she made an inconsistent exception of Byron, whom she regarded as an unfortunate victim of an unrequited youthful love. She extended no such tolerance to Shelley, whose life she considered wicked and whose poetry she considered mawkish. Of Keats I do not think she had ever heard. While she was well-read in Continental classics down to Goethe and Schiller, she knew nothing of the Continental writers of her own time. Turgeniev once gave her one of his novels, but she never read it, or regarded him as anything but the cousin of some friends of hers. She was aware that he wrote books, but so did almost everybody else.

Of psychology in the modern sense, she had, of course, no vestige. Certain motives were known to exist: love of country, public spirit, love of one's children, were laudable motives; love of money, love of power, vanity, were bad motives. Good men acted from good motives always; bad men, however, even the worst, had moments when they were not wholly bad. Marriage was a puzzling institution. It was clearly the duty of husbands and wives to love one another, but it was a duty they ought not to perform too easily, for if sex attraction drew them together there must be something not quite nice about them. Not, of course, that she would have phrased the matter in these terms. What she would have said, and in fact did say, was: 'You know, I never think that the affection of husbands and wives is quite such a good thing as the affection of parents for their children, because there is sometimes something a little selfish about it.' That was as near as her thoughts could come to such a topic as sex. Perhaps once I heard her approach a little nearer to the forbidden topic: that was when she said that Lord Palmerston had been peculiar among men through the fact that he was not quite a good man. She disliked wine, abhorred tobacco, and was always on the verge of becoming a vegetarian. Her life was austere. She ate only the plainest food, breakfasted at eight, and until she reached the age of eighty, never sat in a comfortable chair until after tea. She was completely unworldly, and despised those who thought anything of worldly honours. I regret to say that her attitude to Queen Victoria was far from respectful. She used to relate with much amusement how one time when she was at Windsor and feeling rather ill, the Queen had been graciously pleased to say: 'Lady Russell may sit down. Lady So-and-So shall stand in front of her.'

After I reached the age of fourteen, my grandmother's intellectual limitations became trying to me, and her Puritan morality began to seem to me to be excessive; but while I was a child her great affection for me, and her intense care for my welfare, made me love her and gave me that feeling of safety that children need. I remember when I was about four or five years old lying awake thinking how dreadful it would be when my grandmother was dead. When she did in fact die, which was after I was married, I did not mind at all. But in retrospect, as I have grown older, I have realized more and more the importance she had in moulding my outlook on life. Her fearlessness, her public spirit, her contempt for convention, and her indifference to the opinion of the majority have always seemed good to me and have impressed themselves upon me as worthy of imitation. She gave me a Bible with her favourite texts written on the fly-leaf. Among these was 'Thou shalt not follow a multitude to do evil'. Her emphasis upon this text led me in later life to be not afraid of belonging to small minorities.

My grandmother, when I was a boy, had four surviving brothers and two surviving sisters, all of whom used to come to Pembroke Lodge from time to time. The oldest of the brothers was Lord Minto, whom I knew as Uncle William. The second was Sir Henry Elliot, who had had a respectable diplomatic career, but of whom I remember little. The third, my Uncle Charlie, I remember chiefly because of the length of his name on an envelope: he was Admiral the Hon. Sir Charles Elliot, KCB, and he lived at Devonport. I was told that he was Rear Admiral and that there is a grander sort of admiral called Admiral of the Fleet. This rather pained me and I felt he should have done something about it. The youngest, who was a bachelor, was George Elliot, but was known to me as Uncle Doddy. The chief thing that I was asked to notice about him was his close resemblance to his and my grandmother's grandfather, Mr Brydon, who had been led into regrettable heresy by the lava on Etna. Otherwise, Uncle Doddy was undistinguished. Of Uncle William I have a very painful recollection: He came to Pembroke Lodge one June evening at the end of a day of continual sunshine, every moment of which I had enjoyed. When it became time for me to say good-night, he gravely informed me that the human capacity for enjoyment decreases with the years and that I should never again enjoy a summer's day as much as the one that was now ending. I burst into floods of tears and continued to weep long after I was in bed. Subsequent experience has shown me that his remark was as untrue as it was cruel.

The grown-ups with whom I came in contact had a remarkable incapacity for understanding the intensity of childish emotions. When, at the age of four, I was taken to be photographed in Richmond, the photographer had difficulty in getting me to sit still, and at last promised me a sponge cake if I would remain motionless. I had, until that moment, only had one sponge cake in all my life and it had remained as a high point of ecstasy. I therefore stayed as quiet as a mouse and the photograph was wholly successful. But I never got the sponge cake.

On another occasion I heard one of the grown-ups saying to another 'When is that young Lyon coming?' I pricked up my ears and said 'Is there a lion coming?' 'Yes,' they said, 'he's coming on Sunday. He'll be quite tame and you shall see him in the drawing room.' I counted the days till Sunday and the hours through Sunday morning. At last I was told the young lion was in the drawing room and I could come and see him. I came. And he was an ordinary young man named Lyon. I was utterly overwhelmed by the disenchantment and still remember with anguish the depths of my despair.

To return to my grandmother's family, I remember little of her sister Lady Elizabeth Romilly except that she was the first person from whom I heard of Rudyard Kipling, whose *Plain Tales from the Hills* she greatly admired. The other sister, Lady Charlotte Portal, whom I knew as Aunt Lottie, was more colourful. It was said of her that as a child she had tumbled out of bed and without waking up had murmured, 'My head is laid low, my pride has had a fall'. It was also said that having heard the grown-ups talking about somnambulism she had got up during the following night and walked about in what she hoped was a sleep-walking manner. The grown-ups, who saw that she was wide awake, decided to say nothing about it. Their silence next morning so disappointed her that at last she said, 'did no one see me walking in my sleep last night?' In later life she was apt to express herself unfortunately. On one occasion when she had to order a cab for three people, she thought a hansom would be too small and a four-wheeler too large, so she told the footman to fetch a three-wheeled cab. On another occasion, the footman, whose name was George, was seeing her off at the station when she was on her way to the Continent. Thinking that she might have to write to him about some household matter she suddenly remembered that she did not know his surname. Just after the train had started she put her head out of the window and called out, 'George, George, what's your name?' 'George, My Lady', came the answer. By that time he was out of earshot.

Besides my grandmother there were in the house my Uncle Rollo and my Aunt Agatha, both unmarried. My Uncle Rollo had some importance in my early development, as he frequently talked to me about scientific matters, of which he had considerable knowledge. He suffered all his life from a morbid shyness so intense as to prevent him from achieving anything that involved contact with other human beings. But with me, so long as I was a child, he was not shy, and he used to display a vein of droll humour of which adults would not have suspected him. I remember asking him once why they had coloured glass in church windows. He informed me very gravely that in former times this had not been so, but that once, just after the clergyman had gone up into the pulpit, he saw a man walking along with a pail of whitewash on his head and the bottom of the pail fell out and the man was covered with whitewash. This caused in the poor clergyman such an uncontrollable fit of laughter that he was unable to proceed with the sermon, and ever since this they had had coloured glass in church windows. He had been in the Foreign Office, but he had trouble with his eyes, and when I first knew him he was unable to read or write. His eyes improved later, but he never again attempted any kind of routine work. He was a meteorologist, and did valuable investigations of the effects of the Krakatoa eruption of 1883, which produced in England strange sunsets and even a blue moon. He used to talk to me about the evidence that Krakatoa had caused the sunsets, and I listened to him with profound attention. His conversation did a great deal to stimulate my scientific interests.

My Aunt Agatha was the youngest of the grown-up people at Pembroke Lodge. She was, in fact, only nineteen years older than I was, so when I came there she was twenty-two. During my first years at Pembroke Lodge, she made various attempts to educate me, but without much success. She had three brightly coloured balls, one red, one yellow, and one blue. She would hold up the red ball and say: 'What colour is that?' and I would say, 'Yellow'. She would then hold it against her canary and say: 'Do you think that it is the same colour as the canary?' I would say, 'No', but as I did not know the canary was yellow it did not help much. I suppose I must have learned the colours in time, but I can only remember not knowing them. Then she tried to teach me to read, but that was quite beyond me. There was only one word that I ever succeeded in reading so long as she taught me, and that was the word 'or'. The other words, though equally short, I could never remember. She must have become discouraged, since shortly before I was five years old I was handed over to a kindergarten, which finally succeeded in teaching me the difficult art of reading. When I was six or seven she took me in hand again and taught me English Constitutional history. This interested me very much indeed, and I remember to this day much of what she taught me.

I still possess the little book in which I wrote down her questions and answers, both dictated. A few samples will illustrate the point of view.

Q. What did Henry II and Thomas Becket quarrel about?
A. Henry wished to put a stop to the evils which had arisen in consequence of the Bishops having courts of their own, so that the church law was separated from the common law of the land. Becket refused to lessen the power of the Bishops' Courts, but at last he was persuaded to agree to the Constitutions of Clarendon (the provisions of which are then given).

Q. Did Henry II try to improve the government of the country or not?
A. Yes, throughout his busy reign he never forgot his work of reforming the law. The itinerant justices grew in importance, and not only settled money matters in the counties as at first, but heard pleas and judged cases. It is to Henry II's reforms that we owe the first clear beginnings of trial by jury.

The murder of Becket is not mentioned. The execution of Charles I is mentioned, but not blamed.

She remained unmarried, having once become engaged to a curate and suffered from insane delusions during her engagement, which led to its being broken off. She became a miser, living in a large house, but using few of the rooms in order to save coal, and only having a bath once a week for the same reason. She wore thick woollen stockings which were always coming down in rumples over her ankles, and at most times talked sentimentally about the extreme goodness of certain people and the extreme wickedness of certain others, both equally imaginary. Both in my brother's case and in mine, she hated our wives so long as we lived with them, but loved them afterwards. When I first took my second wife to see her, she put a photograph of my first wife on the mantelpiece, and said to my second wife: 'When I see you I cannot help thinking of dear Alys, and wondering what would happen should Bertie desert you, which God forbid.' My brother said to her once:

'Auntie, you are always a wife behind.' This remark, instead of angering her, sent her into fits of laughter, and she repeated it to everybody. Those who thought her sentimental and doddering were liable to be surprised by a sudden outburst of shrewdness and wit. She was a victim of my grandmother's virtue. If she had not been taught that sex is wicked, she might have been happy, successful, and able.

My brother was seven years older than I was, and therefore not much of a companion to me. Except in holiday time he was away at school. I admired him in the way natural to a younger brother, and was always delighted when he returned at the beginning of the holidays, but after a few days I began to wish the holidays were over. He teased me, and bullied me mildly. I remember once when I was six years old he called in a loud voice: 'Baby!' With great dignity I refused to take any notice, considering that this was not my name. He afterwards informed me that he had had a bunch of grapes which he would have given me if I had come. As I was never in any circumstances allowed to eat any fruit at all, this deprivation was rather serious. There was also a certain small bell which I believed to be mine, but which he at each return asserted to be his and took from me, although he was himself too old to derive any pleasure from it. He still had it when he was grown-up, and I never saw it without angry feelings. My father and mother, as appears from their letters to each other, had considerable trouble with him, but at any rate my mother understood him, as he was in character and appearance a Stanley. The Russells never understood him at all, and regarded him from the first as a limb of Satan.[1] Not unnaturally, finding himself so viewed, he set out to live up to his reputation. Attempts were made to keep him away from me, which I resented as soon as I became aware of them. His personality was, however, very overpowering, and after I had been with him some time I began to feel as if I could not breathe. I retained throughout his life an attitude towards him consisting of affection mixed with fear. He passionately longed to be loved, but was such a bully that he never could keep the love of anyone. When he lost anyone's love, his heart was wounded and he became cruel and unscrupulous, but all his worst actions sprang from sentimental causes.

During my early years at Pembroke Lodge the servants played a larger part in my life than the family did. There was an old housekeeper named Mrs Cox who had been my grandmother's nursery-maid when my grandmother was a child. She was straight and vigorous and strict and devoted to the family and always nice to me. There was a butler named MacAlpine who was very Scotch. He used to take me on

[1] My grandfather on one occasion wrote to my father telling him not to take my brother's naughtiness too seriously, in view of the fact that Charles James Fox had been a very naughty boy, but had nevertheless turned out well.

his knee and read me accounts of railway accidents in the newspaper. As soon as I saw him I always climbed up on him and said: 'Tell me about an accident-happen.' Then there was a French cook named Michaud, who was rather terrifying, but in spite of her awe-inspiring qualities I could not resist going to the kitchen to see the roast meat turning on the old-fashioned spit, and to steal lumps of salt, which I liked better than sugar, out of the salt box. She would pursue me with a carving knife, but I always escaped easily. Out-of-doors there was a gardener named MacRobie of whom I remember little as he left when I was five years old, and the lodge-keeper and his wife, Mr and Mrs Singleton, of whom I was very fond, as they gave me baked apples and beer, both of which were strictly forbidden. MacRobie was succeeded by a gardener named Vidler, who informed me that the English are the lost Ten Tribes, though I do not think I quite believed him. When I first came to Pembroke Lodge, I had a German nursery governess named Miss Hetschel, and I already spoke German as fluently as English. She left a few days after my arrival at Pembroke Lodge, and was succeeded by a German nurse named Wilhelmina, or Mina for short. I remember vividly the first evening when she bathed me, when I considered it prudent to make myself stiff, as I did not know what she might be up to. She finally had to call in outside assistance, as I frustrated all her efforts. Very soon, however, I became devoted to her. She taught me to write German letters. I remember, after learning all the German capitals and all the German small letters, saying to her: 'Now it only remains to learn the numbers', and being relieved and surprised to find that they were the same in German. She used to slap me occasionally, and I can remember crying when she did so, but it never occurred to me to regard her as less of a friend on that account. She was with me until I was six years old. During her time I also had a nursery maid called Ada who used to light the fire in the morning while I lay in bed. She would wait till the sticks were blazing and then put on coal. I always wished she would not put on coal, as I loved the crackle and brightness of the burning wood. The nurse slept in the same room with me, but never, so far as my recollection serves me, either dressed or undressed. Freudians may make what they like of this.

In the matter of food, all through my youth I was treated in a very Spartan manner, much more so, in fact, than is now considered compatible with good health. There was an old French lady living in Richmond, named Madame D'Etchegoyen, a niece of Talleyrand, who used to give me large boxes of the most delicious chocolates. Of these I was allowed only one on Sundays, but Sundays and week-days alike I had to hand them round to the grown-ups. I was very fond of crumbling my bread into my gravy, which I was allowed to do in the nursery, but not in the dining-room. I used often to have a sleep before my dinner, and if I slept late I had dinner in the nursery, but if I woke up in time I had it in the dining-room. I used to pretend to sleep late in order to have dinner in the nursery. At last they suspected that I was pretending, and one day, as I was lying in my bed, they poked me about. I made myself quite stiff, imagining that was how people would be if they were asleep, but to my dismay I heard them saying: 'He is not asleep, because he is making himself stiff.' No one ever discovered why I had pretended to be asleep. I remember an occasion at lunch when all the plates were changed and everybody except me was given an orange. I was not allowed an orange as there was an unalterable conviction that fruit is bad for children. I knew I must not ask for one as that would be impertinent, but as I had been given a plate I did venture to say, 'a plate and nothing on it'. Everybody laughed, but I did not get an orange. I had no fruit, practically no sugar, and an excess of carbo-hydrates. Nevertheless, I never had a day's illness except a mild attack of measles at the age of eleven. Since I became interested in children, after the birth of my own children, I have never known one nearly as healthy as I was, and yet I am sure that any modern expert on children's diet would think that I ought to have had various deficiency diseases. Perhaps I was saved by the practice of stealing crab-apples, which, if it had been known, would have caused the utmost horror and alarm. A similar instinct for self-preservation was the cause of my first lie. My governess left me alone for half an hour with strict instructions to eat no blackberries during her absence. When she returned I was suspiciously near the brambles. 'You have been eating blackberries', she said. 'I have not', I replied. 'Put out your tongue!' she said. Shame overwhelmed me, and I felt utterly wicked.

I was, in fact, unusually prone to a sense of sin. When asked what was my favourite hymn, I answered 'Weary of earth and laden with my sin'. On one occasion when my grandmother read the parable of the Prodigal Son at family prayers, I said to her afterwards: 'I know why you read that—because I broke my jug.' She used to relate the anecdote in after years with amusement, not realizing that she was responsible for a morbidness which had produced tragic results in her own children.

Many of my most vivid early memories are of humiliations. In the summer of 1877 my grandparents rented from the Archbishop of Canterbury a house near Broadstairs, called Stone House. The journey by train seemed to me enormously long, and after a time I began to think that we must have reached Scotland, so I said: 'What country are we in now?' They all laughed at me and said: 'Don't you know you cannot get out of England without crossing the sea?' I did not venture to explain, and was left overwhelmed with shame. While we were there I went down to the sea one afternoon with my grandmother and my

Aunt Agatha. I had on a new pair of boots, and the last thing my nurse said to me as I went out was: 'Take care not to get your boots wet!' But the in-coming tide caught me on a rock, and my grandmother and Aunt Agatha told me to wade through the water to the shore. I would not do so, and my aunt had to wade through and carry me. They supposed that this was through fear, and I never told them of my nurse's prohibition, but accepted meekly the lecture on cowardice which resulted.

In the main, however, the time that I spent at Stone House was very delightful. I remember the North Foreland, which I believed to be one of the four corners of England, since I imagined at that time that England was a rectangle. I remember the ruins at Richborough which greatly interested me, and the *camera obscura* at Ramsgate, which interested me still more. I remember waving corn-fields which, to my regret, had disappeared when I returned to the neighbourhood thirty years later. I remember, of course, all the usual delights of the seaside—limpets, and sea-anemones, and rocks, and sands, and fishermen's boats, and light-houses. I was impressed by the fact that limpets stick to the rock when one tries to pull them off, and I said to my Aunt Agatha, 'Aunty, do limpets think?' To which she answered, 'I don't know'. 'Then you must learn', I rejoined. I do not clearly remember the incident which first brought me into contact with my friend Whitehead. I had been told that the earth was round, and had refused to believe it. My people thereupon called in the vicar of the parish to persuade me, and it happened that he was Whitehead's father. Under clerical guidance, I adopted the orthodox view and began to dig a hole to the Antipodes. This incident, however, I know only from hearsay.

While at Broadstairs I was taken to see Sir Moses Montefiore, an old and much revered Jew who lived in the neighbourhood. (According to the Encyclopaedia, he had retired in 1824.) This was the first time I became aware of the existence of Jews outside the Bible. My people explained to me carefully, before taking me to see the old man, how much he deserved to be admired, and how abominable had been the former disabilities of Jews, which he and my grandfather had done much to remove. On this occasion the impression made by my grandmother's teaching was clear, but on other occasions I was puzzled. She was a fierce Little Englander, and disapproved strongly of Colonial wars. She told me that the Zulu War was very wicked, and that it was largely the fault of Sir Bartle Frere, the Governor of the Cape. Nevertheless, when Sir Bartle Frere came to live at Wimbledon, she took me to see him, and I observed that she did not treat him as a monster. I found this very difficult to understand.

My grandmother used to read aloud to me, chiefly the stories of Maria Edgeworth. There was one story in the book, called *The False*

Key, which she said was not a very nice story, and she would therefore not read it to me. I read the whole story, a sentence at a time, in the course of bringing the book from the shelf to my grandmother. Her attempts to prevent me from knowing things were seldom successful. At a somewhat later date, during Sir Charles Dilke's very scandalous divorce case, she took the precaution of burning the newspapers every day, but I used to go to the Park gates to fetch them for her, and read every word of the divorce case before the papers reached her. The case interested me the more because I had once been to church with him, and I kept wondering what his feelings had been when he heard the Seventh Commandment. After I had learnt to read fluently I used to read to her, and I acquired in this way an extensive knowledge of standard English literature. I read with her Shakespeare, Milton, Dryden, Cowper's *Task*, Thomson's *Castle of Indolence*, Jane Austen, and hosts of other books.

There is a good description of the atmosphere of Pembroke Lodge in *A Victorian Childhood* by Amabel Huth Jackson (*née* Grant Duff). Her father was Sir Mountstuart Grant Duff, and the family lived in a large house at Twickenham. She and I were friends from the age of four until she died during the second world war. It was from her that I first heard of Verlaine, Dostoevsky, the German Romantics, and many other people of literary eminence. But it is of an earlier period that her reminiscences treat. She says:

My only boy friend was Bertrand Russell, who with his grandmother old Lady Russell, Lord John's widow, lived at Pembroke Lodge, in Richmond Park. Bertie and I were great allies and I had an immense secret admiration for his beautiful and gifted elder brother Frank. Frank, I am sorry to say, sympathized with my brother's point of view about little girls and used to tie me up to trees by my hair. But Bertie, a solemn little boy in a blue velvet suit with an equally solemn governess, was always kind, and I greatly enjoyed going to tea at Pembroke Lodge. But even as a child I realized what an unsuitable place it was for children to be brought up in. Lady Russell always spoke in hushed tones and Lady Agatha always wore a white shawl and looked down-trodden. Rollo Russell never spoke at all. He gave one a handshake that nearly broke all the bones of one's fingers, but was quite friendly. They all drifted in and out of the rooms like ghosts and no one ever seemed to be hungry. It was a curious bringing up for two young and extraordinarily gifted boys.

Throughout the greater part of my childhood, the most important hours of my day were those that I spent alone in the garden, and the most vivid part of my existence was solitary. I seldom mentioned my more serious thoughts to others, and when I did I regretted it. I knew each corner of the garden, and looked year by year for the white primroses in one place, the redstart's nest in another, the blossom of the acacia emerging from a tangle of ivy. I knew where the earliest bluebells were to be found, and which of the oaks came into leaf soonest. I remember that in the year 1878 a certain oak tree was in leaf as early as the four-teenth of April. My window looked out upon two Lombardy poplars, each about a hundred feet high, and I used to watch the shadow of the house creeping up them as the sun set. In the morning I woke very early and sometimes saw Venus rise. On one occasion I mistook the planet for a lantern in the wood. I saw the sunrise on most mornings, and on bright April days I would sometimes slip out of the house for a long walk before breakfast. I watched the sunset turn the earth red and the clouds golden; I listened to the wind, and exulted in the lightning. Throughout my childhood I had an increasing sense of loneliness, and of despair of ever meeting anyone with whom I could talk. Nature and books and (later) mathematics saved me from complete despondency.

The early years of my childhood, however, were happy, and it was only as adolescence approached that loneliness became oppressive. I had governesses, German and Swiss, whom I liked, and my intelligence was not yet sufficiently developed to suffer from the deficiency of my people in this respect. I must, however, have felt some kind of unhappiness, as I remember wishing that my parents had lived. Once, when I was six years old, I expressed this feeling to my grandmother, and she proceeded to tell me that it was very fortunate for me that they had died. At the time her remarks made a disagreeable impression upon me and I attributed them to jealousy. I did not, of course, know that from a Victorian point of view there was ample ground for them. My grand-mother's face was very expressive, and in spite of all her experience of the great world she never learned the art of concealing her emotions. I noticed that any allusion to insanity caused her a spasm of anguish, and I speculated much as to the reason. It was only many years later that I discovered she had a son in an asylum. He was in a smart regiment, and went mad after a few years of it. The story that I have been told, though I cannot vouch for its complete accuracy, is that his brother officers teased him because he was chaste. They kept a bear as a regimental pet, and one day, for sport, set the bear at him. He fled, lost his memory, and being found wandering about the country, was put in a workhouse infirmary, his identity being unknown. In the middle of the night, he jumped up shouting 'the bear!—the bear!' and strangled a tramp in the next bed. He never recovered his memory, but lived till over eighty.

When I try to recall as much as I can of early childhood, I find that the first thing I remember after my arrival at Pembroke Lodge is walking in melting snow, in warm sunshine, on an occasion which must have been about a month later, and noticing a large fallen beech tree which was being sawn into logs. The next thing I remember is my fourth birthday, on which I was given a trumpet which I blew all day long, and had tea with a birthday cake in a summer-house. The next thing that I remember is my aunt's lessons on colours and reading, and then, very vividly, the kindergarten class which began just before I was five and continued for about a year and a half. That gave me very intense delight. The shop from which the apparatus came was stated on the lids to be in Berners Street, Oxford Street, and to this day, unless I pull myself together, I think of Berners Street as a sort of Aladdin's Palace. At the kindergarten class I got to know other children, most of whom I have lost sight of. But I met one of them, Jimmie Baillie, in 1929 at Vancouver as I stepped out of the train. I realize now that the good lady who taught us had had an orthodox Froebel training, and was at that time amazingly up-to-date. I can still remember almost all the lessons in detail, but I think what thrilled me most was the discovery that yellow and blue paints made green.

When I was just six my grandfather died, and shortly afterwards we went to St Fillans in Perthshire for the summer. I remember the funny old inn with nobbly wooden door-posts, the wooden bridge over the river, the rocky bays on the lake, and the mountain opposite. My re-collection is that the time there was one of great happiness. My next recollection is less pleasant. It is that of a room in London at No. 8, Chesham Place, where my governess stormed at me while I endeavoured to learn the multiplication table but was continually impeded by tears. My grandmother took a house in London for some months when I was seven years old, and it was then that I began to see more of my mother's family. My mother's father was dead, but my mother's mother, Lady Stanley of Alderley, lived in a large house, No. 40, Dover Street,[1] with her daughter Maude. I was frequently taken to lunch with her, and though the food was delicious, the pleasure was doubtful, as she had a caustic tongue, and spared neither age nor sex. I was always consumed with shyness while in her presence, and as none of the Stanleys were shy, this irritated her. I used to make desperate endeav-ours to produce a good impression, but they would fail in ways that I could not have foreseen. I remember telling her that I had grown $2\frac{1}{2}$ inches in the last seven months, and that at that rate I should grow $4\frac{4}{7}$ inches in a year. 'Don't you know', she said, 'that you should never talk about any fractions except halves and quarters?—it is pedantic!' 'I know it now', I replied. 'How like his father!' she said, turning to my

[1] Completely destroyed in the Blitz.

Aunt Maude. Somehow or other, as in this incident, my best efforts always went astray. Once when I was about twelve years old, she had me before a roomful of visitors, and asked me whether I had read a whole string of books on popular science which she enumerated. I had read none of them. At the end she sighed, and turning to the visitors, said: 'I have no intelligent grandchildren.' She was an eighteenth-century type, rationalistic and unimaginative, keen on enlightenment, and contemptuous of Victorian goody-goody priggery. She was one of the principal people concerned in the foundation of Girton College, and her portrait hangs in Girton Hall, but her policies were abandoned at her death. 'So long as I live', she used to say, 'there shall be no chapel at Girton.' The present chapel began to be built the day she died. As soon as I reached adolescence she began to try to counteract what she considered namby-pamby in my upbringing. She would say: 'Nobody can say anything against *me*, but I always say that it is not so bad to break the Seventh Commandment as the Sixth, because at any rate it requires the consent of the other party.' I pleased her greatly on one occasion by asking for *Tristram Shandy* as a birthday present. She said: 'I won't write in it, because people will say what an odd grandmother you have!' Nevertheless she did write in it. It was an autographed first edition. This is the only occasion I can remember on which I succeeded in pleasing her.

She had a considerable contempt for everything that she regarded as silly. On her birthday she always had a dinner-party of thirteen, and made the most superstitious member of the party go out first. I remember once an affected granddaughter of hers came to see her, bringing a lap dog which annoyed my grandmother by barking. Her granddaughter protested that the dog was an angel. 'Angel?—angel?' said my grandmother indignantly, what nonsense! Do you think he has a soul?' 'Yes, grandmama', replied the young woman pluckily. Throughout the rest of the afternoon, during which her granddaughter remained with her, she informed each visitor in turn: 'What do you think that silly girl Grisel says? She says dogs have souls.' It was her practice to sit in her large drawing-room every afternoon while streams of visitors, including the most eminent writers of the time, came to tea. When any of them left the room, she would turn to the others with a sigh and say: 'Fools are so fatiguin'.' She had been brought up as a Jacobite, her family being Irish Dillons, who fled to France after the Battle of the Boyne and had a private regiment of their own in the French army. The French Revolution reconciled them to Ireland, but my grandmother was brought up in Florence, where her father was Minister. In Florence she used to go once a week to visit the widow of the Young Pretender. She used to say that the only thing she regarded as stupid about her ancestors was their having been Jacobites. I never knew my maternal grandfather, but I heard it said that he used to brow-beat my grandmother, and felt that, if so, he must have been a very remarkable man.[1] She had an enormous family of sons and daughters, most of whom came to lunch with her every Sunday. Her eldest son was a Mohammedan, and almost stone deaf. Her second son, Lyulph, was a free-thinker, and spent his time fighting the Church on the London School Board. Her third son, Algernon, was a Roman Catholic priest, a Papal Chamberlain and Bishop of Emmaus. Lyulph was witty, encyclopaedic, and caustic. Algernon was witty, fat, and greedy. Henry, the Mohammedan, was devoid of all the family merits, and was, I think, the greatest bore I have ever known. In spite of his deafness, he insisted upon hearing everything said to him. At the Sunday luncheons there would be vehement arguments, for among the daughters and sons-in-law there were representatives of the Church of England, Unitarianism, and Positivism, to be added to the religions represented by the sons. When the argument reached a certain pitch of ferocity, Henry would become aware that there was a noise, and would ask what it was about. His nearest neighbour would shout a biased version of the argument into his ear, whereupon all the others would shout 'No, no, Henry, it isn't that!' At this point the din became truly terrific. A favourite trick of my Uncle Lyulph at Sunday luncheons was to ask: 'Who is there here who believes in the literal truth of the story of Adam and Eve?' His object in asking the question was to compel the Mohammedan and the priest to agree with each other, which they hated doing. I used to go to these luncheons in fear and trembling, since I never knew but what the whole pack would turn upon me. I had only one friend whom I could count on among them, and she was not a Stanley by birth. She was my Uncle Lyulph's wife, sister of Sir Hugh Bell. My grandmother always considered herself very broad-minded because she had not objected to Lyulph marrying into what she called 'trade', but as Sir Hugh was a multi-millionaire I was not very much impressed.

Formidable as my grandmother was, she had her limits. Once when Mr Gladstone was expected to tea, she told us all beforehand how she was going to explain to him exactly in what respects his Home Rule policy was mistaken. I was present throughout his visit, but not one word of criticism did she utter. His hawk's eye could quell even her. Her son-in-law, Lord Carlisle, told me of an even more humiliating episode which occurred at Naworth Castle on one occasion when she was staying there. Burne-Jones, who was also staying there, had a tobacco pouch which was made to look like a tortoise. There was also a real tortoise, which strayed one day by mistake into the library. This

[1] It was true. See *The Ladies of Alderley*, by Nancy Mitford, 1938.

suggested a prank to the younger generation. During dinner, Burne-Jones's tobacco pouch was placed near the drawing-room fire, and when the ladies returned from dinner it was dramatically discovered that this time the tortoise had got into the drawing-room. On its being picked up, somebody exclaimed with astonishment that its back had grown soft. Lord Carlisle fetched from the library the appropriate volume of the Encyclopaedia, and read out a pretended passage saying that great heat sometimes had this effect. My grandmother expressed the greatest interest in this fact of natural history, and frequently alluded to it on subsequent occasions. Many years later, when she was quarrelling with Lady Carlisle about Home Rule, her daughter maliciously told her the truth of this incident. My grandmother retorted: 'I may be many things, but I am not a fool, and I refuse to believe you.'

My brother, who had the Stanley temperament, loved the Stanleys and hated the Russells. I loved the Russells and feared the Stanleys. As I have grown older, however, my feelings have changed. I owe to the Russells shyness, sensitiveness, and metaphysics; to the Stanleys vigour, good health, and good spirits. On the whole, the latter seems a better inheritance than the former.

Reverting to what I can remember of childhood, the next thing that is vivid in my memory is the winter of 1880-81, which we spent at Bournemouth. It was there that I first learned the name of Thomas Hardy, whose book *The Trumpet Major*, in three volumes, was lying on the drawing-room table. I think the only reason I remember it is that I wondered what a trumpet major might be, and that it was by the author of *Far from the Madding Crowd*, and I did not know either what a madding crowd was. While we were there, my German governess told me that one got no Christmas presents unless one believed in Father Christmas. This caused me to burst into tears, as I could not believe in such a personage. My only other recollections of the place are that there was an unprecedented snow-storm, and that I learned to skate—an amusement of which I was passionately fond throughout my boyhood. I never missed an opportunity of skating, even when the ice was unsafe. Once when I was staying in Dover Street I went skating in St James's Park and fell in. I had a feeling of disgrace in having to run through the streets dripping wet, but I nevertheless persisted in the practice of skating on thin ice. Of the following year I remember nothing whatever, but my tenth birthday is still as vivid to me as if it were yesterday. The weather was bright and warm, and I sat in a blossoming laburnum tree, but presently a Swiss lady, who had come to be interviewed, and subsequently became my governess, was sent out to play ball with me. She said she had 'catched' the ball, and I corrected her. When I had to cut my own birthday cake, I was much ashamed because I could not get the first slice to come out. But what stays most in my mind is the impression of sunshine.

At the age of eleven, I began Euclid, with my brother as my tutor. This was one of the great events of my life, as dazzling as first love. I had not imagined that there was anything so delicious in the world. After I had learned the fifth proposition, my brother told me that it was generally considered difficult, but I had found no difficulty whatever. This was the first time it had dawned upon me that I might have some intelligence. From that moment until Whitehead and I finished *Principia Mathematica*, when I was thirty-eight, mathematics was my chief interest, and my chief source of happiness. Like all happiness, however, it was not unalloyed. I had been told that Euclid proved things, and was much disappointed that he started with axioms. At first I refused to accept them unless my brother could offer me some reason for doing so, but he said: 'If you don't accept them we cannot go on', and as I wished to go on, I reluctantly admitted them *pro tem*. The doubt as to the premisses of mathematics which I felt at that moment remained with me, and determined the course of my subsequent work.

The beginnings of Algebra I found far more difficult, perhaps as a result of bad teaching. I was made to learn by heart: 'The square of the sum of two numbers is equal to the sum of their squares increased by twice their product.' I had not the vaguest idea what this meant, and when I could not remember the words, my tutor threw the book at my head, which did not stimulate my intellect in any way. After the first beginnings of Algebra, however, everything else went smoothly. I used to enjoy impressing a new tutor with my knowledge. Once, at the age of thirteen, when I had a new tutor, I spun a penny, and he said to me: 'Why does that penny spin?' and I replied: 'Because I make a couple with my fingers.' 'What do you know about couples?' he said. 'Oh, I know all about couples', I replied airily. My grandmother was always afraid that I should overwork, and kept my hours of lessons very short. The result was that I used to work in my bedroom on the sly with one candle, sitting at my desk in a night-shirt on cold evenings, ready to blow out the candle and pop into bed at the slightest sound. I hated Latin and Greek, and thought it merely foolish to learn a language that nobody speaks. I liked mathematics best, and next to mathematics I liked history. Having no one with whom to compare myself, I did not know for a long time whether I was better or worse than other boys, but I remember once hearing my Uncle Rollo saying goodbye to Jowett, the Master of Balliol, at the front door, and remarking: 'Yes, he's getting on very well indeed', and I knew, though how I cannot tell, that he was speaking of my work. As soon as I realized that I was intelligent, I determined to achieve something of intellectual importance if it should be at all possible, and throughout my youth I let nothing whatever stand in the way of this ambition.

It would be completely misleading to suggest that my childhood was all solemnity and seriousness. I got just as much fun out of life as I could, some of it I am afraid of a somewhat mischievous kind. The family doctor, an old Scotchman with mutton-chop whiskers, used to come in his brougham which waited at the front door while the man of healing spoke his piece. His coachman had an exquisite top-hat, calculated to advertise the excellence of the practice. I used to get on the roof above this splendid head-piece and drop rotten rosebuds out of the gutter on to its flat top. They spread all over with a delicious squish and I withdrew my head quickly enough for the coachman to suppose that they had fallen from heaven. Sometimes I did even worse. I threw snowballs at him when he was driving, thereby endangering the valuable lives of him and his employer. I had another amusement which I much enjoyed. On a Sunday, when the Park was crowded, I would climb to the very top of a large beech tree on the edge of our grounds. There I would hang upside down and scream and watch the crowd gravely discussing how a rescue should be effected. When I saw them nearing a decision I would get the right way up and quietly come down. During the time when Jimmie Baillie stayed with me I was led into even more desperate courses. The bath chair in which I remembered my grandfather being wheeled about had been lodged in a lumber room. We found it there and raced it down whatever hills we could find. When this was discovered it was considered blasphemy and we were reproached with melancholy gravity. Some of our doings, however, never came to the ears of the grown-ups. We tied a rope to a branch of a tree and learnt by long practice to swing in a complete circle and return to our starting point. It was only by great skill that one could avoid stopping half-way and bumping one's back painfully into the rough bark of the tree. When other boys came to visit us, we used to carry out the correct performance ourselves and when the others attempted to imitate us we maliciously exulted in their painful failure. My Uncle Rollo, with whom for a while we used to spend three months each year, had three cows and a donkey. The donkey was more intelligent than the cows and learnt to open the gates between the fields with his nose, but he was said to be unruly and useless. I did not believe this and, after some unsuccessful attempts, I learnt to ride him without saddle or bridle. He would kick and buck but he never got me off except when I had tied a can full of rattling stones to his tail. I used to ride him all round the country, even when I went to visit the daughter of Lord Wolseley who lived about three miles from my uncle's house.

CHAPTER II

ADOLESCENCE

M Y CHILDHOOD was, on the whole, happy and straightforward, and I felt affection for most of the grown-ups with whom I was brought in contact. I remember a very definite change when I reached what in modern child psychology is called the 'latency period'. At this stage, I began to enjoy using slang, pretending to have no feelings, and being generally 'manly'. I began to despise my people, chiefly because of their extreme horror of slang and their absurd notion that it was dangerous to climb trees. So many things were forbidden me that I acquired the habit of deceit, in which I persisted up to the age of twenty-one. It became second nature to me to think that whatever I was doing had better be kept to myself, and I have never quite overcome the impulse to concealment which was thus generated. I still have an impulse to hide what I am reading when anybody comes into the room, and to hold my tongue generally as to where I have been, and what I have done. It is only by a certain effort of will that I can overcome this impulse, which was generated by the years during which I had to find my way among a set of foolish prohibitions.

The years of adolescence were to me very lonely and very unhappy. Both in the life of the emotions and in the life of the intellect, I was obliged to preserve an impenetrable secrecy towards my people. My interests were divided between sex, religion, and mathematics. I find the recollection of my sexual preoccupation in adolescence unpleasant. I do not like to remember how I felt in those years, but I will do my best to relate things as they were and not as I could wish them to have been. The facts of sex first became known to me when I was twelve years old, through a boy named Ernest Logan who had been one of my kindergarten companions at an earlier age. He and I slept in the same room one night, and he explained the nature of copulation and its part in the generation of children, illustrating his remarks by funny stories. I found what he said extremely interesting, although I had as yet no physical response. It appeared to me at the time self-evident that free love was the only rational system, and that marriage was bound up with Christian superstition. (I am sure this reflection occurred to me only a very short time after I first knew the facts.) When I was fourteen, my tutor mentioned to me that I should shortly undergo an important physical change. By this time I was more or less able to understand what he meant. I had at that time another boy, Jimmie Baillie, staying with me, the same whom I met at Vancouver in 1929, and he and I used to talk things over, not only with each other, but with the page-boy, who was about our own age or perhaps a year older, and rather more knowing than we were. When it was discovered that we had spent a certain afternoon in doubtful conversation with the page-boy, we were spoken to in tones of deep sorrow, sent to bed, and kept on bread and water. Strange to say, this treatment did not destroy my interest in sex. We spent a great deal of time in the sort of conversation that is considered improper, and in endeavouring to find out things of which we were ignorant. For this purpose I found the medical dictionary very useful. At fifteen, I began to have sexual passions, of almost intolerable intensity. While I was sitting at work, endeavouring to concentrate, I would be continually distracted by erections, and I fell into the practice of masturbating, in which, however, I always remained moderate. I was much ashamed of this practice, and endeavoured to discontinue it. I persisted in it, nevertheless, until the age of twenty, when I dropped it suddenly because I was in love.

The same tutor who told me of the approach of puberty mentioned, some months later, that one speaks of a man's breast, but of a woman's breasts. This remark caused me such an intolerable intensity of feeling that I appeared to be shocked, and he rallied me on my prudery. Many hours every day were spent in desiring to see the female body, and I used to try to get glimpses through windows when the maids were dressing, always unsuccessfully, however. My friend and I spent a winter making an underground house, which consisted of a long tunnel, through which one crawled on hands and knees, and then of a room 6 ft. cube. There was a housemaid whom I used to induce to accompany me to this underground house, where I kissed her and hugged her. Once I asked her whether she would like to spend a night with me, and she said she would die rather, which I believed. She also expressed surprise, saying that she had thought I was good. Consequently this affair proceeded no further. I had by this time quite lost the rationalist outlook on sex which I had had before puberty, and accepted entirely the conventional views as quite sound. I became morbid, and regarded myself as very wicked. At the same time, I took a considerable interest in my own psychology, which I studied carefully and not unintelligently, but I was told that all introspection is morbid, so that I regarded this interest in my own thoughts and feelings as another proof of mental aberration. After two or three years of introspection, however, I suddenly realized that, as it is the only method of obtaining a great deal of important knowledge, it ought not to be condemned as morbid. This relieved my feelings on this point.

Concurrently with this physical preoccupation with sex, went a great intensity of idealistic feeling, which I did not at that time recognize as sexual in origin. I became intensely interested in the beauty of sunsets and clouds, and trees in spring and autumn, but my interest was of a very sentimental kind, owing to the fact that it was an unconscious sublimation of sex, and an attempt to escape from reality. I read poetry widely, beginning with very bad poetry such as *In Memoriam*. While I was sixteen and seventeen, I read, as far as I can remember, the whole of Milton's poetry, most of Byron, a great deal of Shakespeare, large parts of Tennyson, and finally Shelley. I came upon Shelley by accident. One day I was waiting for my Aunt Maude in her sitting-room at Dover Street. I opened it at *Alastor*, which seemed to me the most beautiful poem I had ever read. Its unreality was, of course, the great element in my admiration for it. I had got about half-way through when my Aunt arrived, and I had to put the volume back in the shelf. I asked the grown-ups whether Shelley was not considered a great poet, but found that they thought ill of him. This, however, did not deter me, and I spent all my spare time reading him, and learning him by heart. Knowing no one to whom I could speak of what I thought or felt, I used to reflect how wonderful it would have been to know Shelley, and to wonder whether I should ever meet any live human being with whom I should feel so much in sympathy.

Alongside with my interest in poetry, went 'an intense interest in religion and philosophy. My grandfather was Anglican, my grandmother was a Scotch Presbyterian, but gradually became a Unitarian. I was taken on alternate Sundays to the (Episcopalian) Parish Church at Petersham and to the Presbyterian Church at Richmond, while at home I was taught the doctrines of Unitarianism. It was these last that I believed until about the age of fifteen. At this age I began a systematic investigation of the supposed rational arguments in favour of fundamental Christian beliefs. I spent endless hours in meditation upon this subject; I could not speak to anybody about it for fear of giving pain. I suffered acutely both from the gradual loss of faith and from the need of silence. I thought that if I ceased to believe in God, freedom and immortality, I should be very unhappy. I found, however, that the reasons given in favour of these dogmas were very unconvincing. I considered them one at a time with great seriousness. The first to go was freewill. At the age of fifteen, I became convinced that the motions of matter, whether living or dead, proceeded entirely in accordance with the laws of dynamics, and therefore the will can have no influence upon the body.

I used at this time to write down my reflections in English written in Greek letters in a book headed 'Greek Exercises'.[1] I did this for fear lest someone should find out what I was thinking. In this book I recorded my conviction that the human body is a machine. I should have found intellectual satisfaction in becoming a materialist, but on grounds almost identical with those of Descartes (who was unknown to me except as the inventor of Cartesian co-ordinates), I came to the conclusion that consciousness is an undeniable datum, and therefore pure materialism is impossible. This was at the age of fifteen. About two years later, I became convinced that there is no life after death, but I still believed in God, because the 'First Cause' argument appeared to be irrefutable. At the age of eighteen, however, shortly before I went to Cambridge, I read Mill's *Autobiography*, where I found a sentence to the effect that his father taught him that the question 'Who made me?' cannot be answered, since it immediately suggests the further question 'Who made God?'. This led me to abandon the 'First Cause' argument, and to become an atheist. Throughout the long period of religious doubt, I had been rendered very unhappy by the gradual loss of belief, but when the process was completed, I found to my surprise that I was quite glad to be done with the whole subject.

Throughout this time, I read omnivorously. I taught myself enough Italian to read Dante and Machiavelli. I read Comte, of whom, however, I did not think much. I read Mill's *Political Economy* and *Logic*, and made elaborate abstracts of them. I read Carlyle with a good deal of interest, but with a complete repudiation of his purely sentimental arguments in favour of religion. For I took the view then, which I have taken ever since, that a theological proposition should not be accepted unless there is the same kind of evidence for it that would be required for a proposition in science. I read Gibbon, and Milman's *History of Christianity*, and *Gulliver's Travels* unexpurgated. The account of the Yahoos had a profound effect upon me, and I began to see human beings in that light.

It must be understood that the whole of this mental life was deeply buried; not a sign of it showed in my intercourse with other people. Socially I was shy, childish, awkward, well-behaved, and good-natured. I used to watch with envy people who could manage social intercourse without anguished awkwardness. There was a young man called Cattermole who, I suppose, must have been a bit of a bounder; but I watched him walking with a smart young woman with easy familiarity and evidently pleasing her. And I would think that never, never, never should I learn to behave in a manner that could possibly please any woman in whom I might be interested. Until just before my sixteenth

[1] Some portions of this book are included on pp. 47 to 55.

41

birthday, I was sometimes able to speak of some things to my tutors. Until that date I was educated at home, but my tutors seldom stayed more than three months. I did not know why this was, but I think it was because whenever a new tutor arrived, I used to induce him to enter into a conspiracy with me to deceive my people wherever their demands were absurd. One tutor I had was an agnostic, and used to allow me to discuss religion with him. I imagine that he was dismissed because this was discovered. The tutor whom my people liked best and who stayed the longest with me was a man dying of consumption whose breath stank intolerably. It never occurred to them that it was unwise, from a health point of view, to have me perpetually in his neighbourhood.

Just before my sixteenth birthday, I was sent to an Army crammer at Old Southgate, which was then in the country. I was not sent to him in order to cram for the Army, but in order to be prepared for the scholarship examination at Trinity College, Cambridge. Almost all of the other people there, however, were going into the Army, with the exception of one or two reprobates who were going to take Orders. Everybody, except myself, was seventeen or eighteen, or nineteen, so that I was much the youngest. They were all of an age to have just begun frequenting prostitutes, and this was their main topic of conversation. The most admired among them was a young man who asserted that he had had syphilis and got cured, which gave him great kudos. They would sit round telling bawdy stories. Every incident gave them opportunities for improper remarks. Once the crammer sent one of them with a note to a neighbouring house. On returning, he related to the others that he had rung the bell and a maid had appeared to whom he had said: 'I have brought a letter' (meaning a French letter) to which she replied: 'I am glad you have brought a letter.' When one day in church a hymn was sung containing the line: 'Here I'll raise my Ebenezer', they remarked: 'I never heard it called that before!'

In spite of my previous silent preoccupation with sex, contact with it in this brutal form deeply shocked me. I became very Puritanical in my views, and decided that sex without deep love is beastly. I retired into myself, and had as little to do with the others as possible. The others, however, found me suitable for teasing. They used to make me sit on a chair on a table and sing the only song I knew, which was:

> Old Abraham is dead and gone,
> We ne'er shall see him more,
> He used to wear an old great coat,
> All buttoned down before.

He also had another coat,
Which was of a different kind.
Instead of buttoning down before,
It buttoned up behind.

I soon realized that my only chance of escape from their attentions was to remain imperturbably good-humoured. After a term or two, another teasable boy arrived, who had the added merit of losing his temper. This caused them to let me alone. Gradually, also, I got used to their conversation and ceased to be shocked by it. I remained, however, profoundly unhappy. There was a footpath leading across fields to New Southgate, and I used to go there alone to watch the sunset and contemplate suicide. I did not, however, commit suicide, because I wished to know more of mathematics. My people would, of course, have been horrified if they had known of the sort of conversation that was habitual, but as I was getting on well with mathematics I wished on the whole to stay, and never told them a word as to the sort of place it was. At the end of the year and a half at the crammer's I was examined for scholarships in December 1889, and obtained a minor scholarship. During the ten months that intervened before my going to Cambridge, I lived at home, and coached with the man whom the crammer had hired to teach me.

For a time at the crammer's I had one friend—a man named Edward FitzGerald. His mother was American, and his father Canadian, and he became well-known in later years as a great mountain climber, performing many exploits in the New Zealand Alps and the Andes. His people were very rich, and lived in a large house, No. 19, Rutland Gate.[1] He had a sister who wrote poetry and was a great friend of Robert Browning whom I frequently met at Rutland Gate.[2] She afterwards became first Lady Edmond Fitzmaurice, and then Signora de Phillippi. His sister was considerably older than he was, and an accomplished classical scholar. I conceived a romantic admiration for her, though when I met her later she seemed an unmitigated bore. He had been brought up in America, and was exceedingly sophisticated. He was lazy and lackadaisical, but had remarkable ability in a great many directions, notably in mathematics. He could tell the year of any reputable wine or cigar. He could eat a spoonful of mixed mustard and Cayenne pepper. He was intimate with Continental brothels. His knowledge of literature was extensive, and while an undergraduate at

[1] It is now pulled down.
[2] I had met Robert Browning once before at the age of two when he came to lunch at Pembroke Lodge and talked unceasingly although everybody wished to hear the actor Salvini whom he had brought with him. At last I exclaimed in a piercing voice, 'I wish that man would stop talking'. And he did.

Cambridge, he acquired a fine library of first editions. When he first came to the crammer's, I took to him at once, because he was at any rate a civilized being, which none of the others were. (Robert Browning died while I was there, and none of the others had ever heard of him.) We used both to go home for the weekend, and on the way he would always take me first to lunch with his people and then to a matinée. My people made enquiries about the family, but were reassured by a testimonial from Robert Browning. Having been lonely so long, I devoted a somewhat absurd amount of affection to FitzGerald. To my great delight, I was invited to go abroad with him and his people in August. This was the first time I had been abroad since the age of two, and the prospect of seeing foreign countries excited me greatly. We went first to Paris, where the Exhibition of 1889 was in progress, and we went to the top of the Eiffel Tower, which was new that year. We then went to Switzerland, where we drove from place to place for about a week, ending up in the Engadine. He and I climbed two mountains, Piz Corvach, and Piz Palü. On both occasions there was a snow-storm. On the first I had mountain sickness, and on the second he did. The second occasion was quite exciting, as one of our guides fell over a precipice, and had to be hauled up by the rope. I was impressed by his *sang froid*, as he swore as he fell over.

Unfortunately, however, FitzGerald and I had a somewhat serious disagreement during this time. He spoke with what I thought unpardonable rudeness to his mother, and being young I reproached him for doing so. He was exceedingly angry, with a cold anger which lasted for months. When we returned to the crammer's, we shared lodgings, and he devoted himself to saying disagreeable things, in which he displayed great skill. I came to hate him with a violence which, in retrospect, I can hardly understand. On one occasion, in an access of fury, I got my hands on his throat and started to strangle him. I intended to kill him, but when he began to grow livid, I relented. I do not think he knew that I had intended murder. After this, we remained fairly good friends throughout his time at Cambridge, which, however, ended with his marriage at the end of his second year.

Throughout this time, I had been getting more and more out of sympathy with my people. I continued to agree with them in politics, but in nothing else. At first I sometimes tried to talk to them about things that I was considering, but they always laughed at me, and this caused me to hold my tongue. It appeared to me obvious that the happiness of mankind should be the aim of all action, and I discovered to my surprise that there were those who thought otherwise. Belief in happiness, I found, was called Utilitarianism, and was merely one among a number of ethical theories. I adhered to it after this discovery, and was rash enough to tell grandmother that I was a utilitarian. She covered me with ridicule, and ever after submitted ethical conundrums to me, telling me to solve them on utilitarian principles. I perceived that she had no good grounds for rejecting utilitarianism, and that her opposition to it was not intellectually respectable. When she discovered that I was interested in metaphysics, she told me that the whole subject could be summed up in the saying: 'What is mind? no matter; what is matter? never mind.' At the fifteenth or sixteenth repetition of this remark, it ceased to amuse me, but my grandmother's animus against metaphysics continued to the end of her life. Her attitude is expressed in the following verses:

> O Science metaphysical
> And very very quizzical,
> You only make this maze of life the mazier;
> For boasting to illuminate
> Such riddles dark as Will and Fate
> You muddle them to hazier and hazier.
>
> The cause of every action,
> You expound with satisfaction;
> Through the mind in all its corners and recesses
> You say that you have travelled,
> And all problems unravelled
> And axioms you call your learned guesses.
>
> Right and wrong you've so dissected,
> And their fragments so connected,
> That which we follow doesn't seem to matter;
> But the cobwebs you have wrought,
> And the silly flies they have caught,
> It needs no broom miraculous to shatter.
>
> You know no more than I,
> What is laughter, tear, or sigh,
> Or love, or hate, or anger, or compassion;
> Metaphysics, then, adieu,
> Without you I can do,
> And I think you'll very soon be out of fashion.

I remember her saying to me once after I was grown-up: 'I hear you are writing *another* book', in the tone of voice in which one might say: 'I hear you have another illegitimate child!' Mathematics she did not positively object to, though it was difficult for her to believe that it could serve any useful purpose. Her hope for me was that I should become a Unitarian minister. I held my tongue as to my religious opinions until I was twenty-one. Indeed, after the age of fourteen I found living at home only endurable at the cost of complete silence about everything that interested me. She practised a form of humour, which, though nominally amusing, was really full of animus. I did not at that time know how to reply in kind, and merely felt hurt and miserable. My Aunt Agatha was equally bad, and my Uncle Rollo at the time had withdrawn into himself through sorrow at his first wife's death. My brother, who was at Balliol, had become a Buddhist, and used to tell me that the soul could be contained in the smallest envelope. I remember thinking of all the smallest envelopes that I had seen, and I imagined the soul beating against them like a heart, but from what I could tell of esoteric Buddhism from my brother's conversation, it did not offer me anything that I found of service. After he came of age, I saw very little of him, as the family considered him wicked, and he therefore kept away from home. I was upheld by the determination to do something of importance in mathematics when I grew up, but I did not suppose that I should ever meet anybody with whom I could make friends, or to whom I could express any of my thoughts freely, nor did I expect that any part of my life would be free from great unhappiness.

Throughout my time at Southgate I was very much concerned with politics and economics. I read Mill's *Political Economy*, which I was inclined to accept completely; also Herbert Spencer, who seemed to me too doctrinaire in *The Man Versus The State*, although I was in broad agreement with his bias.

My Aunt Agatha introduced me to the books of Henry George, which she greatly admired. I became convinced that land nationalization would secure all the benefits that Socialists hoped to obtain from Socialism, and continued to hold this view until the war of 1914–18.

My grandmother Russell and my Aunt Agatha were passionate supporters of Gladstone's Home Rule policy, and many Irish M.P.s used to visit Pembroke Lodge. This was at a time when *The Times* professed to have documentary proof that Parnell was an accomplice in murder. Almost the whole upper class, including the great majority of those who had supported Gladstone till 1886, accepted this view, until, in 1889, it was dramatically disproved by the forger Piggot's inability to spell 'hesitancy'. My grandmother and aunt always vehemently rejected the view that Parnell's followers were in alliance with terrorists. They admired Parnell, with whom I once shook hands. But when he became involved in scandal, they agreed with Gladstone in repudiating him.

Twice I went with my Aunt Agatha to Ireland. I used to go for walks with Michael Davitt, the Irish patriot, and also by myself. The beauty of the scenery made a profound impression on me. I remember especially a small lake in County Wicklow, called Lugala. I have associated it ever since, though for no good reason, with the lines:

> Like as the waves make toward the pebbled shore,
> So do our minutes hasten to their end.

Fifty years later, when visiting my friend Crompton Davies in Dublin, I induced him to take me to Lugala. But he took me to a wood high above the lake, not to the 'pebbled shore' that I had remembered, and I went away convinced that one should not attempt to renew old memories.

In the year 1883 my Uncle Rollo bought a house on the slopes of Hindhead, where, for a long time, we all visited him for three months in every year. At that time there were no houses on Hindhead except two derelict coaching inns, the 'Royal Huts' and the 'Seven Thorns'. (They are not now derelict). Tyndall's house, which started the fashion, was being built. I was frequently taken to see Tyndall, and he gave me one of his books, *The Forms of Water*. I admired him as an eminent Man of Science, and strongly desired to make some impression upon him. Twice I had some success. The first time was while he was talking to my Uncle Rollo, and I balanced on one finger two walking sticks with crooks. Tyndall asked me what I was doing, and I said I was thinking of a practical method of determining the centre of gravity. The second time, some years later, was when I told him that I had climbed the Piz Palü. He had been a pioneer Alpinist. I found inexpressible delight in walks through the heather, over Blackdown, down the Punchbowl, and as far as the Devil's Jumps at Churt. I particularly remember exploring a small road called 'Mother Bunch's Lane' (it is now full of houses, and has a sign saying 'Bunch Lane'). It continually diminished, and at last became a mere path leading to the crest of Hurt Hill. Quite suddenly, when I expected nothing, I came upon an enormous view, embracing half of Sussex and almost all of Surrey. Moments of this sort have been important in my life. In general, I find that things that have happened to me out of doors have made a deeper impression than things that have happened indoors.

APPENDIX: 'GREEK EXERCISES'

1888. March 3. I shall write about some subjects which now interest me. I have in consequence of a variety of circumstances come to look into the very foundations of the religion in which I have been brought up. On some points my conclusions have been to confirm my former creed, while on others I have been irresistibly led to such conclusions as would not only shock my people, but have given me much pain. I have arrived at certainty in few things, but my opinions, even where not convictions, are on some things nearly such. I have not the courage to tell my people that I scarcely believe in immortality. I used to speak freely to Mr Ewen on such matters, but now I cannot let out my thoughts to any one, and this is the only means I have of letting off steam. I intend to discuss some of my problems here.

19th. I mean today to put down my grounds for belief in God. I may say to begin with that I do believe in God and that I should call myself a theist if I had to give my creed a name. Now in finding reasons for believing in God I shall only take account of scientific arguments. This is a vow I have made which costs me much to keep, and to reject all sentiment. To find then scientific grounds for a belief in God we must go back to the beginning of all things. We know that the present laws of nature have always been in force. The exact quantity of matter and energy now in the universe must always have been in existence, but the nebular hypothesis points to no distant date for the time when the whole universe was filled with undifferentiated nebulous matter. Hence it is quite possible that the matter and force now in existence may have had a creation, which clearly could be only divine power. But even granting that they have always been in existence, yet whence came the laws which regulate the action of force on matter? I think they are only attributable to a divine controlling power, which I accordingly call God.

March 22. Now let us look into the reasonableness of the reasoning. Let us suppose that the universe we now see has, as some suppose, grown by mere chance. Should we then expect every atom to act in any given conditions precisely similarly to another atom? I think if atoms be lifeless there is no reason to expect them to do anything without a controlling power. If on the other hand they be endowed with free will we are forced to the conclusion that all atoms in the universe have combined in the commonwealth and have made laws which none of them ever break. This is clearly an absurd hypothesis and therefore we are forced to believe in God. But this way of proving his existence at the same time disproves miracles and other supposed manifestations of divine power. It does not however disprove their possibility, for of course the maker of laws can also unmake them. We may arrive in another way at a disbelief in miracles. For if God is the maker of the laws, surely it would imply an imperfection in the law if it had to be altered occasionally, and such imperfection we can never impute to the divine nature, as in the Bible, God repented him of the work.

April 2. I now come to the subject which personally interests us poor mortals more perhaps than any other. I mean the question of immortality. This is the one in which I have been most disappointed and pained by thought. There are two ways of looking at it, first by evolution and comparing men to animals, second, by comparing men with God. The first is the more scientific, for we know all about the animals but not about God. Well, I hold that, taking free will first, to consider there is no clear dividing line between man and the protozoan, therefore if we give free will to men we must give it also the protozoan; this is rather hard to do. Therefore, unless we are willing to give free will to the protozoan we cannot give it to man. This however is possible but it is difficult to imagine, if, as seems to me probable, protoplasm only came together in the ordinary course of nature without any special providence from God; then we and all living things are simply kept going by chemical forces and are nothing more wonderful than a tree, which no one pretends has free will, and even if we had a good enough knowledge of the forces acting on anyone at any time, the motives pro and con, the constitution of his brain at any time, then we could tell exactly what he will do. Again from the religious point of view free will is a very arrogant thing for us to claim, for of course it is an interruption of God's laws, for by his ordinary laws all our actions would be fixed as the stars. I think we must leave to God the primary establishment of laws which are never broken and determine everybody's doings. And not having free will we cannot have immortality.

Monday, April 6. I do wish I believed in the life eternal, for it makes me quite miserable to think man is merely a kind of machine endowed, unhappily for himself, with consciousness. But no other theory is consistent with the complete omnipotence of God of which science, I think, gives ample manifestations. Thus I must either be an atheist or disbelieve in immortality. Finding the first impossible I adopt the second and let no one know. I think, however disappointing may be this view of men, it does give us a wonderful idea of God's greatness to think that He can in the beginning create laws which by acting on a mere mass of nebulous matter, perhaps merely ether diffused through this part of the universe, will produce creatures like ourselves, conscious not only of our existence but even able to fathom to a certain extent God's mysteries. All this with no more intervention on his part. Now let us think whether this doctrine of want of free will is so absurd. If we talk about it to anyone they kick their legs or something of that sort. But perhaps they cannot help it for they have something to prove and therefore that supplies a motive to them to do it. Thus in anything we do we always have motives which determine us. Also there is no line of demarcation between Shakespeare or Herbert Spencer and a Papuan. But between them and a Papuan there seems as much difference as between a Papuan and a monkey.

April 14th. Yet there are great difficulties in the way of this doctrine that man has not immortality nor free will nor a soul, in short that he is nothing more than a species of ingenious machine endowed with consciousness. For consciousness in itself is a quality quite distinguishing men from dead matter and if they have one thing different from dead matter why not have another, free will? By free will I mean that they do not for example obey the first law of motion, or at least that the direction in which the energy they contain is employed depends not entirely on external circumstances. Moreover it seems impossible to imagine that man, the Great Man, with his reason, his knowledge of the universe, and his ideas of right and wrong, Man with his emotions, his love and hate and his religion, that this Man should be a mere perishable chemical compound whose character and his influence for good or for evil depend solely and entirely on the particular motions of the molecules of his brain and that all the greatest men have been great by reason of some one molecule hitting up against some other a little oftener than in other men. Does not this seem utterly incredible and must not any one be mad who believes in such absurdity? But what is the alternative? That, accepting the evolution theory which is practically proved, apes having gradually increased in intelligence, God suddenly by a miracle endowed one with that wonderful reason which it is a mystery how we possess. Then is man, truly called the most glorious work of God, is man destined to perish utterly after he has been so many ages evolving? We cannot say, but I prefer that idea to God's having needed a miracle to produce man and now leaving him free to do as he likes.

April 18th. Accepting then the theory that man is mortal and destitute of free will, which is as much as ever a mere theory, as of course all these kinds of things are mere speculation, what idea can we form of right and wrong? Many say if you make any mention of such an absurd doctrine as predestination, which comes to much the same thing, though parsons don't think so, why what becomes of conscience etc., which they think has been directly implanted in man by God. Now my idea is that our conscience is in the first place due to evolution, which would of course form instincts of self-preservation. Let us take for example the ten commandments as illustrative of primitive morality. Many o them are conducive to quiet living of the community which is best for the preservation of the species. Thus what is always considered the worst possible crime and the one for which most remorse is felt is murder, which is direct annihilation of the species. Again, as we know, among the Hebrews it was thought a mark of God's favour to have many children, while the childless were considered as cursed of God. Among the Romans also widows were hated and I believe forbidden to remain unmarried in Rome more than a year. Now why these peculiar ideas? Were they not simply because these objects of pity or dislike did not bring forth fresh human beings? We can well understand how such ideas might grow up when men became rather sensible, for if murder and suicide were common in a tribe that tribe would die out and hence one which held such acts in abhorrence would have a great advantage. Of course among more educated societies these ideas are rather modified. My own I mean to give next time.

April 20th. Thus I think that primitive morality always originates in the idea of the preservation of the species. But is this a rule which a civilized community ought to follow? I think not. My rule of life, which I guide my conduct by, and a departure from which I consider as a sin, is to act in the manner which I believe to be most likely to produce the greatest happiness, considering both the intensity of the happiness and the number of people made happy. I know that Granny considers this an impractical rule of life and says that since you can never know the thing which will produce the greatest happiness you do much better in following the inner voice. The conscience, however, can easily be seen to depend mostly upon education, as for example common

Irishmen do not consider lying wrong, which fact alone seems to me quite sufficient to disprove the divine value of conscience. And since, as I believe, conscience is merely the combined product of evolution and education, then obviously it is an absurdity to follow that rather than reason. And my reason tells me that it is better to act so as to produce maximum happiness than in any other way. For I have tried to see what other object I could set before me and I have failed. Not my own individual happiness in particular, but everybody's equally, making no distinction between myself, relations, friends, or perfect strangers. In real life it makes very little difference to me as long as others are not of my opinion, for obviously where there is any chance of being found out it is better to do what one's people consider right. My reason for this view: first that I can find no other, having been forced, as everybody must who seriously thinks about evolution, to give up the old idea of asking one's conscience, next that it seems to me that happiness is the great thing to seek after. As an application of the theory to practical life, I will say that in a case where nobody but myself was concerned, if indeed such a case exist, I should of course act entirely selfishly to please myself. Suppose for another instance that I had the chance of saving a man who would be better out of the world. Obviously I should consult my own happiness best by plunging in after him. For if I lost my life, that would be a very neat way of managing it, and if I saved him I should have the pleasure of no end of praise. But if I let him drown I should have lost an opportunity of death and should have the misery of much blame, but the world would be better for his loss and, as I have some slight hope, for my life.

April 29th. In all things I have made the vow to follow reason, not the instincts inherited partly from my ancestors and gained gradually by them, owing to a process of natural selection, and partly due to my education. How absurd it would be to follow these in the questions of right and wrong. For as I observed before, the inherited part can only be principles leading to the preservation of the species to which I belong, the part due to education is good or bad according to the individual education. Yet this inner voice, this God-given conscience which made Bloody Mary burn the Protestants, this is what we reasonable beings are to follow. I think this idea mad and I endeavour to go by reason as far as possible. What I take as my ideal is that which ultimately produces greatest happiness of greatest number. Then I can apply reason to find out the course most conductive to this end. In my individual case, however, I can also go more or less by conscience owing to the excellence of my education. But it is curious how people dislike the abandonment of brutish impulses for reason. I remember poor Ewen getting a whole dinner of argument, owing to his running down impulse. Today again at tea Miss Buhler and I had a long discussion because I said that I followed reason not conscience in matters of right and wrong. I do hate having such peculiar opinions because either I must keep them bottled up or else people are horrified at my scepticism, which is as bad with people one cares for as remaining bottled up. I shall be sorry when Miss Buhler goes because I can open my heart easier to her than to my own people, strange to say.

May 3rd. Miss Buhler is gone and I am left again to loneliness and reserve. Happily, however, it seems all but settled that I am going to Southgate and probably within the week. That will save me I feel sure from morose cogitations during the week, owing to the amount of activity of my life, and novelty at first. I do not expect that I shall enjoy myself at first, but after a time I hope I shall. Certainly it will be good for my work, for my games and my manners, and my future happiness I expect. . . .

May 8th. What a much happier life mine would be but for these wretched ideas of mine about theology. Tomorrow I go, and tonight Granny prayed a beautiful prayer for me in my new life, in which among other things she said: May he especially be taught to know God's infinite love for him. Well that is a prayer to which I can heartily say Amen, and moreover it is one of which I stand in the greatest need. For according to my ideas of God we have no particular reason to suppose he loves us. For he only set the machine in working order to begin with and then left it to work out its own necessary consequences. Now you may say his laws are such as afford the greatest possible happiness to us mortals, but that is a statement of which there can be no proof. Hence I see no reason to believe in God's kindness towards me, and though I was truly affected by the simple beauty of prayer and her earnest way in saying it. What a thing it is to have such people! What might I be had I been worse brought up!

By the way, to change to a more cheerful subject: Marshall[1] and I had an awfully fine day of it. We went down to the river, marched into Broom Hall,[2] bagged a boat of Frank's we found there, and rowed up the river beyond Kingston Bridge without anybody at Broom Hall having seen us except one old man who was lame. Who the dickens he was I haven't the faintest idea. Marshall was awfully anxious to have some tea and we came to an nth rate inn which he thought would do. Having however like idiots left our jackets in the boat-house at Teddington we had to march in without coats and were served by the cheekiest of maids ever I saw who said she thought we were the carpenters come to mend the house. Then we rowed back as hard as possible and got home perspiring fearfully and twenty minutes late which produced a small row.

May 20th. Here I am home again for the first time from Southgate. It seems a pleasant place but it is sad really to see the kind of boys that are common everywhere. No mind, no independent thought, no love of good books nor of the higher refinements of morality. It is really sad that the upper classes of a civilized and (supposed to be) moral country can produce nothing better. I am glad I didn't go away from home sooner as I should never have come to my present state had I done so, but should have been merely like one of them. (By the way, how terribly pharisaical I am getting.) I think the six months since Baillie went have made a great alteration in me. I have become of a calmer, thoughtfuller, poeticaller nature than I was. One little thing I think illustrates this well. I never before thought much of the views in spring, whereas this year

---

[1] A former tutor.   [2] Where my brother was living.

I was so simply carried away by their beauty that I asked Granny if they were not more beautiful than usual, but she said not. I like poetry much better than I did and have read all Shakespeare's historical plays with great delight, and long to read *In Memoriam.*

May 27th. As I said last time, I attempt to work according to my principles without the smallest expectations of reward, and even without using the light of conscience blindly as an infallible guide. . . . It is very difficult for anyone to work aright with no aid from religion, by his own internal guidance merely. I have tried and I may say failed. But the sad thing is that I have no other resource. I have no helpful religion. My doctrines, such as they are, help my daily life no more than a formula in Algebra. But the great inducement to a good life with me is Granny's love and the immense pain I know it gives her when I go wrong. But she must I suppose die some day and where then will be my stay? I have the very greatest fear that my life hereafter be ruined by my having lost the support of religion. I desire of all things that my religion should not spread, for I of all people ought, owing to my education and the care taken of my moral well-being, to be of all people the most moral. So I believe I might be were it not for these unhappy ideas of mine, for how easy it is when one is much tempted to convince oneself that only happiness will be produced by yielding to temptation, when according to my ideas the course one has been taught to abhor immediately becomes virtuous. If ever I shall become an utter wreck of what I hope to be I think I shall bring forward this book as an explanation. We stand in want of a new Luther to renew faith and invigorate Christianity and to do what do the Unitarians if only they had a really great man such as Luther to lead them. For religions grow old like trees unless reformed from time to time. Christianity of the existing kinds has had its day. We want a new form in accordance with science and yet helpful to a good life.

June 3rd. It is extraordinary how few principles or dogmas I have been able to become convinced of. One after another I find my former undoubted beliefs slipping from me into the region of doubt. For example, I used never for a moment to doubt that truth was a good thing to get hold of. But now I have the very greatest doubt and uncertainty. For the search for truth has led me to these results I have put in this book, whereas had I been content to accept the teachings of my youth I should have remained comfortable. The search for truth had shattered most of my old beliefs and has made me commit what are probably sins where otherwise I should have kept clear of them. I do not think it has in any way made me happier. Of course it has given me a deeper character, a contempt for trifles or mockery, but at the same time it has taken away cheerfulness and made it much harder to make bosom friends, and worst of all it has debarred me from free intercourse with my people, and thus made them strangers to some of my deepest thoughts, which, if by any mischance I do let them out, immediately become the subject for mockery, which is inexpressibly bitter to me though not unkindly meant. Thus in my individual case I should say the effects of a search for truth have been more bad than good. But the truth which I accept as such may be said not to be truth and I may be told that if I get at real truth I shall be made happier by it, but this is a very doubtful proposition. Hence I have great doubt of the unmixed advantage of truth. Certainly truth in biology lowers one's idea of man which must be painful. Moreover, truth estranges former friends and prevents the making of new ones, which is also a bad thing. One ought perhaps to look upon all these things as a martyrdom, since very often truth attained by one man may lead to the increase in the happiness of many others though not to his own. On the whole I am inclined to continue to pursue truth, though truth of the kind in this book, if that indeed be truth, I have no desire to spread but rather to prevent from spreading.

July 15th. My holidays have begun about a week now and I am getting used to home and beginning to regard Southgate as a dream of the past. For although I tell people I like it very much, yet really, though better than I expected, life there has great trials and hardships. I don't suppose anybody hates disturbance as I do or can so ill stand mockery, though to outward appearance I keep my temper all right. Being made to sing, to climb on chairs, to get up for a sponging in the middle of the night, is to me fifty times more detestable than to others. I always have to go through in a moment a long train of reasoning as to the best thing to say or do, for I have sufficient self-control to do what I think best, and the excitement, which to others might seem small, leaves me trembling and exhausted. However, I think it is an excellent thing for me, as it increases my capacity for enjoyment and strengthens me morally to a very considerable extent. I shan't forget in a hurry their amazement that I had never said a 'damn', which with things like it goes near to making me a *fanfaron de crimes*. This, however, is a bad thing to be, when only too many real crimes are committed. . . . I am glad I didn't go to school before. I should have wanted strength and have had no time for the original thought, which though it has caused me much pain, is yet my chief stay and support in troubles. I am always kept up by a feeling of contempt, erroneous though it may be, for all who despitefully use me and persecute me. I don't think contempt is misplaced when a chap's habitual language is about something like 'who put me on my cold, cold pot whether I would or not? My mother.' Sung to the tune of 'Thy will be done'. Had my education, however, been the least bit less perfect than it is I should probably have been the same. But I feel I must enjoy myself at home much better than ever before, which with an imaginary feeling of heroism reconciles me to a great deal of unhappiness at Southgate.

July 20th. There are about three different, though converging ways of looking at this question of free will, first, from the omnipotence of God, second, from the reign of law, and third, from the fact that all our actions, if looked into, show themselves as caused by motives. These three ways we see at once to be really identical, for God's omnipotence is the same thing as the reign of law, and the determination of actions by motives is the particular form which the reign of law takes in man. Let us now examine closely each of these ways.

First, from the omnipotence of God. What do we mean, in the first place, by free will? We mean that, where several courses are open to us, we can choose any one. But according to this definition, we are not ruled by God, and alone of created things, we are independent of him. That appears unlikely, but is by no means impossible, since his omnipotence is only an inference. Let us then pass on to the Second, from the reign of law. Of all the things we know, except perhaps the higher animals, it is obvious that law is completely the master. That man is also under its dominion appears from a fact such as Grimm's Law, and again from the fact that it is possible sometimes to predict human actions. If man, then, be subject to law, does not this mean, that his actions are pre-determined, just as much as the motions of a planet or the growth of a plant? The Duke of Argyll, indeed, speaks of freedom within the bounds of law, but to me that's an unmeaning phrase, for subjection to law must mean a certain consequence always following in given conditions. No doubt different people in the same circumstances act differently, but that is only owing to difference of character, just as two comets in the same position move differently, because of differences in their eccentricities. The third, from the consideration of motives, is about the strongest. For if we examine any action whatsoever, we find always motives, over which we have no more control than matter over the forces acting on it, which produce our actions. The Duke of Argyll says we can present motives to ourselves, but is not that an action, determined by our character, and other unavoidable things? The argument for free will from the fact that we feel it, is worthless, for we do not feel motives which we find really exist, nor that mind depends on brain, etc. But I am not prepared dogmatically to deny free will, for I have often found that good arguments don't present themselves on one side of a question till they are told one. My nature may incline me to disbelieve free will, and there may be very excellent arguments for free will which either I have never thought of, or else have not had their full weight with me. . . . It is difficult not to become reckless and commit suicide, which I believe I should do but for my people.

CHAPTER III

CAMBRIDGE

MY FATHER had been at Cambridge, but my brother was at Oxford. I went to Cambridge because of my interest in mathematics. My first experience of the place was in December 1889 when I was examined for entrance scholarships. I stayed in rooms in the New Court, and I was too shy to enquire the way to the lavatory, so that I walked every morning to the station before the examination began. I saw the Backs through the gate of the New Court, but did not venture to go into them, feeling that they might be private. I was invited to dine with the Master, who had been Headmaster of Harrow in my father's time. I there, for the first time, met Charles and Bob Trevelyan. Bob characteristically had borrowed Charles's second best dress suit, and fainted during dinner because somebody mentioned a surgical operation. I was alarmed by so formidable a social occasion, but less alarmed than I had been a few months earlier when I was left *tête-à-tête* with Mr Gladstone. He came to stay at Pembroke Lodge, and nobody was asked to meet him. As I was the only male in the household, he and I were left alone together at the dinner table after the ladies retired. He made only one remark: 'This is very good port they have given me, but why have they given it me in a claret glass?' I did not know the answer, and wished the earth would swallow me up. Since then I have never again felt the full agony of terror.

I was very anxious to do well in the scholarship examination, and nervousness somewhat interfered with my work. Nevertheless, I got a minor scholarship, which gave me extreme happiness, as it was the first time I had been able to compare myself with able contemporaries.

From the moment that I went up to Cambridge at the beginning of October 1890 everything went well with me. All the people then in residence who subsequently became my intimate friends called on me during the first week of term. At the time I did not know why they did so, but I discovered afterwards that Whitehead, who had examined for scholarships, had told people to look out for Sanger and me. Sanger was a freshman like myself, also doing mathematics, and also a minor scholar. He and I both had rooms in Whewell's Court. Webb, our coach, had a practice of circulating MSS among his classes, and it fell to my lot to deliver a MS to Sanger after I had done with it. I had not seen him before, but I was struck by the books on his shelves. I said: 'I see you have Draper's *Intellectual Development of Europe* which I think a very good book.' He said: 'You are the first person I have ever met who has heard of it!' From this point the conversation proceeded, and at the end of half an hour we were lifelong friends. We compared notes as to how much mathematics we had done. We agreed upon theology and meta-physics. We disagreed upon politics (he was at the time a Conservative, though in later life he belonged to the Labour Party). He spoke of Shaw, whose name was until then unknown to me. We used to work on mathematics together. He was incredibly quick, and would be half-way through solving a problem before I had understood the question. We both devoted our fourth year to moral science, but he did economics, and I did philosophy. We got our Fellowships at the same moment. He was one of the kindest men that ever lived, and in the last years of his life my children loved him as much as I have done. I have never known anyone else with such a perfect combination of penetrating intellect and warm affection. He became a Chancery barrister, and was known in legal circles for his highly erudite edition of Jarman *On Wills*. He used to lament that Jarman's relatives had forbidden him to mention in the pre-face that Jarman died intestate. He was also a very good economist, and he could read an incredible number of languages, including such out-of-the-way items as Magyar and Finnish. I used to go walking tours with him in Italy, and he always made me do all the conversation with inn-keepers, but when I was reading Italian, I found that his knowledge of the language was vastly greater than mine. His death in the year 1930 was a great sorrow to me.

The other friends whom I acquired during my first term I owed chiefly to Whitehead's recommendation. I learned afterwards that in the scholarship examination another man had obtained more marks than I had, but Whitehead had the impression that I was the abler of the two. He therefore burned the marks before the examiners' meeting, and recommended me in preference to the other man. Two of my closest friends were Crompton and Theodore Llewelyn Davies. Their father was vicar of Kirkby Lonsdale, and translator of Plato's *Republic* in the Golden Treasury edition, a distinguished scholar and a Broad Churchman whose views were derived from F. D. Maurice. He had a family of six sons and one daughter. It was said, and I believe with truth, that throughout their education the six sons, of whom Crompton and Theodore were the youngest, managed, by means of scholarships, to go through school and university without expense to their father. Most of them were also strikingly good-looking, including Crompton, who had very fine blue eyes, which sometimes sparkled with fun and at other times had a steady gaze that was deeply serious. The ablest and one of the best loved of the family was the youngest, Theodore, with whom, when I first knew them, Crompton shared rooms in College. They both in due course became Fellows, but neither of them became resident. Afterwards the two lived together in a small house near Westminster Abbey, in a quiet out-of-the-way street. Both of them were able, high-minded and passionate, and shared, on the whole, the same ideals and opinions. Theodore had a somewhat more practical outlook on life than Crompton. He became Private Secretary to a series of Conservative Chancellors of the Exchequer, each of whom in turn he converted to Free Trade at a time when the rest of the Government wished them to think otherwise. He worked incredibly hard and yet always found time to give presents to the children of all his friends, and the presents were always exactly appropriate. He inspired the deepest affection in almost everybody who knew him. I never knew but one woman who would not have been delighted to marry him. She, of course, was the only woman he wished to marry. In the spring of 1905, when he was thirty-four, his dead body was found in a pool near Kirkby Lonsdale, where he had evidently bathed on his way to the station. It was supposed that he must have hit his head on a rock in diving. Crompton, who loved his brother above everyone, suffered almost unendurably. I spent the weeks after Theodore's death with him, but it was difficult to find anything to say.[1] The sight of his unhappiness was agonizing. Ever since, the sound of Westminster chimes has brought back to me the nights I lay awake in misery at this time. On the Sunday after the accident, I was in church when his father, with determined stoicism, took the service as usual, and just succeeded in not breaking down. Gradually Crompton recovered, but not fully until his marriage. After that, for no reason that I could understand, I saw nothing of him for many years, until one evening, when I was living in Chelsea, I heard the front door bell, and found Crompton on the doorstep. He behaved as if we had met the day before, was as charming as ever, and insisted on seeing my children asleep. I think I had become so much associated with his suffering after Theodore's death, that for a long time he found my presence painful.

One of my earliest memories of Crompton is of meeting him in the darkest part of a winding College staircase and his suddenly quoting, without any previous word, the whole of 'Tyger, Tyger, burning bright'. I had never, till that moment, heard of Blake, and the poem affected me so much that I became dizzy and had to lean against the wall. Hardly a day passed without my remembering some incident connected with Crompton—sometimes a joke, sometimes a grimace of disgust at mean-

[1] See my letter to Lucy Donnelly, Appendix p. 178; also Crompton Davies's letter on p. 195.

ness or hypocrisy, most often his warm and generous affection. If I were tempted at any time to any failure of honesty, the thought of his disapproval would still restrain me. He combined wit, passion, wisdom, scorn, gentleness, and integrity, in a degree that I have never known equalled. In addition to all these, his intense and unalterable affection gave to me and others, in later years, an anchor of stability in a disintegrating world.

His loyalties were usually peculiar to himself. He was incapable of following a multitude, either for good or evil. He would profess contempt and amusement for all the causes in which his friends excited themselves, laughing to scorn 'The Society for this' or 'The World League for Promoting that', while all the time he was a crusade in himself, for Ireland against England, for small business against big, for the have-nots against the haves, for competition against monopoly. His chief enthusiasm was for the taxation of land values.

Henry George is now an almost forgotten prophet, but in 1890, when I first knew Crompton, his doctrine that all rent should be paid to the State rather than to private landowners was still an active competitor with Socialism among those who were not satisfied with the economic *status quo*. Crompton, at this time, was already a fanatical adherent of Henry George. He had, as was to be expected, a strong dislike of Socialism, and a strong devotion to the principle of freedom for private enterprise. He had no dislike of the capitalist who made his money in industry, but regarded as a mere incubus the man who is able to levy toll on the industry of others because he owns the land that they need. I do not think he ever asked himself how the State could fail to become immensely powerful if it enjoyed all the revenue to be derived from landownership. In his mind, as in Henry George's, the reform was to be the completion of individualistic liberalism, setting free energies now throttled by monopoly power. In 1909, he believed that Henry George's principles were being carried out by Lloyd George, whose famous budget he helped to perfect.

At the beginning of the 1914–18 War he was solicitor to the Post Office, but his ardent agreement with the opinions of his wife, who was an Irish Nationalist and imprisoned as a Sinn Feiner, made his position untenable. He was dismissed at a moment's notice. In spite of the prejudice of the time he was almost immediately taken in as a partner by Messrs. Coward, Chance & Co., one of the leading firms of City solicitors. In 1921, it was he who drafted the treaty of peace that established Irish self-government, though this was never publicly known. His unselfishness made any important worldly success impossible, since he never stood in the way of others acquiring credit for his work; and he did not care for public recognition and honours. But his ability, though it was not this that made him unforgettable, was very great.

What made Crompton at the same time so admirable and so delightful, was not his ability, but his strong loves and hates, his fantastic humour, and his rock-like honesty. He was one of the wittiest men that I have ever known, with a great love of mankind combined with a contemptuous hatred for most individual men. He had by no means the ways of a saint. Once, when we were both young, I was walking with him in the country, and we trespassed over a corner of a farmer's land. The farmer came running out after us, shouting and red with fury. Crompton held his hand to his ear, and said with the utmost mildness: 'Would you mind speaking a little louder? I'm rather hard of hearing.' The farmer was reduced to speechlessness in the endeavour to make more noise than he was already making. Not long before his death I heard him tell this story, with great detail and exaggeration, attributing his part in it to me, while I interrupted, saying, 'don't believe a word of it. It wasn't me, it was all Crompton,' until finally he dissolved in affectionate chuckles.

He was addicted to extreme shabbiness in his clothes, to such a degree that some of his friends expostulated. This had an unexpected result. When Western Australia attempted by litigation to secede from the Commonwealth of Australia, his law firm was employed, and it was decided that the case should be heard in the King's Robing Room. Crompton was overheard ringing up the King's Chamberlain and saying: 'The unsatisfactory state of my trousers has lately been brought to my notice. I understand that the case is to be heard in the King's Robing Room. Perhaps the King has left an old pair of trousers there that might be useful to me.'

His distastes—which were numerous and intense—were always expressed in a manner that made one laugh. Once, when he and I were staying with his father, a Bishop was also a guest—the mildest and most inoffensive type of cleric, the kind of whom it would be natural to say that he would not hurt a fly. Unfortunately his politics were somewhat reactionary. When at last we were alone, Crompton put on a manner that would have been appropriate to a fellow-captive on a pirate ship, and growled out: 'Seems a *desperate* character.'

When the Liberal Government came into office at the end of 1905, and Lord Haldane, fat, comfortable, and soothing, was put at the War Office, Crompton, very gravely, said he had been chosen to prevent the Generals from having apoplexy when Army reforms were suggested.

Motor traffic annoyed him by its imperiousness. He would cross London streets without paying attention to it, and when cars hooted indignantly he would look round with an air of fastidious vexation, and say, 'don't make that noise!' Although he wandered about with an air of dreamy abstraction, wearing his hat on the back of his head, motorists became convinced that he must be someone of enormous importance, and waited patiently while he went his way.

He loved London as much as Lamb or Dr Johnson did. Once, when he was inveighing against Wordsworth for writing about the lesser celandine, I said, 'do you like him better on Westminster Bridge?' 'Ah, yes,' he answered, 'if only he had treated it on the same scale.' In his last years we often walked together in London after dinner, he and my wife and I. Crompton would take our arms, if he were not holding them already, as we passed Wren's church of St Clement Danes, to remind us to look up at one of his favourite sights, the spire standing out dimly against the glowing blue of the evening sky. On these walks he would sometimes get into conversation with people that we met. I remember him engaging a park-keeper in an earnest discussion, perhaps of land values. The park-keeper was at first determined to remember both his class and his official position, and treated Crompton with respectful disapproval. Strangers ought not to be so ready to talk to strangers, gentlemen should not be so easy with workingmen, and no one should talk to officials on duty. But this stiffness soon melted. Crompton was truly democratic. He always spoke to his clerks or his servants with the same tone that he would have used to an important person such as one of the Indian Rajahs whose affairs he handled, and his manner in a two-roomed Irish cabin was exactly the same as in a party of celebrities. I remember with what grave courtesy he rose to bow and shake hands with our parlourmaid, on hearing that she came from the same district as his family.

By temperament he was inclined to anarchism; he hated system and organization and uniformity. Once, when I was with him on Westminster Bridge, he pointed with delight to a tiny donkey-cart in the middle of the heavy traffic. 'That's what I like,' he said, 'freedom for all sorts.'

On another occasion, when I was walking with him in Ireland, we went to a bus station, where I, without thinking, made for the largest and most comfortable bus. His expression was quite shocked as he took me by the arm and hurried me away to a shabby little 'jalopie' of a bus, explaining gravely that it was pluckily defying the big combines.

His opinions were often somewhat wayward, and he had no objection to giving his prejudices free rein. He admired rebels rather more, perhaps, than was wholly rational. He had a horror of anything that seemed calculating, and I once shocked him deeply by saying that a war could not be justified unless there was a likelihood of victory. To him, heroic and almost hopeless defiance appeared splendid. Many of his prejudices were so consonant to my feelings that I never had the heart to argue with them—which in any case would have been a hopeless task.

With his temperament and opinions, it was natural that he should hate the Sidney Webbs. When they took up Poor Law Reform, he would say that, since everyone else rejected their attempts at regulation, they had at last been driven to organize the defenceless paupers. He would allege, as one of their triumphs of organization, that they employed a pauper with a peg leg to drill holes for the potatoes.

He was my lawyer for many years—a somewhat thankless task which he undertook out of friendship. Most of his practice consisted of affairs of great importance, concerning Indian Princes, Dominion Governments, or leading Banks. He showed, in legal matters, unbending straightforwardness, combined with skill and patience—this last truly astonishing, since nature had made him one of the most impatient of men. By these methods, which inspired confidence even in opponents, he achieved results which ingenious trickery could never have achieved. I remember the stony expression which came over his face during the course of a legal consultation when someone suggested a course that was not entirely straightforward.

With all his underlying seriousness, he was almost invariably gay. At the end of a long day of exhausting and responsible work he would arrive at a dinner party as jolly as if he had already enjoyed a good dose of champagne, and would keep everybody laughing. It was in the middle of a dinner party that he died, quite suddenly, of heart failure. Probably he had known that this was liable to happen, but he had kept the knowledge to himself. Afterwards, his friends remembered slight indications that he had not expected to live long, but they had not been sufficient to cause active anxiety among those who valued him.

In his last years he spent much of his leisure in writing a book on philosophy, which he referred to disparagingly as his 'pie-dish' in allusion to an old man in one of Ibsen's plays who had only one talent, the making of pie-dishes, and only one ambition, to make a really good pie-dish before he died. After Greek poetry, philosophy had been, when he was young, his main intellectual preoccupation; when I first knew him, we spent much time arguing about ethics and metaphysics. A busy professional life had kept him, throughout his middle years, engaged in practical affairs, but at last he was able to spare some time for purely theoretical thinking, to which he returned with wholehearted joy. When the book was nearly finished he lost it, as people do sometimes lose the things they value most. He left it in a train. It was never recovered. Someone must have picked it up in the hope that it had financial value. He mentioned the loss, sadly but briefly, said that there was nothing for it but to begin all over again from the few notes he had, and then changed the subject. We saw less of him during the few months that were left before his death, though when we did see him he was as gay and affectionate as ever. He was spending most of his spare energy on trying to make up the work that was lost; but the pie-dish was never finished.

Another friend of my Cambridge years was McTaggart, the philosopher, who was even shyer than I was. I heard a knock on my door one day—a very gentle knock. I said: 'come in', but nothing happened. I said, 'come in', louder. The door opened, and I saw McTaggart standing on the mat. He was already President of The Union, and about to become a Fellow, and inspired me with awe on account of his metaphysical reputation, but he was too shy to come in, and I was too shy to ask him to come in. I cannot remember how many minutes this situation lasted, but somehow or other he was at last in the room. After that I used frequently to go to his breakfasts, which were famous for their lack of food; in fact, anybody who had been once, brought an egg with him on every subsequent occasion. McTaggart was a Hegelian, and at that time still young and enthusiastic. He had a great intellectual influence upon my generation, though in retrospect I do not think it was a very good one. For two or three years, under his influence, I was a Hegelian. I remember the exact moment during my fourth year when I became one. I had gone out to buy a tin of tobacco, and was going back with it along Trinity Lane, when suddenly I threw it up in the air and exclaimed: 'Great God in boots!—the ontological argument is sound!' Although after 1898 I no longer accepted McTaggart's philosophy, I remained fond of him until an occasion during the first war, when he asked me no longer to come and see him because he could not bear my opinions. He followed this up by taking a leading part in having me turned out of my lectureship.

Two other friends whom I met in my early days in Cambridge and retained ever since, were Lowes Dickinson and Roger Fry. Dickinson was a man who inspired affection by his gentleness and pathos. When he was a Fellow and I was still an undergraduate, I became aware that I was liable to hurt him by my somewhat brutal statement of unpleasant truths, or what I thought to be such. States of the world which made me caustic only made him sad, and to the end of his days whenever I met him, I was afraid of increasing his unhappiness by too stark a realism. But perhaps realism is not quite the right word. What I really mean is the practice of describing things which one finds almost unendurable in such a repulsive manner as to cause others to share one's fury. He told me once that I resembled Cordelia, but it cannot be said that he resembled King Lear.

From my first moment at Cambridge, in spite of shyness, I was exceedingly sociable, and I never found that my having been educated at home was any impediment. Gradually, under the influence of congenial society, I became less and less solemn. At first the discovery that I could say things that I thought, and be answered with neither horror nor derision but as if I had said something quite sensible, was intoxicating. For a long time I supposed that somewhere in the university there were really clever people whom I had not yet met, and whom I should at once recognize as my intellectual superiors, but during my second year, I discovered that I already knew all the cleverest people in the university. This was a disappointment to me, but at the same time gave me increased self-confidence. In my third year, however, I met G. E. Moore, who was then a freshman, and for some years he fulfilled my ideal of genius. He was in those days beautiful and slim, with a look almost of inspiration, and with an intellect as deeply passionate as Spinoza's. He had a kind of exquisite purity. I have never but once succeeded in making him tell a lie, and that was by a subterfuge. 'Moore,' I said, 'do you *always* speak the truth?' 'No', he replied. I believe this to be the only lie he had ever told. His people lived in Dulwich, where I once went to see them. His father was a retired medical man, his mother wore a large china brooch with a picture of the Colosseum on it. He had sisters and brothers in large numbers, of whom the most interesting was the poet, Sturge Moore. In the world of intellect, he was fearless and adventurous, but in the everyday world he was a child. During my fourth year I spent some days walking with him on the coast of Norfolk. We fell in by accident with a husky fellow, who began talking about Petronius with intense relish for his indecencies. I rather encouraged the man, who amused me as a type. Moore remained completely silent until the man was gone, and then turned upon me, saying: 'that man was horrible.' I do not believe that he has ever in all his life derived the faintest pleasure from improper stories or conversation. Moore, like me, was influenced by McTaggart, and was for a short time a Hegelian. But he emerged more quickly than I did, and it was largely his conversation that led me to abandon both Kant and Hegel. In spite of his being two years younger than me, he greatly influenced my philosophical outlook. One of the pet amusements of all Moore's friends was to watch him trying to light a pipe. He would light a match, and then begin to argue, and continue until the match burnt his fingers. Then he would light another, and so on, until the box was finished. This was no doubt fortunate for his health, as it provided moments during which he was not smoking.

Then there were the three brothers Trevelyan. Charles, the eldest, was considered the least able of the three by all of us. Bob, the second, was my special friend. He became a very scholarly, but not very inspired, poet, but when he was young he had a delicious whimsical humour. Once, when we were on a reading party in the Lakes, Eddie Marsh, having overslept himself, came down in his night-shirt to see if breakfast was ready, looking frozen and miserable. Bob christened him 'cold white shape', and this name stuck to him for a long time. George Trevelyan was considerably younger than Bob, but I got to know him well later on. He and Charles were terrific walkers. Once when I went a walking tour with George in Devonshire, I made him promise to be content with twenty-five miles a day. He kept his promise until the last day. Then he left me, saying that now he must have a little walking. On another occasion, when I was walking alone, I arrived at the Lizard one evening and asked if they could give me a bed. 'Is your name Mr. Trevelyan?' they answered. 'No,' I said, 'are you expecting him?' 'Yes,' they said, 'and his wife is here already.' This surprised me, as I knew that it was his wedding day. I found her languishing alone, as he had left her at Truro, saying that he could not face the whole day without a little walk. He arrived about ten o'clock at night, completely exhausted, having accomplished the forty miles in record time, but it seemed to me a somewhat curious beginning for a honeymoon. On August 4, 1914, he and I walked together down the Strand quarrelling. Since then I saw him only once, until I returned to Trinity in 1944, after he had become Master. When he was still an undergraduate he explained to me once that the Trevelyans never make matrimonial mistakes. 'They wait', he said, 'until they are thirty, and then marry a girl who has both sense and money.' In spite of occasional bad times, I have never wished that I had followed this prescription.

Bob Trevelyan was, I think, the most bookish person that I have ever known. What is in books appeared to him interesting, whereas what is only real life was negligible. Like all the family, he had a minute knowledge of the strategy and tactics concerned in all the great battles of the world, so far as these appear in reputable books of history. But I was staying with him during the crisis of the battle of the Marne, and as it was Sunday we could only get a newspaper by walking two miles. He did not think the battle sufficiently interesting to be worth it, because battles in mere newspapers are vulgar. I once devised a test question which I put to many people to discover whether they were pessimists. The question was: 'If you had the power to destroy the world, would you do so?' I put the question to him in the presence of his wife and child, and he replied: 'What? Destroy my library?—Never!' He was always discovering new poets and reading their poems out aloud, but he always began deprecatingly: 'This is not one of his best poems.' Once when he mentioned a new poet to me, and said he would like to read me some of his things, I said: 'Yes, but don't read me a poem which is not one of his best.' This stumped him completely, and he put the volume away.

The dons contributed little to my enjoyment of Cambridge. The Master came straight out of Thackeray's *Book of Snobs*. He generally began his remarks with 'Just thirty years ago today . . .' or with, 'Do you by any chance remember what Mr Pitt was doing one hundred years ago today?', and he would then proceed to relate some very tedious historical anecdote to show how great and good were all the statesmen mentioned in history. His epistolary style is illustrated by the letter that he wrote me after the mathematical tripos in which I was bracketed seventh wrangler:

> Trinity Lodge,
> Cambridge,
> June 13th 1893

My dear B. Russell

I cannot tell you how happy this grand victory has made us. Just 33 years have passed since I placed the Fifth Form Prize for Latin Prose in the hands of your dear Father at Harrow, and now I am permitted to congratulate his son and his own Mother on a remarkable Mathematical success which will be much appreciated in the College.

We knew your Mathematical ability but we knew also that you had not given your whole mind to Mathematics but had bestowed large parts of it on other, possibly even greater, subjects. If this had seriously spoiled your Mathematical position I should of course have regretted it, but I should have understood that there were solid compensations.

Now there is happily nothing but congratulation, and you will look forward quietly to the Moral Science Tripos and the Fellowship without any misgiving that you have left behind you a Mathematical waste.

I must give myself the pleasure of writing just a few lines to Lady Russell and Lady Stanley. This will be a happy day for both of them.

> *Believe me to be,*
> *Most truly yours,*
> H. *Montagu Butler*
> (*Master of Trinity*)

I remember once going to breakfast at the Lodge, and it happened that the day was his sister-in-law's birthday. After wishing her many happy returns, he continued: 'Now, my dear, you have lasted just as long as the Peloponnesian War.' She did not know how long this might be, but feared it was longer than she could wish. His wife took to Christian Science, which had the effect of prolonging his life for some twenty years beyond what might otherwise have been expected. This happened through her lack of sympathy with his ailments. When he was ill, she would send word to the Council Meeting that the Master was in bed and refused to get up. It must be said, however, that the Vice-Master, Aldous Wright, and the Senior Fellow, Joey Prior, lasted almost equally long without the help of Christian Science. I remember when I was an undergraduate watching the three of them standing bare-headed at the Great Gate to receive the Empress Frederick. They were already very old men, but fifteen years later they seemed no older. Aldous Wright was a very dignified figure, standing always as straight as a ramrod, and never appearing out-of-doors without a top hat. Even once when he was roused from sleep at three in the morning by a fire the top hat was duly on his head. He stuck to the English pronunciation of Latin, while the Master adopted the Continental pronunciation. When they read grace in alternate verses, the effect was curious, especially as the Vice-Master gabbled it while the Master mouthed it with unction. While I was an undergraduate, I had regarded all these men merely as figures of fun, but when I became a Fellow and attended College meetings, I began to find that they were serious forces of evil. When the Junior Dean, a clergyman who raped his little daughter and became paralysed with syphilis, had to be got rid of in consequence, the Master went out of his way to state at College Meeting that those of us who did not attend chapel regularly had no idea how excellent this worthy's sermons had been. Next to these three the most important person in the College was the Senior Porter, a magnificent figure of a man, with such royal dignity that he was supposed by undergraduates to be a natural son of the future Edward the Seventh. After I was a Fellow I found that on one occasion the Council met on five successive days with the utmost secrecy. With great difficulty I discovered what their business had been. They had been engaged in establishing the painful fact that the Senior Porter had had improper relations with five bedmakers, in spite of the fact that all of them, by Statute, were *'nec juvenis, nec pulchra'*.

As an undergraduate I was persuaded that the Dons were a wholly unnecessary part of the university. I derived no benefits from lectures, and I made a vow to myself that when in due course I became a lecturer I would not suppose that lecturing did any good. I have kept this vow.

I had already been interested in philosophy before I went to Cambridge, but I had not read much except Mill. What I most desired was to find some reason for supposing mathematics true. The arguments in Mill's *Logic* on this subject already struck me as very inadequate. I read them at the age of eighteen. My mathematical tutors had never shown me any reason to suppose the Calculus anything but a tissue of fallacies. I had therefore two questions to trouble me, one philosophical, and one mathematical. The mathematical question had already in the main been solved on the Continent, though in England the Continental work was little known. It was only after I left Cambridge and began to live abroad that I discovered what I ought to have been taught during my three years as an undergraduate. Philosophy, however, was another matter. I knew in the country Harold Joachim, who taught philosophy at Merton, and was a friend of F. H. Bradley. Joachim's sister had married my Uncle Rollo, and I used to meet him occasionally at tennis-parties and such occasions. I got him to give me a long list of philosophical books that I ought to read, and while I was still working at mathematics I embarked upon them. As soon as I was free to do so, I devoted myself to philosophy with great ardour. During my fourth year I read most of the great philosophers as well as masses of books on the philosophy of mathematics. James Ward was always giving me fresh books on this subject, and each time I returned them, saying that they were very bad books. I remember his disappointment, and his painstaking endeavours to find some book that would satisfy me. In the end, but after I had become a Fellow, I got from him two small books, neither of which he had read or supposed of any value. They were Georg Cantor's *Mannichfaltigkeitslehre*, and Frege's *Begriffsschrift*. These two books at last gave me the gist of what I wanted, but in the case of Frege I possessed the book for years before I could make out what it meant. Indeed, I did not understand it until I had myself independently discovered most of what it contained.

By this time, I had quite ceased to be the shy prig that I was when I first went to Cambridge. I remember a few months before I came into residence, going to see my tutor about rooms, and while I waited in the ante-room I turned over the pages of the *Granta* (the undergraduate newspaper). It was May Week, and I was shocked to read in the paper that during this week people's thoughts were not devoted to work. But by my fourth year I had become gay and flippant. Having been reading pantheism, I announced to my friends that I was God. They placed candles on each side of me and proceeded to acts of mock worship. Philosophy altogether seemed to me great fun, and I enjoyed the curious ways of conceiving the world that the great philosophers offer to the imagination.

The greatest happiness of my time at Cambridge was connected with a body whom its members knew as 'The Society', but which outsiders, if they knew of it, called 'The Apostles'. This was a small discussion society, containing one or two people from each year on the average, which met every Saturday night. It has existed since 1820, and has had as members most of the people of any intellectual eminence who have been at Cambridge since then. It is by way of being secret, in order that those who are being considered for election may be unaware of the fact. It was owing to the existence of The Society that I so soon got to know the people best worth knowing, for Whitehead was a member, and told the younger members to investigate Sanger and me on account of our scholarship papers. With rare exceptions, all the members at any one time were close personal friends. It was a principle in discussion that there were to be no *taboos*, no limitations, nothing considered shocking, no barriers to absolute freedom of speculation. We discussed all manner of things, no doubt with a certain immaturity, but with a detachment and interest scarcely possible in later life. The meetings would generally end about one o'clock at night, and after that I would pace up and down the cloisters of Neville's Court for hours with one or two other members. We took ourselves perhaps rather seriously, for we considered that the virtue of intellectual honesty was in our keeping. Undoubtedly, we achieved more of this than is common in the world, and I am inclined to think that the best intelligence of Cambridge has been notable in this respect. I was elected in the middle of my second year, not having previously known that such a society existed, though the members were all intimately known to me already.

I was elected to The Society early in 1892. The following letters of congratulation require an explanation of some phrases which were adopted in The Society by way of making fun of German metaphysics. The Society was supposed to be The World of Reality; everything else was Appearance. People who were not members of The Society were called 'phenomena'. Since the metaphysicians maintained that Space and Time are unreal, it was assumed that those who were in The Society were exempted from bondage to Space and Time.

c/ Hon. Sir Charles Elliott, KCSI,
Lieut. Gov. of Bengal, India   Weds. March 9, 1892

Dear Russell

I have just heard by this morning's mail that you have joined us— Hurrah. It is good news indeed. I mustn't let the mail go off this afternoon without a few words to say how glad I am, and how sorry not to be at Cambridge now to give you a fraternal handshake. You will of course get your own impressions, but it was certainly a true new life to me, and a revelation of what Cambridge really was.

It is just time for letters to go, so I'm afraid I can't write just now to tell you of my experiences. Theodore will tell you how I am getting on. I was very sorry to hear that you had not been well. Get all right quick. Don't let Webb[1] kill you.

Excuse these hurried lines. Confound those absurd humbugs, space and time, which have the impudence to pretend that they are now separating us. Whereas we know that they have nothing to do with that

---

[1] My mathematical coach.

true existence in the bonds of which I was in the beginning am now and ever shall be

fraternally and affectionately yours
CROMPTON Ll. D.

I haven't time to write to Sanger a proper letter, so would you mind handing him the enclosed scrawl?
Do write to me if you have time.

Devon St., New Plymouth,
Taranaki, New Zealand.   17th May, 1892

Dear Russell

Many congratulations on the delightful news of last February, which —with a bondage to space and time perfectly inexplicable in apostolic matters—has only just reached me via India.

I am most awfully glad. I hope you have been told of our brother Whitehead's penetration, who detected the apostolic nature of yourself and Sanger by your entrance scholarship essays, and put us on the watch for you.

I wish I could get back for a Saturday night or so, and have it out with Theodore about Xtianity being the religion of love—just the one thing which it isn't I should say. I don't see how the ideas of a personal God and real love can coexist with any vigour.

How about the Embryos?[1] I hear that the younger Trevelyan (Bob) is very promising, and Green of Kings.

I have innumerable more letters for the mail. I hope to see you in the middle of next January.

Yours fraternally,
(*Sgd.*) *Ellis McTaggart*

Some things became considerably different in the Society shortly after my time.

The tone of the generation some ten years junior to my own was set mainly by Lytton Strachey and Keynes. It is surprising how great a change in mental climate those ten years had brought. We were still Victorian; they were Edwardian. We believed in ordered progress by means of politics and free discussion. The more self-confident among us may have hoped to be leaders of the multitude, but none of us wished to be divorced from it. The generation of Keynes and Lytton did not seek to preserve any kinship with the Philistine. They aimed rather at a life of retirement among fine shades and nice feelings, and conceived of the good as consisting in the passionate mutual admirations of a clique of

[1] Our name for people we were thinking of electing.

the élite. This doctrine, quite unfairly, they fathered upon G. E. Moore, whose disciples they professed to be. Keynes, in his memoir 'Early Beliefs' has told of their admiration for Moore's doctrine. Moore gave due weight to morals and by his doctrine of organic unities avoided the view that the good consists of a series of isolated passionate moments, but those who considered themselves his disciples ignored this aspect of his teaching and degraded his ethics into advocacy of a stuffy girls-school sentimentalizing.

From this atmosphere Keynes escaped into the great world, but Strachey never escaped. Keynes's escape, however, was not complete. He went about the world carrying with him everywhere a feeling of the bishop *in partibus*. True salvation was elsewhere, among the faithful at Cambridge. When he concerned himself with politics and economics he left his soul at home. This is the reason for a certain hard, glittering, inhuman quality in most of his writing. There was one great exception, *The Economic Consequences of the Peace*, of which I shall have more to say in a moment.

I first knew Keynes through his father, and Lytton Strachey through his mother. When I was young, Keynes's father taught old-fashioned formal logic in Cambridge. I do not know how far the new developments in that subject altered his teaching. He was an earnest Nonconformist who put morality first and logic second. Something of the Nonconformist spirit remained in his son, but it was overlaid by the realization that facts and arguments may lead to conclusions somewhat shocking to many people, and a strain of intellectual arrogance in his character made him find it not unpleasant to *épater les bourgeois*. In his *Economic Consequences of the Peace* this strain was in abeyance. The profound conviction that the Treaty of Versailles spelt disaster so roused the earnest moralist in him that he forgot to be clever—without, however, ceasing to be so.

I had no contact with him in his economic and political work, but I was considerably concerned in his *Treatise on Probability*, many parts of which I discussed with him in detail. It was nearly finished in 1914, but had to be put aside for the duration.

He was always inclined to overwork, in fact it was overwork that caused his death. Once in the year 1904, when I was living in an isolated cottage in a vast moor without roads, he wrote and asked if I could promise him a restful week-end. I replied confidently in the affirmative, and he came. Within five minutes of his arrival the Vice Chancellor turned up full of University business. Other people came unexpectedly to every meal, including six to Sunday breakfast. By Monday morning we had had twenty-six unexpected guests, and Keynes, I fear, went away more tired than he came. On Sunday, August 2, 1914, I met him hurrying across the Great Court of Trinity. I asked him what the hurry was and he said he wanted to borrow his brother-in-law's motorcycle to go to London. 'Why don't you go by train', I said. 'Because there isn't time', he replied. I did not know what his business might be, but within a few days the bank rate, which panic-mongers had put up to ten per cent, was reduced to five per cent. This was his doing.

I do not know enough economics to have an expert opinion on Keynes's theories, but so far as I am able to judge it seems to me to be owing to him that Britain has not suffered from large-scale unemployment in recent years. I would go further and say that if his theories had been adopted by financial authorities throughout the world the great depression would not have occurred. There are still many people in America who regard depressions as acts of God. I think Keynes proved that the responsibility for these occurrences does not rest with Providence.

The last time that I saw him was in the House of Lords when he returned from negotiating a loan in America and made a masterly speech recommending it to their Lordships. Many of them had been doubtful beforehand, but when he had finished there remained hardly any doubters except Lord Beaverbrook and two cousins of mine with a passion for being in the minority. Having only just landed from the Atlantic, the effort he made must have been terrific, and it proved too much for him.

Keynes's intellect was the sharpest and clearest that I have ever known. When I argued with him, I felt that I took my life in my hands, and I seldom emerged without feeling something of a fool. I was sometimes inclined to feel that so much cleverness must be incompatible with depth, but I do not think this feeling was justified.

Lytton Strachey, as mentioned before, I first got to know through his mother. She and I were fellow members of a committee designed to secure votes for women. After some months she invited me to dinner. Her husband, Sir Richard Strachey, was a retired Indian official, and the British Raj was very much in the air. My first dinner with the family was a rather upsetting experience. The number of sons and daughters was almost beyond computation, and all the children were to my unpractised eyes exactly alike except in the somewhat superficial point that some were male and some were female. The family were not all assembled when I arrived, but dropped in one by one at intervals of twenty minutes. (One of them, I afterwards discovered, was Lytton.) I had to look round the room carefully to make sure that it was a new one that had appeared and not merely one of the previous ones that had changed his or her place. Towards the end of the evening I began to doubt my sanity, but kind friends afterwards assured me that things had really been as they seemed.

Lady Strachey was a woman of immense vigour, with a great desire that some at least of her children should distinguish themselves. She had an admirable sense of prose and used to read South's sermons aloud to her children, not for the matter (she was a free thinker), but to give them a sense of rhythm in the writing of English. Lytton, who was too delicate to be sent to a conventional school, was seen by his mother to be brilliant, and was brought up to the career of a writer in an atmosphere of dedication. His writing appeared to me in those days hilariously amusing. I heard him read *Eminent Victorians* before it was published, and I read it again to myself in prison. It caused me to laugh so loud that the officer came round to my cell, saying I must remember that prison is a place of punishment.

Lytton was always eccentric and became gradually more so. When he was growing a beard he gave out that he had measles so as not to be seen by his friends until the hairs had reached a respectable length. He dressed very oddly. I knew a farmer's wife who let lodgings and she told me that Lytton had come to ask her if she could take him in. 'At first, Sir,' she said, 'I thought he was a tramp, and then I looked again and saw he was a gentleman, but a very queer one.' He talked always in a squeaky voice which sometimes contrasted ludicrously with the matter of what he was saying. One time when I was talking with him he objected first to one thing and then to another as not being what literature should aim at. At last I said, 'Well, Lytton, what should it aim at?' And he replied in one word—'Passion'. Nevertheless, he liked to appear lordly in his attitude towards human affairs. I heard someone maintain in his presence that young people are apt to think about Life. He objected, 'I can't believe people think about Life. There's nothing in it.' Perhaps it was this attitude which made him not a great man.

His style is unduly rhetorical, and sometimes, in malicious moments, I have thought it not unlike Macaulay's. He is indifferent to historical truth and will always touch up the picture to make the lights and shades more glaring and the folly or wickedness of famous people more obvious. These are grave charges, but I make them in all seriousness.

It was in The Society that I first became aware of Moore's excellence. I remember his reading a paper which began: 'In the beginning was matter, and matter begat the devil, and the devil begat God.' The paper ended with the death first of God and then of the devil, leaving matter alone as in the beginning. At the time when he read this paper, he was still a freshman, and an ardent disciple of Lucretius.

On Sunday it was our custom to breakfast late, and then spend the whole day till dinner-time walking. I got to know every road and footpath within ten miles of Cambridge, and many at much greater distances, in this way. In general I felt happy and comparatively calm while at

Cambridge, but on moonlight nights I used to career round the country in a state of temporary lunacy. The reason, of course, was sexual desire, though at that time I did not know this.

After my time The Society changed in one respect. There was a long drawn out battle between George Trevelyan and Lytton Strachey, both members, in which Lytton Strachey was on the whole victorious. Since his time, homosexual relations among the members were for a time common, but in my day they were unknown.

Cambridge was important in my life through the fact that it gave me friends, and experience of intellectual discussion, but it was not important through the actual academic instruction. Of the mathematical teaching I have already spoken. Most of what I learned in philosophy has come to seem to me erroneous, and I spent many subsequent years in gradually unlearning the habits of thought which I had there acquired. The one habit of thought of real value that I acquired there was intellectual honesty. This virtue certainly existed not only among my friends, but among my teachers. I cannot remember any instance of a teacher resenting it when one of his pupils showed him to be in error, though I can remember quite a number of occasions on which pupils succeeded in performing this feat. Once during a lecture on hydrostatics, one of the young men interrupted to say: 'Have you not forgotten the centrifugal forces on the lid?' The lecturer gasped, and then said: 'I have been doing this example that way for twenty years, but you are right.' It was a blow to me during the War to find that, even at Cambridge, intellectual honesty had its limitations. Until then, wherever I lived, I felt that Cambridge was the only place on earth that I could regard as home.

CHAPTER IV

ENGAGEMENT

IN THE SUMMER of 1889, when I was living with my Uncle Rollo at his house on the slopes of Hindhead, he took me one Sunday for a long walk. As we were going down Friday's Hill, near Fernhurst, he said: 'Some new people have come to live at this house, and I think we will call upon them.' Shyness made me dislike the idea, and I implored him, whatever might happen, not to stay to supper. He said he would not, but he did, and I was glad he did. We found that the family were Americans, named Pearsall Smith, consisting of an elderly mother and father, a married daughter and her husband, named Costelloe, a younger daughter at Bryn Mawr home for the holidays, and a son at Balliol. The father and mother had been in their day famous evangelistic preachers, but the father had lost his faith as the result of a scandal which arose from his having been seen to kiss a young woman, and the mother had grown rather too old for such a wearing life. Costelloe, the son-in-law, was a clever man, a Radical, a member of the London County Council. He arrived fresh from London while we were at dinner, bringing the latest news of a great dock strike which was then in progress. This dock strike was of considerable interest and importance because it marked the penetration of Trade Unionism to a lower level than that previously reached. I listened open-mouthed while he related what was being done, and I felt that I was in touch with reality. The son from Balliol conversed in brilliant epigrams, and appeared to know everything with contemptuous ease. But it was the daughter from Bryn Mawr who especially interested me. She was very beautiful, as appears from the following extract from the *Bulletin*, Glasgow, May 10, 1921: 'I remember meeting Mrs Bertrand Russell at a civic reception or something of the kind (was it a reception to temperance delegates?) in Edinburgh twenty odd years ago. She was at that time one of the most beautiful women it is possible to imagine, and gifted with a sort of imperial stateliness, for all her Quaker stock. We who were present admired her so much that in a collected and dignified Edinburgh way we made her the heroine of the evening.' She was more emancipated than any young woman I had known, since she

75

was at college and crossed the Atlantic alone, and was, as I soon discovered, an intimate friend of Walt Whitman. She asked me whether I had ever read a certain German book called *Ekkehard*, and it happened that I had finished it that morning. I felt this was a stroke of luck. She was kind, and made me feel not shy. I fell in love with her at first sight. I did not see any of the family again that summer, but in subsequent years, during the three months that I spent annually with my Uncle Rollo, I used to walk the four miles to their house every Sunday, arriving to lunch and staying to supper. After supper they would make a camp fire in the woods, and sit round singing negro spirituals, which were in those days unknown in England. To me, as to Goethe, America seemed a romantic land of freedom, and I found among them an absence of many prejudices which hampered me at home. Above all, I enjoyed their emancipation from good taste. It was at their house that I first met Sidney Webb, then still unmarried.

Sidney and Beatrice Webb, whom I knew intimately for a number of years, at times even sharing a house with them, were the most completely married couple that I have ever known. They were, however, very averse from any romantic view of love or marriage. Marriage was a social institution designed to fit instinct into a legal framework. During the first ten years of their marriage, Mrs Webb would remark at intervals, 'as Sidney always says, marriage is the waste-paper basket of the emotions'. In later years there was a slight change. They would generally have a couple to stay with them for the week-end, and on Sunday afternoon they would go for a brisk walk, Sidney with the lady and Beatrice with the gentleman. At a certain point, Sidney would remark, 'I know just what Beatrice is saying at this moment. She is saying, "as Sidney always says, marriage is the waste-paper basket of the emotions".' Whether Sidney ever really did say this is not known.

I knew Sidney before his marriage. But he was then much less than half of what the two of them afterwards became. Their collaboration was quite dove-tailed. I used to think, though this was perhaps an undue simplification, that she had the ideas and he did the work. He was perhaps the most industrious man that I have ever known. When they were writing a book on local government, they would send circulars to all local government officials throughout the country asking questions and pointing out that the official in question could legally purchase their forthcoming book out of the rates. When I let my house to them, the postman, who was an ardent socialist, did not know whether to be more honoured by serving them or annoyed at having to deliver a thousand answers a day to their circulars. Webb was originally a second division clerk in the civil service, but by immense industry succeeded in rising into the first division. He was somewhat earnest and did not like jokes on sacred subjects such as political theory. On one occasion I remarked to him that democracy has at least one merit, namely, that a Member of Parliament cannot be stupider than his constituents, for the more stupid he is, the more stupid they were to elect him. Webb was seriously annoyed and said bitingly, 'that is the sort of argument I don't like'.

Mrs Webb had a wider range of interests than her husband. She took considerable interest in individual human beings, not only when they could be useful. She was deeply religious without belonging to any recognized brand of orthodoxy, though as a socialist she preferred the Church of England because it was a State institution. She was one of nine sisters, the daughters of a self-made man named Potter who acquired most of his fortune by building huts for the armies in the Crimea. He was a disciple of Herbert Spencer, and Mrs Webb was the most notable product of that philosopher's theories of education. I am sorry to say that my mother, who was her neighbour in the country, described her as a 'social butterfly', but one may hope that she would have modified this judgment if she had known Mrs Webb in later life. When she became interested in socialism she decided to sample the Fabians, especially the three most distinguished, who were Webb, Shaw and Graham Wallas. There was something like the Judgment of Paris with the sexes reversed, and it was Sidney who emerged as the counterpart of Aphrodite.

Webb had been entirely dependent upon his earnings, whereas Beatrice had inherited a competence from her father. Beatrice had the mentality of the governing class, which Sidney had not. Seeing that they had enough to live on without earning, they decided to devote their lives to research and to the higher branches of propaganda. In both they were amazingly successful. Their books are a tribute to their industry, and the School of Economics is a tribute to Sidney's skill. I do not think that Sidney's abilities would have been nearly as fruitful as they were if they had not been backed by Beatrice's self-confidence. I asked her once whether in her youth she had ever had any feeling of shyness. 'O no,' she said, 'if I ever felt inclined to be timid as I was going into a room full of people, I would say to myself, "you're the cleverest member of one of the cleverest families in the cleverest class of the cleverest nation in the world, why should you be frightened".'

I both liked and admired Mrs Webb, although I disagreed with her about many very important matters. I admired first and foremost her ability, which was very great. I admired next her integrity: she lived for public objects and was never deflected by personal ambition, although she was not devoid of it. I liked her because she was a warm and kind friend to those for whom she had a personal affection, but I disagreed with her about religion, about imperialism, and about the worship of the State. This last was of the essence of Fabianism. It led both the Webbs and also Shaw into what I thought an undue tolerance of Mussolini and Hitler, and ultimately into a rather absurd adulation of the Soviet Government.

But nobody is all of a piece, not even the Webbs. I once remarked to Shaw that Webb seemed to me somewhat deficient in kindly feeling. 'No,' Shaw replied, 'you are quite mistaken. Webb and I were once in a tram-car in Holland eating biscuits out of a bag. A handcuffed criminal was brought into the tram by policemen. All the other passengers shrank away in horror, but Webb went up to the prisoner and offered him biscuits.' I remember this story whenever I find myself becoming unduly critical of either Webb or Shaw.

There were people whom the Webbs hated. They hated Wells, both because he offended Mrs Webb's rigid Victorian morality and because he tried to dethrone Webb from his reign over the Fabian Society. They hated Ramsay MacDonald from very early days. The least hostile thing that I ever heard either of them say about him was at the time of the formation of the first Labour Government, when Mrs Webb said he was a very good substitute for a leader.

Their political history was rather curious. At first they co-operated with the Conservatives because Mrs Webb was pleased with Arthur Balfour for being willing to give more public money to Church Schools. When the Conservatives fell in 1906, the Webbs made some slight and ineffectual efforts to collaborate with the Liberals. But at last it occurred to them that as socialists they might feel more at home in the Labour Party, of which in their later years they were loyal members.

For a number of years Mrs Webb was addicted to fasting, from motives partly hygienic and partly religious. She would have no breakfast and a very meagre dinner. Her only solid meal was lunch. She almost always had a number of distinguished people to lunch, but she would get so hungry that the moment it was announced she marched in ahead of all her guests and started to eat. She nevertheless believed that starvation made her more spiritual, and once told me that it gave her exquisite visions. 'Yes,' I replied, 'if you eat too little, you see visions; and if you drink too much, you see snakes.' I am afraid she thought this remark inexcusably flippant. Webb did not share the religious side of her nature, but was in no degree hostile to it, in spite of the fact that it was sometimes inconvenient to him. When they and I were staying at a hotel in Normandy, she used to stay upstairs in the mornings since she could not bear the painful spectacle of us breakfasting. Sidney, however, would come down for rolls and coffee. The first morning Mrs Webb sent a message by the maid, 'we do not have butter for Sidney's breakfast'. Her use of 'we' was one of the delights of their friends.

Both of them were fundamentally undemocratic, and regarded it as the function of a statesman to bamboozle or terrorize the populace. I realized the origins of Mrs Webb's conceptions of government when she repeated to me her father's description of shareholders' meetings. It is the recognized function of directors to keep shareholders in their place, and she had a similar view about the relation of the Government to the electorate.

Her father's stories of his career had not given her any undue respect for the great. After he had built huts for the winter quarters of the French armies in the Crimea, he went to Paris to get paid. He had spent almost all his capital in putting up the huts, and payment became important to him. But, although everybody in Paris admitted the debt, the cheque did not come. At last he met Lord Brassey who had come on a similar errand. When Mr Potter explained his difficulties, Lord Brassey laughed at him and said, 'my dear fellow, you don't know the ropes. You must give fifty pounds to the Minister and five pounds to each of his underlings.' Mr Potter did so, and the cheque came next day.

Sidney had no hesitation in using wiles which some would think unscrupulous. He told me, for example, that when he wished to carry some point through a committee where the majority thought otherwise, he would draw up a resolution in which the contentious point occurred twice. He would have a long debate about its first occurrence and at last give way graciously. Nine times out of ten, so he concluded, no one would notice that the same point occurred later in the same resolution.

The Webbs did a great work in giving intellectual backbone to British socialism. They performed more or less the same function that the Benthamites at an earlier time had performed for the Radicals. The Webbs and the Benthamites shared a certain dryness and a certain coldness and a belief that the waste-paper basket is the place for the emotions. But the Benthamites and the Webbs alike taught their doctrines to enthusiasts. Bentham and Robert Owen could produce a well-balanced intellectual progeny and so could the Webbs and Keir Hardie. One should not demand of anybody all the things that add value to a human being. To have some of them is as much as should be demanded. The Webbs pass this test, and indubitably the British Labour Party would have been much more wild and woolly if they had never existed. Their mantle descended upon Mrs Webb's nephew Sir Stafford Cripps, and but for them I doubt whether the British democracy would have endured with the same patience the arduous years through which we have been passing.

When I mentioned at home that I had met Sidney Webb, my grand-mother replied that she had heard him lecture once in Richmond, and that he was 'not quite. . . .' 'Not quite what?' I persisted. 'Not quite a gentleman in mind or manners,' she finally said.

Among the Pearsall Smiths I escaped from this sort of thing. Among them I was happy and talkative and free from timidity. They would draw me out in such a way as to make me feel quite intelligent. I met interesting people at their house, for instance William James. Logan Pearsall Smith indoctrinated me with the culture of the nineties—Flaubert, Walter Pater, and the rest. He gave me rules for good writing, such as 'Put a comma every four words; never use "and" except at the beginning of a sentence'. I learned to make sentences full of paren-theses in the style of Walter Pater. I learned the right thing to say about Manet, and Monet, and Degas, who were in those days what Matisse and Picasso were at a later date.

Logan Pearsall Smith was seven years older than I was, and gave me much moral advice. He was in a state of transition between the ethical outlook of Philadelphia Quakerism and that of Quartier-Latin Bohemia. Politically he was a socialist, having been converted by Graham Wallas, one of the founders of the Fabian Society (who, however, at a later date reverted to Liberalism). Logan tried to adapt the philanthropic practice of the Quakers to the socialist creed. In sexual morality he was at that time very ascetic, in fact almost Mani-chaean, but in religion he was agnostic. He wished to persuade free-thinking young people to preserve a high standard of personal dis-cipline and self-denial. With this object, he created what he called humorously 'The Order of Prigs', which I joined, and whose rules I obeyed for several years.[1]

With each year that passed I became more devoted to Alys, the unmarried daughter. She was less flippant than her brother Logan, and less irresponsible than her sister, Mrs Costelloe. She seemed to me to possess all the simple kindness which I still cherished in spite of Pembroke Lodge, but to be devoid of priggery and prejudice. I won-dered whether she would remain unmarried until I grew up, for she was five years older than I was. It seemed unlikely, but I became increasingly determined that, if she did, I would ask her to marry me. Once, I remember, I drove with her and her brother to Leith Hill to visit Judge Vaughan Williams, whose wife wore an Elizabethan ruff and was otherwise surprising. On the way they elicited from me that I believed in love at first sight, and chaffed me for being so sentimental. I felt deeply wounded, as the time had not yet come to say why I believed

---

[1] I give the rules in the Appendix on p. 88, and these are followed by fragments of some of the letters received from L. P. S. during my years at Cambridge.

in it. I was aware that she was not what my grandmother would call a lady, but I considered that she resembled Jane Austen's Elizabeth Bennett. I think I was conscious of a certain pleasurable broadmindedness in this attitude.

I came of age in May 1893, and from this moment my relations with Alys began to be something more than distant admiration. In the following month I was Seventh Wrangler in the mathematical Tripos, and acquired legal and financial independence. Alys came to Cambridge with a cousin of hers, and I had more opportunities of talking with her than I had ever had before. During the Long Vacation, she came again with the same cousin, but I persuaded her to stay for the inside of a day after the cousin was gone. We went on the river, and discussed divorce, to which she was more favourable than I was. She was in theory an advocate of free-love, which I considered admirable on her part, in spite of the fact that my own views were somewhat more strict. I was, however, a little puzzled to find that she was deeply ashamed of the fact that her sister had abandoned her husband for Berenson, the art critic. Indeed, it was not till after we were married that she consented to know Berenson. I was very much excited by her second visit to Cambridge, and began to correspond regularly with her. I was no longer spending the summers at Haslemere, because my grandmother and my Aunt Agatha did not get on with my Uncle Rollo's second wife. But on the 13th of September, I went to Friday's Hill for a two days' visit. The weather was warm and golden. There was not a breath of wind, and in the early morning there were mists in the valleys. I remember that Logan made fun of Shelley for speaking of 'golden mists', and I in turn made fun of Logan, saying there had been a golden mist that very morning, but before he was awake. For my part I was up and about early, having arranged with Alys to go for a walk before breakfast. We went and sat in a certain beech-wood on a hill, a place of extraordinary beauty looking like an early Gothic cathedral, and with a glimpse of distant views through the tree trunks in all directions. The morning was fresh and dewy, and I began to think that perhaps there might be happiness in human life. Shyness, however, prevented me from getting beyond feeling my way while we sat in the wood. It was only after breakfast, and then with infinite hesitation and alarm, that I arrived at a definite proposal, which was in those days the custom. I was neither accepted nor rejected. It did not occur to me to attempt to kiss her, or even take her hand. We agreed to go on seeing each other and corresponding, and to let time decide one way or the other. All this happened out-of-doors, but when we finally came in to lunch, she found a letter from Lady Henry Somerset, inviting her to the Chicago World's Fair to help in preaching temperance, a virtue of which in those days America was supposed not to have enough. Alys had inherited from her mother an ardent belief in total abstinence, and was much elated to get this invitation. She read it out triumphantly, and accepted it enthusiastically, which made me feel rather small, as it meant several months of absence, and possibly the beginning of an interesting career.

When I came home, I told my people what had occurred, and they reacted according to the stereotyped convention. They said she was no lady, a baby-snatcher, a low-class adventuress, a designing female taking advantage of my inexperience, a person incapable of all the finer feelings, a woman whose vulgarity would perpetually put me to shame. But I had a fortune of some £20,000 inherited from my father, and I paid no attention to what my people said. Relations became very strained, and remained so until after I was married.

At this time I kept a locked diary, which I very carefully concealed from everyone. In this diary I recorded my conversations with my grandmother about Alys and my feelings in regard to them. Not long afterwards a diary of my father's, written partly in shorthand (obviously for purposes of concealment), came into my hands. I found that he had proposed to my mother at just the same age at which I had proposed to Alys, that my grandmother had said almost exactly the same things to him as she had to me, and that he had recorded exactly the same reflections in his diary as I had recorded in mine. This gave me an uncanny feeling that I was not living my own life but my father's over again, and tended to produce a superstitious belief in heredity.[1]

Although I was deeply in love, I felt no conscious desire for any physical relations. Indeed, I felt that my love had been desecrated when one night I had a sexual dream, in which it took a less ethereal form. Gradually, however, nature took charge of this matter.

The next occasion of importance was on January 4, 1894, when I came up from Richmond for the day to visit Alys at her parents' house, 44 Grosvenor Road. It was a day on which there was a heavy snow-storm. All London was buried under about six inches of snow, and I had to wade through it on foot from Vauxhall. The snow brought a strange effect of isolation, making London almost as noiseless as a lonely hill top. It was on this occasion that I first kissed Alys. My only previous experience in this direction was with the housemaid mentioned in an earlier chapter, and I had not foreseen how great would be the ecstasy of kissing a woman whom I loved. Although she still

[1] In a letter to Alys, September 2, 1894, I wrote: 'My Aunt Georgy [the Lady Georgiana Peel, my grandmother's step-daughter] yesterday was very kind, but too inquisitive (as indeed most women are); she said even in old times at the slightest thought of a marriage my grandmother used to get into a sort of fever and be fussy and worried about it.'

said that she had not made up her mind whether to marry me or not, we spent the whole day, with the exception of meal-times, in kissing, with hardly a word spoken from morning till night, except for an interlude during which I read *Epipsychidion* aloud. I arrived home quite late, having walked the mile and a half from the station through a blizzard, tired but exultant.

Throughout my next term at Cambridge, there were alternations in her feelings. At some moments she seemed eager to marry me, and at other moments determined to retain her freedom. I had to work very hard during this time, as I was taking the second part of the Moral Sciences Tripos in one year, but I never found that love, either when it prospered or when it did not, interfered in the slightest with my intellectual concentration. When the Easter Vacation came, I went first with my Aunt Maude to Rome to stay with my uncle the Monsignor. And from there I went to Paris, where Logan had an apartment, and his mother and Alys were staying close by. It was my first experience of the life of American art students in Paris, and it all seemed to me very free and delightful. I remember a dance at which Alys appeared in a dress designed by Roger Fry. I remember, also, some rather unsuccessful attempts to instil culture into me by taking me to see Impressionist pictures in the Luxembourg. And I remember floating on the Seine at night near Fontainebleau with Alys beside me, while Logan filled the night with unbending cleverness. When I got back to Cambridge, James Ward spoke to me gravely about wasting my last vacation on the Continent when I ought to have been working. However, I did not take him seriously, and I got a First with distinction.

About the time that I finished with Triposes, Alys consented to become definitely engaged to me. At this, my people, who had never ceased from opposition, began to feel that something drastic must be done. They had no power to control my actions, and their strictures on her character had naturally remained without effect. Nevertheless, they found a weapon which very nearly gave them the victory. The old family doctor, a serious Scotsman with mutton-chop whiskers, began to tell me all the things that I had dimly suspected about my family history: how my Uncle William was mad, how my Aunt Agatha's engagement had had to be broken off because of her insane delusions, and how my father had suffered from epilepsy (from what medical authorities have told me since, I doubt whether this was a correct diagnosis). In those days, people who considered themselves scientific tended to have a somewhat superstitious attitude towards heredity, and of course it was not known how many mental disorders are the result of bad environment and unwise moral instruction. I began to feel as if I was doomed to a dark destiny. I read Ibsen's *Ghosts* and

Björnson's *Heritage of the Kurts*. Alys had an uncle who was rather queer. By emphasizing these facts until they rendered me nearly insane, my people persuaded us to take the best medical opinion as to whether, if we were married, our children were likely to be mad. The best medical opinion, primed by the family doctor, who was primed by the family, duly pronounced that from the point of view of heredity we ought not to have children. After receiving this verdict in the house of the family doctor at Richmond, Alys and I walked up and down Richmond Green discussing it. I was for breaking off the engagement, as I believed what the doctors said and greatly desired children. Alys said she had no great wish for children, and would prefer to marry, while avoiding a family. After about half an hour's discussion, I came round to her point of view. We therefore announced that we intended to marry, but to have no children. Birth control was viewed in those days with the sort of horror which it now inspires only in Roman Catholics. My people and the family doctor tore their hair. The family doctor solemnly assured me that, as a result of his medical experience, he knew the use of contraceptives to be almost invariably gravely injurious to health. My people hinted that it was the use of contraceptives which had made my father epileptic. A thick atmosphere of sighs, tears, groans, and morbid horror was produced, in which it was scarcely possible to breathe. The discovery that my father had been epileptic, my aunt subject to delusions, and my uncle insane, caused me terror, for in those days everybody viewed the inheritance of mental disorders superstitiously. I had sensed something of the kind, though without definite knowledge. On July 21, 1893 (which I subsequently learnt to be Alys's birthday), I dreamed that I discovered my mother to be mad, not dead, and that, on this ground, I felt it my duty not to marry. After the facts had been told to me, I had great difficulty in shaking off fear, as appears from the following reflections, which I showed to nobody, not even Alys, until a much later date.

July 20–21 (1894). Midnight. This night is the anniversary of my dream about Alys, and also of her birth. Strange coincidence, which, combined with the fact that most of my dream has come true, very strongly impresses my imagination. I was always superstitious, and happiness has made me more so; it is terrifying to be so utterly absorbed in one person. Nothing has any worth to me except in reference to her. Even my own career, my efforts after virtue, my intellect (such as it is), everything I have or hope for, I value only as gifts to her, as means of shewing how unspeakably I value her love. And I am happy, divinely happy. Above all, I can still say, thank God, lust has absolutely no share in my passion. But just when I am happiest, when joy is purest, it seems to transcend itself and fall suddenly to haunting terrors of loss —it would be so easy to lose what rests on so slender and unstable a foundation! My dream on her birthday; my subsequent discovery that my people *had* deceived me as in that dream; their solemn and reiterated warnings; the gradual discovery, one by one, of the tragedies, hopeless and unalleviated, which have made up the lives of most of my family; above all, the perpetual gloom which hangs like a fate over PL,[1] and which, struggle as I will, invades my inmost soul whenever I go there, taking all joy even out of Alys's love; all these, combined with the fear of heredity, cannot but oppress my mind. They make me feel as though a doom lay on the family and I were vainly battling against it to escape into the freedom which seems the natural birthright of others. Worst of all, this dread, of necessity, involves Alys too. I feel as tho' darkness were my native element, and a cruel destiny had compelled me, instead of myself attaining to the light, to drag her back with me into the gulf from which I have partially emerged. I cannot tell whether destiny will take the form of a sudden blow or of a long-drawn torture, sapping our energies and ruining our love; but I am haunted by the fear of the family ghost, which seems to seize on me with clammy invisible hands to avenge my desertion of its tradition of gloom.

All these feelings of course are folly, solely due to chocolate cake and sitting up late; but they are none the less real, and on the slightest pretence they assail me with tremendous force. Painful as it will necessarily be to them, I must for some time avoid seeing more than a very little of my people and of PL, otherwise I really shall begin to fear for my sanity. PL is to me like a family vault haunted by the ghosts of maniacs—especially in view of all that I have recently learnt from Dr Anderson. Here, thank heaven, all is bright and healthy, my Alys especially; and as long as I can forget PL and the ghastly heritage it bequeaths to me I have no forebodings, but only the pure joy of mutual love, a joy so great, so divine, that I have not yet ceased to wonder how such a thing can exist in this world which people abuse. But oh I *wish* I could know it would bring joy to her in the end, and not teach her further, what alas it has already begun to teach her, how terrible a thing life may be and what depths of misery it can contain.

The fears generated at that time have never ceased to trouble me subconsciously. Ever since, but not before, I have been subject to violent nightmares in which I dream that I am being murdered, usually by a lunatic. I scream out loud, and on one occasion, before waking, I nearly

[1] Pembroke Lodge.

strangled my wife, thinking that I was defending myself against a murderous assault.

The same kind of fear caused me, for many years, to avoid all deep emotion, and live, as nearly as I could, a life of intellect tempered by flippancy. Happy marriage gradually gave me mental stability, and when, at a later date, I experienced new emotional storms, I found that I was able to remain sane. This banished the conscious fear of insanity, but the unconscious fear has persisted.

Whatever indecision I had felt as to what we ought to do was ended when Alys and I found another doctor, who assured me breezily that he had used contraceptives himself for many years, that no bad effects whatever were to be feared, and that we should be fools not to marry. So we went ahead, in spite of the shocked feelings of two generations. As a matter of fact, after we had been married two years we came to the conclusion that the medical authorities whom we had consulted had been talking nonsense, as indeed they obviously were, and we decided to have children if possible. But Alys proved to be barren, so the fuss had been all about nothing.

At the conclusion of this *fracas* I went to live at Friday's Hill with Alys's people, and there I settled down to work at a Fellowship dissertation, taking non-Euclidean Geometry as my subject. My people wrote almost daily letters to me about 'the life you are leading', but it was clear to me that they would drive me into insanity if I let them, and that I was getting mental health from Alys. We grew increasingly intimate.

My people, however, were not at the end of their attempts. In August they induced Lord Dufferin, who was then our Ambassador in Paris, to offer me the post of honorary attaché. I had no wish to take it, but my grandmother said that she was not much longer for this world, and that I owed it to her to see whether separation would lessen my infatuation. I did not wish to feel remorse whenever she came to die, so I agreed to go to Paris for a minimum of three months, on the understanding that if that produced no effect upon my feelings, my people would no longer actively oppose my marriage. My career in diplomacy, however, was brief and inglorious. I loathed the work, and the people, and the atmosphere of cynicism, and the separation from Alys. My brother came over to visit me, and although I did not know it at the time, he had been asked to come by my people, in order to form a judgment on the situation. He came down strongly on my side, and when the three months were up, which was on November 17th, I shook the dust of Paris off my feet, and returned to Alys. I had, however, first to make my peace with her, as she had grown jealous of her sister, of whom I saw a good deal during the latter part of my time in Paris. It must be said that making my peace only took about ten minutes.

The only thing of any permanent value that I derived from my time in Paris was the friendship of Jonathan Sturges, a man for whom I had a very great affection. Many years after his death, I went to see Henry James's house at Rye, which was kept at that time as a sort of museum. There I suddenly came upon Sturges's portrait hanging on the wall. It gave me so great a shock that I remember nothing else whatever about the place. He was a cripple, intensely sensitive, very literary, and belonging to what one must call the American aristocracy (he was a nephew of J. P. Morgan). He was a very witty man. I took him once into the Fellows' Garden at Trinity, and he said: 'Oh yes! This is where George Eliot told F. W. H. Myers that there is no God, and yet we must be good; and Myers decided that there is a God, and yet we need not be good.' I saw a great deal of him during my time in Paris, which laid the foundations of a friendship that ended only with his death.

LETTERS

15 rue du Sommerard
Paris
Oct. 25 '9?

My dear Bertie

I have been meaning to write to you before, to tell you how much I enjoyed my visit to Cambridge, but I have been through such a season of woe in settling myself here! It is all due to that bothersome new order, for it is very hard to get rooms within the fixed margin, and I am much too proud to confess an excess so soon. So I have at last settled myself in the Latin Quarter, up seven flights of stairs, and I find that the spiritual pride that fills my breast more than amply compensates for all the bother. It *is* nice to feel better than one's neighbours! I met a friend yesterday who is living in cushioned ease across the river, and I felt so very superior, I am rather afraid that when I write to my adviser, I shall receive a hair shirt by return of post. Have you tried to observe the discipline? I do not speak evil, for I have no one to speak it to, though I think it of my landlady. And the other day, I was so reduced by the state of my things when I moved here that I could do nothing but eat a bun and read Tid-bits.

I have begun to write a novel, but be assured, it is not religious, and is not to be rejected by the publishers for a year or two yet.

My journey here after I left you was most amusing. On the steamer we sat in rows and glared at each other, after the pleasant English manner. There was a young married couple who stood out as a warning and a lesson to youth. He was a puzzled looking, beardless young man, and she was a limp figure of a woman, and there was a baby. The husband poured his wife into an arm-chair, and then walked up and down with the baby. Then he stood for a long while, looking at the watery horizon as if he were asking some question of it. But the dismal unwellness of his wife and baby soon put an end to his meditations. What a warning to youth! And I might have been in his place!

I hope you went to the debate to prove that the upper classes are un-educated—those broad generalizations are so stimulating—there is so much that one can say.

I hope you mean to join our order, and if you do, make me your adviser. I will set you nice penances, and then I shall be sure to hear from you—for there must be some rules that you will break—some rift in your integrity.

Give my regards to Sheldon Amos if you see him.

> *Yours ever,*
> *Logan Pearsall Smith*

15 Rue du Sommerard
Paris
Nov. 1891

Dear Bertie

I enclose the rules—the general outlines—we must have a meeting of the Order before long to settle them definitely. As for rule one, you had better fix a sum, and then keep to that. By the account you enclosed to me, you appear to be living on eggs and groceries—I should advise you to dine occasionally. Then at College one ought to entertain more or less—and that ought not to count as board and lodging. As to rule 4—I should say at College it is perhaps better not to do too much at social work.

What you say about changing one's self denial is only too true and terrible —it went to my heart—one does form a habit, and then it is no bother. I will write to the Arch Prig about it.

Of course you must consider yourself a member, and you must confess to me, and I will write you back some excellent ghostly advice. And you must get other members. We shall expect to enroll half of Trinity.

I am living as quietly as an oyster, and I find it pleasant to untangle oneself for a while from all social ties, and look round a bit. And there is so much to look at here!

> *Yours ever,*
> *Logan Pearsall Smith*

Here are the rules of The Order of Prigs as Logan Pearsall Smith drew them up.

Maxims: Don't let anyone know you are a prig.

1. Deny yourself in inconspicuous ways and don't speak of your economies.
2. Avoid all vain and unkind criticism of others.[1]
3. Always keep your company manners on—keep your coat brushed and your shoe-laces tied.

---

[1] Logan was the most malicious scandal-monger I have ever known.

4. Avoid the company of the rich and the tables of the luxurious—all those who do not regard their property as a trust.
5. Don't be a Philistine! Don't let any opportunities of hearing good music, seeing good pictures or acting escape you.
6. Always let others profit as much as possible by your skill in these things.
7. Do what you can to spread the order.

Specific Rules:

1. Don't let your board and lodging exceed two pounds a week.
2. Keep a strict account of monies spent on clothes and pleasure.
3. If your income provides more than the necessities of Life, give at least a tenth of it in Charity.
4. Devote an evening a week, or an equivalent amount of time, to social work with the labouring Classes, or visiting the sick.
5. Set apart a certain time every day for examination of conscience.
6. Abstain entirely from all intoxicating liquors, except for purposes of health.
7. Practise some slight self-denial every day, for instance—Getting up when called, No cake at tea, No butter at breakfast, No coffee after dinner.
8. Observe strictly the rules of diet and exercise prescribed by one's doctor, or approved by one's better reason.
9. Read some standard poetry or spiritual book every day, for at least half an hour.
10. Devote $\frac{1}{2}$ hour every other day, or $1\frac{1}{2}$ hours weekly, to the keeping fresh of learning already acquired—going over one's scientific or classical work.
11. Keep all your appointments punctually, and don't make any engagements or promises you are not likely to fulfil.

The Arch Prig[1] or the associate Prig is empowered to give temporary or permanent release from any of these rules, if he deem it expedient.

All neglect of the rules and maxims shall be avowed to the Arch Prig, or one's associate, who shall set a penance, if he think it expedient.

Suggested penances:

Pay a duty call.
Write a duty letter.
Learn some poetry or prose.
Translate English into another language.
Tidy up your room.
Extend your hospitality to a bore.
(Hair shirts can be had of the Arch Prig on application.)

[1] I don't know who the Arch Prig was, or even whether he existed outside Logan's imagination.

15 Rue du Sommerard
Paris
Dec. 3 1891

My dear Bertie

I think you make an excellent **Prig**, and you have lapses enough to make it interesting. I was shocked however by the price, 12/6 you paid for a stick. There seems an odour of sin about that. 2/6 I should think ought to be the limit, and if the morality of Cambridge is not much above that of Oxford, I should think that your 12/6 stick would not keep in your possession long.

I know nothing about tobacco and meerschaums, so I cannot follow you into these regions of luxury. I must ask some one who smokes pipes about it. Well, I think you'd better impose one of the penances out of the list on yourself and then if you continue in sin I shall become more severe.

I find Priggishness, like all forms of excellence, much more difficult than I had imagined—by-the-by—let me tell you that if one simply *thinks* one has read one's half hour, one has probably read only a quarter of an hour. Human nature, at least my nature, is invariably optimistic in regard to itself.

No, the rule as to 1½ hrs. a week need not apply to you—but you *ought* to go to concerts, unless you are too busy. As to charities—there are an infinite number that are good—but why not save what money you have for such purposes for the Prig fund? And then when we have a meeting we can decide what to do with it. It will be most interesting when we all meet, to compare experiences. I am afraid it may lead however to reflexions of a pessimistic angle.

My adviser the Arch Prig, has failed me—if it were not speaking evil I should insinuate the suspicion that he had got into difficulties with the rules himself, which would be very terrible.

I live alone here with the greatest contentment. One inherits, when one comes here, such a wealth of tradition and civilization! The achievements of three or four centuries of intelligence and taste—that is what one has at Paris. I was bewildered at first, and shivered on the brink, and was homesick for England, but now I have come to love Paris perfectly.

Do write again when you have collected more sins, and tell me whether the fear of penance acts on you in the cause of virtue. It does on a cowardly nature like mine.

Yours ever,
Logan Pearsall Smith

15 Rue du Sommerard
Paris
Jan. 11th 1892

My dear Bertie

I have just read through your letter again to see if I could not find some excuse for imposing a penance on you, for having hurt my foot this afternoon, I feel in a fierce mood. But I am not one of those who see sin in a frock coat— if it be well fitting. But wait a bit—are you sure you told me what you had read in order, as you say, to confound my scepticism—was there not a slight infringement of maxim 1 lurking in your mind? If upon severe self-examination you find there was, I think you had better finish learning the 'Ode to the West Wind' which you partly knew last summer.

So far I have written in my official capacity as your adviser. But as your friend I was shocked and startled by your calm statement that you indulge in 'all the vices not prohibited by the rules'. These I need not point out are numerous, extending from Baccarat to biting one's finger nails—I hesitate to believe that you have abandoned yourself to them all. I think you must have meant that you read a great deal of Browning.

I am living in great quiet and contentment. A certain portion of the day I devote to enriching the English language with rules and moralities, the rest of the time I contemplate the mind of man as expressed in art and literature. I am thirsting of course for that moment—and without doubt the moment will come—when I shall hear my name sounded by all Fame's tongues and trumpets, and see it misspelled in all the newspapers. But I content myself in the meantime, by posing as a poet in the drawing rooms of credulous American ladies.

As a novelist or 'fictionist' to use the Star expression, I make it my aim to show up in my tales, in which truth is artistically mingled with morality, 'Cupid and all his wanton snares'. I also wish to illustrate some of the incidents of the eternal war between the sexes. What will the whited sepulchres of America say? Je m'en fiche.

Well, it is pleasant thus to expatiate upon my own precious identity.

I suppose you are 'on the threshold'—as one says, when one wishes to write high style—the threshold of another term—and so resuming my character of moral adviser I will salt this letter with some sententious phrase, if I can find one that is both true and fresh—but I cannot think of any—the truth is always so banal—that is why the paradox has such a pull over it.

Yours ever,
Logan Pearsall Smith

14 Rue de la Grande Chaumière
Paris
March 19 '92

Dear Bertie

I think members ought to be admitted to the Order, who are moderate drinkers, if they are satisfactory in other ways. Good people are so rare. But on all these points we must debate when we meet. We are going to Haslemere sometime in Easter Week, I think, and I hope you will keep a few days free to pay us a visit then. But I will write to you again when I get to England. As you see by my address, I have moved again, and I am at last settled in a little apartment furnished by myself. I am in Bohemia, a most charming country, inhabited entirely by French Watchmen and American and English art students, young men and women, who live in simple elegance and deshabille. My £2.0.0 a week seems almost gross extravagance here, and one's eyes are never wounded by the sight of clean linen and new coats. Really you can't imagine how charming it is here—everybody young poor and intelligent and hard at work.

When I came here first, I knew some 'society' people on the other side of the river, and used to go and take tea and talk platitudes with them, but how their lives seem so empty, their minds so waste and void of sense, that I cannot approach them without a headache of boredom. How dull and un-intelligent people can make themselves if they but try.

Yours ever,
L. P. Smith

Friday's Hill
Haslemere
Nov. 24 '92

Ça va bien à Cambridge, Bertie? I wish I could look in on you—only you would be startled at my aspect, as I have shaved my head till it is as bald as an egg, and dressed myself in rags, and retired to the solitude of Fernhurst, where I am living alone, in the Costelloe Cottage.[1] Stevens wrote to me, asking me to send something to the *Cambridge Observer*[2] and, prompted by Satan (as I believe) I promised I would. So I hurried up and wrote an article on Henry James, and when I had posted it last night, it suddenly came over me how stupid and bad it was. Well, I hope the good man won't print it.

There are good things in the *Observer* he sent me. I was quite surprised—it certainly should be encouraged. Only I don't go with it in its enthusiasm for impurity—its jeers at what Milton calls 'The sage and serious doctrine of virginity'. It is dangerous for Englishmen to try to be French, they never catch the note—the accent. A Frenchman if he errs, does it 'dans un moment d'oubli', as they say—out of absentmindedness, as it were—while the English-man is much too serious and conscious. No, a civilization must in the main develop on the lines and in the ways of feeling already laid down for it by those who founded and fostered it. I was struck with this at the 'New English Art Club' I went up to see. There are some nice things, but in the mass it bore the same relation to real art—French art—as A Church Congress does to real social movements.

So do show Sickert and his friends that a gospel of impurity, preached with an Exeter Hall zeal and denunciation, will do much to thicken the sombre fogs in which we live already.

I shall stay in England for a while longer—when does your vac. begin and where do you go?

Yrs
Lo L. P. Smith

---

[1] This was a cottage close to Friday's Hill, inhabited by the family of Logan's married sister Mrs Costelloe (afterwards Mrs Berenson).

[2] This was a high-brow undergraduate magazine, mainly promoted by Oswald Sickert (brother of the painter), who was a close friend of mine.

14 rue de la Grande Chaumière
Paris
Feb. 14th '93

My dear Bertie

I was sorry that Musgrave and I could not get to Richmond, but I was only a short time in London. I shall hope to go at Easter, if I am back. Paris welcomed me as all her own, when I got here and I have been living in the charm of this delightful and terrible place. For it is pretty terrible in many ways, at least the part of Paris I live in. Perhaps it is the wickedness of Paris itself, perhaps the fact that people live in this quarter without conventions or disguises or perhaps—which I am inclined to believe—the life of artists is almost always tragical—or not wanting at least in elements of Tragedy—that gives me the sense of the wretchedness and the fineness of life here. Just think, this very morning I discovered that a girl here I know had gone mad. She came in to see me, begged me to help her write a book to attack French immorality and now I am waiting to see the doctor I sent for, to see if we must shut her up.

As for 'morality' well—one finds plenty of the other thing, both in women and men. I met the other day one of the Young Davies' at Studd's studio—and my heart sank a little at the sight of another nice young Englishman come to live in Paris. But he I suppose can take care of himself.

But I must not abuse Paris too much, for after all this, and perhaps on account of it, Paris is beyond measure interesting. There are big stakes to be won or lost and everybody is playing for them.

Yours,
L. Pearsall Smith

44 Grosvenor Road
Westminster
Oct. 29 '93

My dear Bertie

You I suppose are watching the yellowing of the year at Cambridge, and indulging in the sentiments proper to the season. I am still kept unwillingly in London, and see no present prospect of getting away. I have tried to like London, for its grimy charms have never yet been adequately commended;— and charms it certainly has—but I have decided that if ever I 'do' London hatred and not love must be my inspiration, and for literary purposes hatred is an excellent theme. All French realism is rooted in hatred of life as it is, and according to Harold Joachim's rude but true remark, such pessimism must be based somehow on optimism. 'No shadow without light', and the bright dream of what London might be, and Paris already, to a small extent is— makes the present London seem ignoble and dark. Then I have been going a little into literary society—not the best literary society, but the London Bohemia of minor novelists, poets and journalists—and it does not win one to enthusiasm. No; the London Bohemia of minor novelists, poets and journalists is wanting in just that quality which would redeem Bohemia—disinterested-ness—it is a sordid, money-seeking Bohemia, conscious of its own meanness and determined to see nothing but meanness in the world at large. They sit about restaurant tables, these pale-faced little young men, and try to show that all the world is as mean and sordid as they themselves are—and indeed they do succeed for the moment in making the universe seem base.

How do you like your philosophy work? Don't turn Hegelian and lose yourself in perfumed dreams—the world will never get on unless a few people at least will limit themselves to believing what has been proved, and keep clear the distinction between what we really know and what we don't.

Yours ever,
Logan Pearsall Smith

Queen's Hotel
Barnsley
Nov. 16 1893

Dear Bertie

Thanks so much for your generous cheque[1]—the need here is very great, but thanks to the money coming in, there is enough to keep the people going in some sort of way. They are splendid people certainly—and it is hard to believe they will ever give in. It seems pretty certain to me that the Masters brought on the strike very largely for the purpose of smashing the Federation. Of course the Federation is often annoying—and I daresay the owners have respectable grievances, but their profits are very great and no one seems to think that they could not afford the 'living wage'. Within the last year a good deal of money has been invested in collieries here, and several new pits started, showing that the business is profitable. Well, it does one good to see these people, and the way they stick by each other, men and women, notwithstanding their really dreadful privations.

Yrs.
Logan Pearsall Smith

44 Grosvenor Road
Westminster Embankment
S.W.
Nov. 1893

Dear Bertie

You forgot to endorse this—write your name on the back, and send it to J. T. Drake, 41 Sheffield Road. It will be weeks before many of the Barnsley people will be able to get to work, and this money will come in most usefully. Every 10/- gives a meal to 240 children! I am very glad that I went to Barnsley, though I went with groans, but it does one good to see such a fine democracy. I wish you could have seen a meeting of miners I went to; a certain smart young Tory MP came with some courage, but very little sense to prove to the miners that they were wrong. They treated him with good-natured contempt and when he told them that their wages were quite sufficient they replied 'Try it lad yourself'—'it wouldn't pay for your bloody starched

[1] In support of a miners' strike.

clothes'. 'Lad, your belly's full' and other playful remarks. 'Noo redooction' a woman shouted and everyone cheered. Then a miner spoke with a good deal of sense and sarcasm, and the young M P was in about as silly a position as one could be in—well-fed well-dressed and rosy. The combat between him and the man to whom he preached contentment was what you call striking. But he had to smile and look gracious, as only Tories can, and pretend he was enjoying it immensely.

Yrs.
L. Pearsall Smith

44 Grosvenor Road
Westminster Embankment
S.W.
Dec. 2nd (1893)

My dear Bertie

Of course I know how matters stand, and naturally being as fond of my sister as I am, I do not regard your way of feeling as folly. And if you remain of the same mind after several years, I can assure you that I don't know of anyone who I should like better as a brother-in-law—nor indeed do I think there is anyone who would make a better husband for Alys. But sincerely I think you would make a mistake by engaging yourself too soon—but I dare say you don't intend to do that. One never knows what one will develop into, and anyhow the first few years after 21 should be given to self education, and the search for one's work, and marriage, or even a settled engagement, interferes sadly with all that.

Yes I *do* believe in you, Bertie, though the faculty for belief is not one of those most developed in me—only I shall believe more in your decision when I see that after a few years of good work and experience of the world you still remain the same. Win your spurs, *mon cher*—let us see that you are good and sensible—as indeed we believe you are—your friends all have the highest ideas of your ability and promise, only keep yourself free and interested in your work. Love should be the servant, and not the master of life.

Yours affy.
L. P. S.

The following letters were written to Alys during our three-months separation.

Pembroke Lodge
Richmond, Surrey
July 31st 1894

My darling Alys

As was to be expected there is nothing particular to be told, as nothing has happened. So far, however, it has not been particularly odious. When I arrived I found my Grandmother on a sofa in her sitting-room, looking very pale and sad; still, I was relieved to find her out of bed. Our meeting was *very* affectionate, though silent. We have talked only of indifferent subjects; she obviously realizes that it is bad for her health to talk of anything agitating.

The Doctor does not allow her to have any correspondence but what my Aunt thinks good for her (though she herself doesn't know this), however she was given my letter this morning and seems to have been pleased with it. My false conscience has been rather subdued by thee and the atmosphere of Friday's Hill, so that I find it far more endurable than last time in spite of my grandmother's illness; perhaps because of it too, in a way, because it sets everything in a kindlier and more natural key.

My aunt has been cross-questioning me about all my plans, but her comments, though *most* eloquent, have been silent. I told her about America, and she seemed to think it odd we should go unmarried: I said 'Well we thought it would be better than marrying before going out there', but to that she made no answer. All she said was 'I shan't tell Granny about that just yet'. She will probably have to go away for her health in September and she fished for me to offer to stay here with my grandmother; but I said I should be at Friday's Hill. I said I might in the following months come here every now and then, but should mainly live at Friday's Hill. She looked thunder, but said nothing. She has realized the uselessness of advice or criticism. She spoke about my grandmother seeing thee, but I said it would be better not without me.

My grandmother unfortunately is not so well this evening; she has to take sleeping-draughts and medicines for her digestion constantly and they are afraid both of stopping them and of her becoming dependent on them. She is very affecting in her illness, but having steeled my conscience I don't mind so much. She has been writing verses about Arthur to try and distract her mind from this one topic; she has also been reading a good deal with the same end in view; but apparently she has not succeeded very well.

But really it isn't half so bad here as it might be, so thee needn't make thyself unhappy about me or imagine I shall come back in the state of mind I was in yesterday fortnight. However I don't want—if I can help it, to make any promises as to when I shall come back. Goodnight Dearest. I am really happy but for being unutterably bored and I hope thee is enjoying the country even without me to force thee to do so.

Thine devotedly
Bertie

Ramsbury Manor
Wiltshire
Aug. 30th 1894

My Darling

I am very much perplexed by this offer of a post in Paris. If I were sure it wouldn't last beyond Xmas, and then would not tie me down to the same sort of post in future, I should feel inclined to accept it: it would pass the time of our separation very enjoyably (for I should certainly enjoy being at the Paris Embassy immensely); it would give me about as much of the world as could well be crammed into the time; it would give me some knowledge of the inside of diplomacy, and would certainly be a valuable experience, if it could remain an isolated episode. I don't know whether it would necessarily postpone our meeting and marriage; I fear it would; and that would be an argument against it. Also I am afraid of the world and its tone, as they are very bad for me, especially when I enjoy them, and I am very much afraid that such a career, once entered on, would be very hard to leave. Besides it would mean a number of aristocratic ties, which would hamper our future activity. And hardly any home appointment could induce me to give up the year of travel we propose, as I am sure that would not only be *far* the pleasantest way of spending our first year of marriage, but would also have great educational value. I wish my grandmother had given me more particulars: all that is clear from her letter is that it would give her great satisfaction if I accepted it. I should probably offend Lord Dufferin if I refused it, though perhaps that could be avoided. I *do* wish we could meet to discuss it; and I should like to have Logan's opinion.

2 p.m. The more I think of it, the more it seems to me that it would be the first step in a career I wish to avoid; but I cannot be sure till I hear more. And if I refuse, it would of course definitely cut me off from Secretaryships etc., as people wouldn't want to offer things to so fastidious and apparently capricious a young man. That is an advantage or the reverse according as you look at it. My brain is in a whirl and it is too hot to think.

Pembroke Lodge
Richmond, Surrey
Sep. 1, 9 p.m. '94

My darling Alys

Now that I am home again I have time to write a really long letter, and I feel tonight as if I could write for ever: I am made sentimental and full of thoughts by the place. I am reminded so vividly of last September that it seems as if I had all my work still before me. I went out today and sat by the fountain and thought of the long solitary days I used to spend there, meditating, wishing, scarcely daring to hope; trying to read the minutest indications in the bare, dry little letters thee used to write me, and in the number of days thee waited before answering mine; miserable in a way, mad with impatience, and yet full of a new life and vigour, so that I used to start with surprise at finding I no longer wished to die, as I had done for 5 years, and had supposed I always should do. How I counted the hours till Dunrozel came to visit here, and I was free to leave my Grandmother! Being here alone again I feel as if the intervening year had been a dream; as if thee still were to me a distant, scarcely possible, heaven; indifferent, as heaven must be, to mere earthly strugglers. But there is a strange weariness, like that of a troublesome dream, which forms an undercurrent to all my thoughts and makes the dream-feelings different in tone from those of last September; a weariness compounded of all the struggles and anxieties and pains of the past year, of all the strain and all the weary discussions and quarrels which winning thee has cost me. I am not unhappy, however, far from it; but for the moment it seems as if I had lived my life, and it had been good; it reached a climax, a supreme moment, and now there seems no more need to care about it: it can have nothing better in store, and therefore there would be no bitterness in death.

I suppose thee will think these feelings morbid, but I don't know that they are particularly so. I got into a dreamy mood from reading Pater: I was immensely impressed by it, indeed it seemed to me almost as beautiful as anything I had ever read (except here and there, where his want of humour allowed him to fall into a discordant note, as with the valetudinarian cat); especially I was struck by the poplars and another passage I can't find again. It recalled no definite childish memories, because since the age of definite memories I have not lived in a world of sensuous impressions like that of Florian; but rather in the manner of Wordsworth's Ode, I dimly feel again the very early time before my intellect had killed my senses. I have a vague confused picture of the warm patches of red ground where the setting summer sun shone on it, and of the rustling of the poplars in front of the house when I used to go to bed by daylight after hot days, and the shadow of the house crept slowly up them. I have a vague feeling of perpetual warm sunny weather, when I used to be taken driving and notice the speckled shadows moving across the carriage, before it occurred to me that they were caused by the leaves overhead. (As soon as I discovered this, the scientific interest killed the impression, and I began speculating as to why the patches of light were always circular and so on.) But very early indeed I lost the power of attending to impressions per se, and always abstracted from them and sought the scientific and intellectual and abstract that lay behind them, so that it wouldn't have occurred to me, as to Florian, to need a philosophy for them; they went bodily into my mental waste-paper basket. (That is why the book made me so dreamy, because it carried me back to my earliest childhood, where nothing seems really real.) I didn't begin to need such a philosophy till the age of puberty, when the sensuous and emotional reasserted itself more strongly than before or since, so that I felt carried back for a time to my infancy; then I made a sort of religion of beauty, such as Florian might have had; I had a passionate desire to find some link between the true and the beautiful, so strong that beauty gave me intense pain (tho' also a tingling sensuous thrill of tremendous strength), from the constant sense of this unfulfilled requirement of harmony between it and fact. I read Alastor after I had lived some time in this state, and there I found the exact mood I had experienced, vividly described. It was only gradually, as I came to care less and less for beauty, as I got through the natural period of morbidness (for in me so intense a passion for the beautiful was necessarily abnormal), only as I became more purely intellectual again, that I ceased to suffer from this conflict. Of course my taste of real life in the Fitz episode got me out of such mere sentimentality, and since then it has been only by moments I have suffered from it. If I could believe in Bradley, as I do most days, I should never suffer from it again. . . .

Sunday morning Sep. 2

I sent thee a wire from Reading early yesterday morning to say 'Shan't come since Nov. 17 is unchanged', but I suppose thee was already gone from Chichester before it arrived. Thee says thee will come to Paris if I can't come to England, but I rather gather from my Grandmother that I shall be able to chuck this post when I like. Will thee send my hat in my hat-box, as I need both? And please write by the 1st post tomorrow, otherwise I may be gone.

I shall probably go the day after hearing from Lord Kimberley. But I can't go and see Edith and Bryson, as they surely are staying in Britanny till Nov? Shall I send the Pater to Mariechen, or straight to Carey Thomas? All these details are tiresome, and I am sorry not to have remembered all the things I want sent in one batch, but my memory works that way unavoidably.

I like the Tragic Muse immensely, it is such fun; besides, it is singularly appropriate to my present situation.—My Aunt Georgy yesterday was very kind, but too inquisitive (as indeed most women are); she said even in old times at the slightest thought of a marriage my Grandmother used to get into a sort of fever and be fussy and worried about it. . . .

. . . I am grown quite glad of the Paris plan, and shall make a great effort not to hate my companions too much. At any rate I ought to be able to write amusing letters from there. Give me literary criticisms of my descriptions, so that I may make them as vivid as possible.—It is sad thee should have grown bored with thy friend's talk, but it is difficult to throw oneself into other people's petty concerns when one's own are very absorbing and interesting. I am *not* sorry thee has come to understand why I minded thy going right away to America more than a separation with thee still in London. Thee thought it very silly then, and so no doubt it is, but it is natural.

I hope this letter is long enough to satisfy thee: it has been a great satisfaction to write it, and I shall expect a *very* long one in return. If thee hears from Edith Thomas, thee will send me her letter, won't thee? I will wire as soon as I know when I'm going to Paris.

Goodbye my Darling. It was much better not to meet again and have the pain of a real parting.

> *Thine devotedly*
> *Bertie*

> Pembroke Lodge
> Richmond, Surrey
> Sep. 3 '94, 10 a.m.

Dearest Alys

I got three letters from thee by the 1st post this morning, one of them forwarded from Ramsbury, a particularly charming one. I am returning the documents it contained, which amused me much.

I have quite settled to accept the Paris offer (owing to thy urging me to do so), and I fancy Lord Kimberley's confirmation of it is purely formal. I am only waiting here for another letter from Lord Dufferin, and then I shall be off immediately. But I am rather sorry thee makes so very light of the dangers and drawbacks of aristocracy; I begin to fear thee will never understand why I dread them, and that it is not a mere superstition. Thee and Logan could mix with aristocrats to any extent (before thy engagement at any rate) without ever coming across the stumbling-blocks they put in the way of one of their own class who wishes to 'escape'. Americans are liked in society just because they are for the most part queer specimens, and don't do the things other people do or abstain from the things other people abstain from; people expect a sort of spectacular amusement from them, and therefore tolerate anything, though all but a *very* small minority make up for it by bitterly abusing them behind their backs. It thus comes about that you would never see aristocrats as they are with one of themselves; rigid and stiff and conventional, and horrified at the minutest divergence from family tradition. Besides they are mostly my relations and my Grandmother's friends: unless I make a fool of myself in Paris, this offer will lead to others, at home; any refusal will give great pain to my Grandmother (whose death is by no means to be counted on) and will offend and annoy the whole set of them. Also being my relations they all feel they have a right to advise; when I am trying to work quietly and un-obtrusively, in a way which seems to me honest, but is very unlikely to bring me the slightest fame or success till I'm 50 at least, they will come and badger me to go in for immediate success; from my many connections and the good will most of them unfortunately bear me, it will probably be easily within my reach, and I shall be pestered and worried almost out of my life by their insistence. And (I must confess it) horrible as such a thought is, I do not *entirely* trust thee to back me up. I have a passion for experience, but if I am to make anything of the talents I have, I must eschew a vast deal of possible experience, shut myself up in my study, and live a quiet life in which I see only people who approve of such a life (as far as possible); I know myself well enough to be sure (though it is a confession of weakness) that if thee insists on my having a lot of experience, on my seeing a heterogeneous society and going out into the world, and perhaps having episodes of an utterly different, worldly sort of life, my nervous force will be unequal to the strain; I shall either have to give up the work my conscience approves of, or I shall be worn out and broken down by the time I'm 30. In short, know my own needs, much better than thee does; and it is *very* important to me that thee should back me up in insisting on them. Casual experience of life is of very little use to a specialist, such as I aspire to be; good manners are *absolutely* useless. Thee has a sort of illogical kindness (not to call it weakness), which prevents thy seeing the application of a general rule to a particular case, if anybody is to derive a little pleasure from its infraction, so that thee is quite capable, while protesting that in general thee wishes me to lead a quiet student's life, of urging me in every particular case to accept offers, and go in for practical affairs, which really are hindrances to me. Both of us, too, are in danger of getting intoxicated by cheap success, which is the most damning thing on earth; if I waste these years, which ought to be given almost *entirely* to theoretic work and the acquisition of ideas by thought (since that is scarcely possible except when one is young), my conscience will reproach me through-out the rest of my life. Once for all, G. A. [God Almighty] has made me a theorist, not a practical man; a knowledge of the world is therefore of very little value to me. One hour spent in reading Wagner's statistics is probably of more value than 3 months in casual contact with society. *Do* be stern and consistent in accepting this view of myself, as otherwise (if I have to fight thee as well as my relations and the world) I shall certainly miss what I *hope* it lies in me to do. Thee may read what thee likes of this to Logan and see if he doesn't agree with me. The needs of a theorist are so utterly different from thine that it seems impossible for thee to realize how things of the greatest importance to thee may be utterly worthless to me. Beatrice Webb's case is very different, for she married a man whom all her smart relations hated, while thee with thy damnably friendly manner cannot help ingratiating thyself with them all! Besides I should imagine she was a person who feels it less than I do when she has to go against the wishes of those who are fond of her. And besides, all the early years of her life were wasted, so that she can never become first-rate,[1] or more than a shadow of her husband.—Excuse the tone of this letter: the fact is I have had the fear a long time that thee would ruin my career by wishing me to be too practical, and it has now at last come to a head. . . .

> Pembroke Lodge
> Richmond, Surrey
> Sep. 3 1894

Dearest Alys

. . . It was hardly in *early* boyhood I wished to harmonize the true and the beautiful, but rather when I was 16 and 17. I was peculiar chiefly because I was so constantly alone—when I had a spell of the society of other boys I soon became much more like them. I think when I was *Quite* a child I was more thoughtful than rather later. I remember vividly a particular spot on the gravel walk outside the dining-room here, where a great uncle of mine told me one fine summer's afternoon at tea time that I should never enjoy future fine afternoons quite so much again. He was half in joke half in earnest, and went on to explain that one's enjoyments grow less and less intense and unmixed as one grows older. I was only 5 years old at the time, but, being a pessimistic theory about life, it impressed me profoundly; I remember arguing against it then, and almost weeping because I felt I probably knew better and was likely to be right; however I know now that he certainly wasn't, which is a consolation. Then as now, I hugged my enjoyments with a sort of personal affection, as tho' they were something outside of me. Little did he think what a profound impression his chance careless words had made! . . .

> Pembroke Lodge
> Richmond, Surrey
> Sunday morning
> September 9th 1894

Dearest Alys

. . . It is strange, but I'm really in some ways happier than during the month at Friday's Hill; I realize that thee and I together were trying to stamp out my affection for my Grandmother, and that the attempt was a failure. My conscience was bad, so that I dreamt about her every night, and always had an uneasy consciousness of her in the background of even the happiest moments. Now, if she dies, I shall have a good conscience towards her: otherwise I should have had, I believe for life, that worse sort of remorse, the remorse for cruelty to a person whom death has removed from one's longing to make up for past deficiencies. My love for her is altogether too real to be ignored with impunity. . . .

---

[1] What a mistaken judgment!

Victoria, 9 a.m.
September 10th

Dearest Alys

I have got off after all today! I got thy two letters at breakfast: they will sustain me during the voyage. I feel too journeyfied to be sentimental or to have anything at all to say. I am very glad to be off, of course. But I was a little put off by my visit to the d'Estournelles yesterday. All the people were French except the Spanish Ambassador and the Italian Ambassadress, and I was not much impressed by their charms or even their manners: except the Spaniard, they were all oppressively and too restlessly polite for English taste: there was none of the repose and unobtrusiveness which constitutes good breeding to the British mind. I am to see three of them again in Paris, worse luck. It is very hard to live up to their incessant compliments and always have one ready to fire off in return. . . .

British Embassy
Paris
Friday, October 12th, 1894
9.45 a.m.

My dearest Alys

. . . I had a perfectly delightful evening with Miss Belloc[1] last night—from 7 till 12—as she stayed so late I suppose she enjoyed it too. I believe she was really very nice but to me she was surrounded by the halo of Friday's Hill and I should have thought her charming if she'd been the devil incarnate, or anything short of human perfection. We met at 7 at Neal's Library, Rue Rivoli—then we walked some time in the Tuilleries Gardens and elsewhere, and then dined at a queer quiet place in the Palais Royal. Then we walked about again for a long time, and both smoked an enormous number of cigarettes, and finally I left her at the door of her hotel at midnight, with hopes of another meeting today or tomorrow. We talked of thee and all the family, of French and English people, of Grant Allen, Stead and Mrs Amos, of the Embassy and its dreariness—of the various French poets who'd been in love with her and whom she'd been in love with—of her way of getting on with her French conventional relations and of their moral ideas (always incomprehensible and therefore interesting to me)—of Lady Henry and Pollen (whom we agreed to loathe) and Miss Willard—of vice in general and the difference between Parisian and London vice in particular and of her experiences in the way of being spoken to—and many other things. I found her talk very interesting and I think she enjoyed herself too—though not of course as much as I did, because she was the first congenial person I'd seen since I was at Vétheuil,[2] and the first to whom I could talk about thee. Her French sentiments come in

[1] Afterwards Mrs Lowndes. She was a sister of Hilaire Belloc.

[2] I stayed a week-end at Vétheuil with three sisters named Kinsella, who were friends of the Pearsall Smiths. I there met Condor the painter, whose only remark was: 'Wouldn't it be odd if one were so poor that one had to give them shaving soap instead of cream with their tea?' It was there also that I made the acquaintance of Jonathan Sturges, who was in love with one of the sisters.

very oddly—it is difficult to fit them in with her love of Stead—altogether being of two nations has made her not so much of a piece as she ought to be. But I *did* enjoy my evening—far more than anything since I left Friday's Hill—for the first time I was able to admire the Seine at night (which is *perfectly* lovely) without growing maudlin. . . .

> Monday, October 15th, 1894
> 12.30 a.m.

My Beloved

Don't say thee thinks of me from my letters as 'brains in the abstract', it does sound *so* cold and dry and lifeless. Letters *are* bad, but they ought to have more reality than that. To me too tonight five weeks seems a long time— that is because my brother is with me. I *shall* be glad when he goes. I hate him and half fear him—he dominates me when he is with me because I dread his comments if he should know me as I am. Thee hasn't made me less sensitive but more so—because I have had to embody one result of my real self in a form in which all the world can see it, which gives every one a hold for attacking me—I dread the moment when the Embassy people will discover it. Even the joy of getting away from all the people who annoy me would be enough by itself to be an intense source of joy. . . .

> British Embassy, Paris
> Wednesday, October 17th 1894
> 10 a.m.

My darling Alys

. . . I don't at all wish to alarm people—but my brother, of his own accord yesterday, while we were dining at La Perouse, said he could well imagine it, that *he* was afraid of me, though of hardly anyone else, because I never let myself go, and one felt me coldly critical inside.—Of course that *is* what I feel with my brother, but I'm sorry if I'm that way with people like Miss Belloc. He thinks himself a person of universal Whitmaniac sympathy; but if you sympathize with *everybody* it comes to much the same as sympathizing with none, or at any rate not with those who are hated! . . .

My brother won't want to come to Germany—I don't think he likes thee, which is a mercy—he thinks thee has the American hardness, by which he means not submitting completely to the husband and not being sensual. He says American women only love from the waist upwards. Thee can imagine I don't open my soul to him! It seems hard on thee to give thee a second objectionable brother-in-law called Frank. . . .

> British Embassy
> October 20th 1894
> 3 p.m.

My darling Alys

I think the real use of our separation is to give me a good conscience and to hasten our marriage. Thee doesn't think my good conscience will last, but

I think it will if I don't see too much of my Grandmother. I feel no duties now, only a mild irritation when I think of her and Aunt Agatha, and it will be a good thing to continue to feel so. And all this separation is well worth while, for we should never have been really happy together without the knowledge we had really done something serious for my Grandmother. . . . I enclose Sanger's two letters—I have answered saying I would probably do two Dissertations—the second letter is much more encouraging than the first. I said I would make the Geometry the chief one my first shot and the Economics my second shot. . . .

I have been reading more Mill and beginning an Essay on Axioms for the Moral Science Club at Cambridge, of which Trotter, the hard-working Scotsman I beat and despise, is Secretary. It will be an immense pleasure to go to Cambridge and read a paper and enjoy the Society again. The Society is a real passion to me—after thee, I know no greater joy. I shall read them a paper on controlling our passions, in which I shall point out that we can't, and that the greater they are the less we ought to though the more easily we can.—This sounds paradoxical but isn't. I take refuge in intellectual activity which has always been rather of the nature of a dissipation and opiate to me.

Goodbye my Darling, my Joy. I will write again tomorrow.

> *Thine heart and soul*
> Bertie

British Embassy, Paris
October 22nd 1894, 9 p.m.

My darling Alys

. . . I don't think thee'll be tempted to grow too dependent on me, because thee'll find I shall be bored if thee always agrees with me, and shall want an argument now and them to give my brain a little exercise. I feel a real and solid pleasure when anybody points out a fallacy in any of my views, because I care much less about my opinions than about their being true. But thee *Must* think for thyself instead of merely taking scraps from different people—that is what makes thy opinions so disjointed, because thee takes different opinions from different people, thinking the two subjects independent—but no two subjects are really independent, so that people with different Popes for different things have an extraordinary hotch-potch of views. Logan, thee and Mariechen all have that vice, Logan least, M. most.

Logan once told me thee had better taste in pictures than M., and yet thee seldom opens thy mouth, but leaves all the talking on such subjects to her dogmatizing. This is an example how thee wastes thy mind, not from modesty, but from a combination of laziness and pride, the same pride that kept thee silent so long about thy real opinions.—What M. says about getting ideas from somewhere is true of herself but by no means of everybody—e.g. in my paper on space which I'm writing now, there is a whole section of close reasoning which I have seen nowhere, and which, for ought I know, may be quite original. It is like the rule of speak when you're spoken to—if everyone followed it, there could be no ideas in the world: they have to come from someone originally. And even when one's ideas are got from others, they have quite a different complexion when one has fought against them and wrestled with them and struggled to understand the process by which they are acquired than when one lazily accepts them because one thinks the man a good man. I fought every inch of the way against Idealism in Metaphysic and Ethics—and that is why I was forced to understand it thoroughly before accepting it, and why when I came to write it out, Ward used to be enchanted at my lucidity. But having lapsed into mere bragging, perhaps this homily had better stop! ...

British Embassy, Paris
Wednesday, October 31st 1894
9.30 p.m.

My darling Alys

... I shan't mind being 'run' in the unimportant details of practical things —where to dine, what to eat, etc.—in important practical matters, when I've had a little practice in them, I maintain that I'm not incompetent and I should sit on thee vigorously if thee tried to dictate to me! But Evelyn Nordhoff is right that thee wouldn't be likely to do so. As long as I remain a student or a theorist of any sort, I *shall* have no duties to the outside world. I remember saying to thee on the Chelsea Embankment last November what Logan is always repeating, that that sort of person *ought* to lead a selfish life in small things, because it increases one's efficiency, and the work is so *vastly* more important than any good one does by little politenesses and so forth. Fortunately my needs are simple—tea and quiet are all I require. I enjoyed my lunch with the Dufferins very much. I was alone with Lord and Lady Dufferin and he was perfectly charming, though he appeared to have forgotten all about my engagement, at least nothing was said about it. He is really a delicious man—so perfect and well-rounded. He was very gracious—said it had been the greatest pleasure to him to find he could please my Grandmother by giving me this place—asked if there had been much work: so I said not so much lately, and he smiled and said there was always less with an Ambassador than a Minister. I told them Phipps was in raptures over Sarah's new play, and they smiled again and said they had no very high opinion of Phipps's taste. They seem to share the general contempt. He treated me so affectionately that my heart quite warmed to him, in spite of its being due to my Grandparents, not to myself. I was not the least shy, and did and said exactly what was proper. Thee will be glad to know that Lady Dufferin was *atrociously* dressed, in a sort of grey serge. Lord Dufferin had just come in from bicycling: he rides right up to the very Embassy door and wheels his machine in himself. The French used to be shocked but now, largely owing to him I believe, it has become far more fashionable for swells than it is in England. When he was in Petersburg there was quite a scandal because one night, by way of Dum-crambo or some similar game, he acted a pig and hopped and grunted, and everyone thought it very shocking for an Ambassador. He treats his wife with a curious formal polite affection, which I believe is perfectly genuine, only that the habit of formal politeness has made that his only possible manner: but it sounds odd to hear 'my Love' and such terms in the tone in which he might say Your Majesty or Your Excellency. It was a glorious day and I went all round the Bois with Dodson, which I also enjoyed immensely—all the autumn tints were at their very finest, and I can't imagine more ideal weather. Coming back he was vastly impressed by my nerve in the traffic. I suppose it is mathematics or something, but I know I'm singularly good at riding through crowded streets! I quite won his respect, as he is of the type that worships 'nerve' in any form. He came lumbering on behind. He is a nice simple innocent youth, who thinks everybody else stupendously clever. Harford and I smile over him, but we both like him and I think he likes both of us.

I didn't mean to go on to a 2nd sheet but I'm not sleepy enough to go to bed, though it's 10.30, and I can't settle down to any other occupation than writing to thee—It's nice riding with Dodson, because it makes him mad with envy to see me go without using my hands on the handles! . . .[1]

Cambridge[2]
November 3rd, 1.30

My dearest Alys

. . . I have been wildly happy all morning: ever since I left King's Cross I've felt as if we'd just parted and I were coming back as I did so often by that train last winter. It's perfectly delightful seeing my friends again—I never knew before how fond I am of them and how *infinitely* nicer (and cleverer!) they are than the ordinary run of young men. I've just been seeing Ward who says there's nothing philosophical for me to do in Economics but I might very well take some mathematical job of pure theory, only then I should have to begin specializing almost at once. He advised me to take in time and motion too in my other Dissertation, and discuss Newton's 3 laws, which would be interesting. It is lovely weather, and the yellow elms are heavenly, and all the people are good and nice, and it is perfect paradise after the hell of Paris. I had a glorious long talk with Sanger and revelled in his intellectual passion. . . . I will write again by Lion[3] tomorrow, a longer letter telling all that happens. Ward is to be shewn my paper on Space and I shall be wildly eager to hear what he says about it. Short of love, his praise is about the most delightful thing in the world to me. I got none today, but enjoyed seeing him, he's such a delightful man. Now I must hunt up someone to lunch. Less than a fortnight thank heaven! Fare thee well my Beloved.

Thine ever most devotedly
Bertie

[1] I find myself shocked by the conceit and complacency of the above letter and of some of the others written about the same time. I wonder that Alys endured them.
[2] I went to Cambridge for the week-end, but did not see Alys as the three months had not expired.
[3] Lion FitzPatrick—afterwards Mrs Phillimore.

In the train—Cambridge
Sunday November 4th 1894
5.15 p.m.

My dearest Alys

It is a great pity all my letters come in a lump and I'm very sorry to have addressed Friday's Hill. I hope it won't happen again. I'm *so* glad thee's happy and busy too—if I were imagining thee unhappy it would be unendurable not to see thee tonight—as it is it gives me pleasure to think thee is near. It has been *perfectly* delightful to be at Cambridge again. Moore and Sanger and Marsh were *so* nice to see again. I love them all far more than I supposed before. We had a large meeting last night. McT. and Dickinson and Wedd came, at which I could not help feeling flattered. Thee will be glad to hear that several of them thought my paper too theoretical, though McT. and I between us persuaded them in time that there was nothing definite to be said about practical conduct. I have left my paper behind as Marsh and Sanger want to read it over again. McT. spoke first and was excessively good, as I had hoped. I said in my paper I would probably accept anything he said, and so I did. For my sake he left out immortality, and reconciled my dilemma at the end without it. I can't put what he said in a letter, but I dare say I shall bring it out in conversation some day. We had a delightful dinner at Marsh's before the meeting, and I was *so* glad just to be with them again that I didn't talk a bit too much. Moore though he didn't say much looked and was as glorious as ever—I almost worship him as if he were a god. I have never felt such an extravagant admiration for anybody. I always speak the truth to Marsh, so I told him we were separated three months to please my grandmother; the rest asked no inconvenient questions. Most of them were pleased with my paper, and were glad of my making Good and less good my terms instead of right and wrong. The beginning also amused them a good deal. I stayed up till 2 talking to Marsh and then slept till 10.30, when I went to breakfast with Sanger. I lunched with Marsh, and talked shop with Amos and saw my rooms. As he has furnished them—they're brighter but not *near* so nice. Sanger thought my bold idea in my Space paper 'colossal'—I hope Ward will think so too! Amos tells me Ward said I was so safe for a Fellowship that it didn't matter a bit what I wrote on—but this must be taken cum grano salis—it is slightly coloured by Amos's respect for me. They *all* urged me to do what I'm good at, rather than fly off to Economics, tho' all of them greatly respect Economics and would be delighted to have me do them ultimately. I have great respect for their judgments because they are honest and know me. So I shall do 2 Dissertations next year and only Space this—or Space and Motion, as Ward suggests. But of course I shall work at Economics at once. Sanger is working at Statistics, and explained several hideous difficulties in the theory, important for practice too, since the whole question of Bimetallism and many others turn on them. I had never suspected such difficulties before, and they inspired me with keen intellectual delight from the thought of obstacles to be overcome. My intellectual pleasures during the last years have been growing very rapidly keener, and I feel as if I might make a great deal out of them when we're married and all our difficulties are settled. I am convinced since reading

Bradley that all knowledge is good, and therefore shouldn't need to bother about immediate practical utility—though of course, when I come to Economics, that will exist too. I'm very glad to find that passion developing itself, for without it no one *can* accomplish good thinking on abstract subjects—one can't think hard from a mere sense of duty. Only I need little successes from time to time to keep it a source of energy. My visit to Cambridge has put me in very good conceit with myself and I feel very happy to think we are within our fortnight and that Mariechen will make it fly. I laughed more than in all the time since I left Friday's Hill and I talked well and made others laugh a great deal too. . . .

Trinity College, Cambridge
December 9th 1894, 2 a.m.

My dearest Alys

I will write a little letter tonight though it *is* late. Sanger met me at the station and took me to tea with Marsh, where I found Crompton who is as charming as ever and in better spirits than I ever saw him before, delighted with the law and very glad to feel settled for life. Moore read about lust and set forth exactly thy former ideal which he got from me when we met the normal man on the walking-tour. His paper did not give any good arguments, but was beautifully written in parts, and made me very fond of him. A year ago I should have agreed with every word—as it was, I spoke perfectly frankly and said there need be nothing lustful in copulation where a spiritual love was the predominant thing, but the spiritual love might seek it as the highest expression of union. Everybody else agreed with me, except McT. who came in after the discussion was over. Crompton was very good indeed and quite worsted Moore, though Moore would not admit it. I am going to see all the dons tomorrow. I have been arguing with Amos, who is much incensed at my advocacy of hyper-space, and is not coming to the wedding (not as a consequence of our differences!). . . .

Thine ever devotedly
Bertie

I was at this time very intimate with Eddie Marsh (afterwards Sir Edward Marsh), so I told him about Alys and got him to go and see her. She was engaged in a crusade to induce daughters to rebel against their parents. This is alluded to in Marsh's letter.

Cold Ash, Newbury
March 25, '94

My dear Russell

I want to thank you for two very pleasant occasions last week. I went on Sunday and found the room full of two American girls, one of whom went away to write home and the other to do political economy. Then we had a delightful talk for an hour or two, about you and other matters. I think we shall be great friends. I'm very happy about you, still more so than I was before.

She wanted to make my sister revolt, and accordingly asked me to bring her to lunch last Wednesday wh. was exceedingly kind. My sister also seemed to make great friends, and was most enthusiastic when we went away. I don't know if she'll revolt or not. Mr Pearsall Smith is a dear old boy. I think he was very sarcastic to me but I'm not really sure if he was or not. Among other things he said I talked exactly like old Jowett, wh. I don't believe. What funny grammar they talk to one another.

It isn't much worth while telling you what you know already, I don't mean about the grammar, so perhaps this letter ought to come to an end here but it would be rather short so I'll go on with my own affairs. The most interesting thing is that I've been seeing a certain amount of Robert Bridges, he's a charming man, with thick dark hair which grows like thatch and a very attract-ive imped. in his sp. He reminded me curiously of Verrall, though he's much bigger all over and his face has funny bumps like Furness. I went for a walk with him on Friday; he talked in a very interesting way, tho' not quite as Coleridge talked to Hazlitt; after lunch he got a headache or something and seemed to get somehow much older (he's 49) and talked about his own plays a good deal. He had a perfect right to, as of course I was interested, but it was very funny how openly he praised them. He said 'I think I've given blank verse all the pliability it's capable of in the Humours of the Court, don't you?'—'the Feast of Bacchus is amusing from beginning to end: it's sure to find its way to the stage and when it gets there it'll keep there'.

This isn't vanity in the least, he's quite free from that. I'm just going over there to church, I hear he's trained the choir with remarkable success.

I suppose you're having an awfully good time in Rome. Don't bother to write till you come back. I thought you'd like to hear about Sunday. I should go on writing, except that I'm not sure how much goes for 2½d. Please remember me to Miss Stanley.

Yr. affectionate friend
Edward Marsh

Heidelberg
Neuenheimer Landstr. 52
Sept. 15

My dear Russell

I was just going comfortably to sleep over my Grammatik when I unluckily fell to wondering whether the opposite to an icicle was called an isinglass or bicicle; and the shock of remembering that I was thinking about stalactite and stalagmite woke me up completely; but I'm not going to do any more Gram-matik; so here is the answer to your letter, though it was so far from proper as to be quite shocking.

I should have thought Paris was a very good exchange for Dresden, as the separation would have taken place in either case wouldn't it? I'm very sorry not to see you, though in some ways it's a good thing, as I'm not in the least either solemn or suitable, and it's quite enough to have been seen by Sanger. I'm not going to give you an account of all my wickednesses, as I'm tired of doing that; I resolved to write to all my friends and see who'd be shocked first, beginning at the most likely end with Barran, G. Trevy, Conybeare; to my utter astonishment they contented themselves one after the other with telling me not to get fat, and the first person who thought of being horror-struck was Moore.

I'm getting on pretty well with German, though I haven't arrived at the stage of finding it a reasonable medium for the expression of thought. I think the original couple who spoke it must have died rather soon after the Tower of Babel, leaving a rather pedantically-minded baby, who had learnt all the words of one syllable, and had to make up the long ones with them—at least how else can you account for such words as Handschule and be-ab-sicht-igen? I never knew a language so little allusive—comparative coarseness of 'sich kleiden' with the elegance of 'se mettre'—English gains by having so many Latin words—their literalness is concealed—for instance independence is exactly the same as Unabhängigkeit, yet the one seems quite respectable, while the other is unspeakably crude. I can read pretty well by now, and can mostly find some way or other of expressing what I mean, but I can't under-stand when people talk at their natural pace. Unluckily all the plays they've done yet at Mannheim are too unattractive to go to; but I've seen more operas since I've been here than in my whole previous life, though that isn't saying much. The performances aren't quite satisfactory, as the actors are so dreadful to look at. I went to Fidelio yesterday. The heroine was played by a lady whom I mistook at first for Corney Grain—you know she is disguised as a page. Fat women are in a sad dilemma—either they must have their bodices all of the same stuff, in which case they look as if they were just going to burst, or they must have an interval of some other stuff, in which case they look as if they had. For instance Fidelio had a brown—jerkin? it was my idea of a jerkin—open in front, with something white showing underneath; and puffs of white in the sleeves, which had just that effect. I've seen innumerable sights since I've been here (anything does for a sight in Germany) I scandal-ized everybody the other day by going to sleep in the middle of being driven slowly round Frankfort in a fly. I don't think even the Frenchmen find the sight quite so funny as I do—but they're mostly rather young (I ought to explain it's a big pension full of Frenchmen learning German and Germans teaching them. I'm the only Englishman). They're mostly also very delightful —I've made great friends with one German, who is a very charming, but not Apostolic, and one Frenchman who is, very; I've hardly ever seen a Frenchman who hadn't a charm of his own, quite apart from his merits. . . .

Here came Mittagessen, after which I'm as learned to say I find myself almost incapable of further exertion (by the way the Frau Professor says I'm viel angenehmer in that respect than most Englishmen—I mean in respect of my general habit of 'eating what's set before me', according to the nursery rule). So I've read through what I've written already. I'm afraid it reads rather leichtsinnig—but consider that it's an exquisite day and I'd spent the rest of the morning in the garden saying to myself 'behold how good and how pleasant a thing it is for persons of different nationalities to sit together in chairs'—with an interval for my German lesson, which was as usual very funny, the Professor who talks English very badly, makes up examples out of the rules; and I had to translate such sentences as 'Rid yourself of your whimps', 'Do you remember my?' and 'He posted off all his wretches'—which, when I heard the German, I recognized as 'He boasted of all his riches'.

Write me a postcard now and then when your brain is for the moment off the boil—I'm here till the end of the month—I should like very much to come back by Paris, but I'm debarred by 2 considerations, both insurmountable—I) I shan't have any money left—II) I haven't any clothes in which I could come within a mile of an Embassy, or be seen about with anyone connected with one—I hope you're getting on all right.

Yrs. fraternally
E. H. M.

Heidelberg
(1894)

My dear Russell

I've got just ½ an hour before Abendessen, and I can think of 7 people on the spur of the moment whom I ought to write to rather than you—however you seem to 'feel it more', as Mrs Gummidge says. I'm awfully sorry you aren't enjoying yourself more in Paris. I should have thought the mere feel of the place would be enough—but your account of your people's letters is most depressing—the idea of consoling oneself with a bad hymn when one might console oneself with the Walrus and the Carpenter, say—however the 10th of December isn't very far off.

I don't quite understand your not liking Frenchmen—is it simply because they're unchaste? It is very disgusting—all the ones here for instance fornicate pretty regularly from 16 years old, and talk about it in a way that would sicken me in England—but it's merely a matter of education, and one can't object to individual people because they behave in the way they've been brought up to. . . .

Yours fraternally
Edward Marsh

Heidelberg
Oct. 1 (1894)

Dear Russell

Barran sent me the enclosed letter for you today, and I accompany it with the greatest of all the treasures I found in 'Zion's Herald'—When one follows out the similitude in its details, it becomes too delightful especially the tact with which God has got over the little awkwardness caused by the 'Great superiority of his Social Station'. 'As is usual with lovers' is a good touch—and so is the coyness with which mankind is represented as 'wondering what God can see in us'. The whole thing is an 'Editorial'.

I got your letter this morning, and I'm very glad you're a little happier. I wondered for a long time if I could get in a day at Paris on my way back, but time money and clothes were all inexorably against it.

The Frenchmen I've known here were nearly all too young to be repulsively bestial; some of them will become so no doubt, others, I think, will not. My chief friend for instance went to a brothel only to see what it was like and was so much sickened he could hardly 'baiser', as they call it.

I shall write you a very serious letter some day, for the sake of my character, but till then, I'll go on being frivolous if you like.

My last great adventure was meeting O. B.[1] accidentally at the station—he was on his way to Elfiel to buy German champagne (!) and had come here for German cigars. I brought him for a night to the Pension—he made a great impression on every one, and was very jolly. Almost the first thing he told me was that the Duchesses of York and Teck are going to pay him a visit at Cambridge next term—which, as he remarked, would give people a great deal to talk about, but it wasn't his fault, as they'd practically invited themselves.

What news of your brother?

Yours fraternally
E. H. Marsh

40 Dover Street, W
May 11 1894

Dearest Bertrand

I have been back[2] 3 weeks but have been overwhelmed with arrears of work and now I write because I have heard that a report is going about that you are probably going to be engaged to Miss Pearsall Smith. I hope this is not so, for if you thought you wd. be too young to enter Parliament before you were 29 I must think it would be a great pity for you to engage yr. self and take such an important step at 21 or 22. I forget which you are—It would stop you in so many things and you have seen so very little of the world 'of Young Women' as Lady Russell puts it, that I shall be very sorry if you have bound yr. self thus early. But all this may be idle gossip and you may be sure I shall not spread it, but could not help writing to say what a pity I think it wd. be at the very outset of life to enter on such an engagement and with a girl a good bit older than yourself. Do not answer my letter unless you wish it, but I shall hope that what I have is merely gossip founded perhaps on yr. having been at the Wild Duck with the young lady.

Yrs. afft.
Maude Stanley

Clandeboye
Co. Down
Septr. 5, '94

My dear Bertie

Lady Russell will have told you that everything has been arranged for your going to Paris. I am sure you will like it, and the climate is charming at this time of the year: and though perhaps there may be a certain amount of work,

---

[1] Oscar Browning.   [2] From Rome, where I had accompanied her.

I hope it will not be too much to prevent you taking advantage of your stay to see all that is to be seen in Paris, for the autumn is the best time for that.

I think, if it could be arranged, that it would be very desirable from our official point of view that you should stay for at least three months, though I hope we shall tempt you to remain longer and to go out a little into Paris society, which would amuse you very much.

I have written to all the authorities at Paris to warn them of your arrival, and to tell them to do everything they can to make you feel at home.

Yours very sincerely
Dufferin and Ava

Hotel du Prince de Galles
Paris
Sep. 11, 1894

Dear Lord Dufferin

I have waited till I was established here to thank you warmly for your two kind letters to me. It is very good of you to take so much trouble about me, and I have indeed been most cordially received by everybody. I arrived in Paris last night and spent this morning at the Embassy. I am sure I shall like the work, and that the life generally will be very agreeable.

I will certainly stay the three months which you speak of as officially desirable, indeed under ordinary circumstances I should have been glad to stay any length of time; but I am engaged to be married, and had hoped that the wedding might be in December; so you will, I am sure, understand that I should be glad to be free then, if that is possible without any inconvenience. I hope you will not think this wish ungracious on my part—no lesser inducement could have made me wish to shorten my stay here, and I am deeply obliged to you for having given me the appointment—but as I do not intend to take up the diplomatic service as my career, it seemed perhaps needless to postpone my wedding, for which I feel a natural impatience.

Yours gratefully and sincerely
Bertrand Russell

The following letters have to do with a project, which I entertained for a short time, of abandoning mathematical philosophy for economics, and also with the affairs of The Society. It was the practice for one member, in rotation, to read a short paper, chosen by the others the previous Saturday out of four suggested subjects. In the subsequent discussion it was a rule that everyone must say something.

Trinity College, Cambridge
Oct. 18th, '94

Dear Russell

When I first read your letter I thought that you had gone raving mad. I took it round to Marsh, and he did not take such a serious view of the case. I will, of course, ask Ward about it directly. I don't know how far it would be possible for you to do much good at the subject, but I am fairly certain that the amount of economics which you would have to read, would not be more than you could easily do. But I expect that, as well as Psychology and Ethics that you would have to learn some politics and law. I doubt whether you will really find much life in trying to find out whether the word 'Utility' can have any meaning and what is meant by a man's 'demand for tobacco'. Surely you have a very excellent opportunity of being of some service to the Universe by writing about space whereas I doubt if you will quickly increase human happiness by doing the basis of economics. For, on the one hand, owing chiefly to the spread of democracy, it is distrusted and despised, and on the other hand the few people who, like myself, think that it is or ought to be a science naturally do not much mind whether it means anything or not. I expect McTaggart will have a fit if I tell him what you say. Trotter would like a paper from you (if it is possible) for the Moral Science Club. Last Saturday we chose subjects and Marsh is reading on Saturday on, I think, 'Why we like nature'. Please let someone know as soon as possible which day you are coming up on. It is splendid of you to come. We are thinking about George Trevvy but are not quite decided. I hear that Edward Carpenter has published yet another pamphlet on 'Marriage'. I will send you a copy as soon as I get one.

Have you got Erdmann's book on the Axioms of Geometry or do you know of anyone up here who has it; as I rather want to read it and can't find it in the 'Varsity library. Do you see the English papers? Some women have been raising hell about the prostitutes at the Empire and it is probably going to be closed. I wish they would protest against those in the streets instead.

I can't find anything to write about in Economics and I find law somewhat dull so I should be depressed if it were not that I am going to hear the 9th Symphony on the day after tomorrow.

Yours frat.
Charles Percy Sanger

Trinity College, Cambridge
Oct. 19th, '94

Dear Russell

I went to Ward and asked him about you. He said immediately that you had better do economics, if you thought that you would like it better. That the important thing was to work at what you liked and that though your dissertation would have to go in by August, yet you worked very fast and would probably have enough time. He also said that there was not the slightest objection to your sending in two or more dissertations, or that if you write an article on space in 'Mind' or elsewhere that you could count that in with your dissertation on Economics. But that, as one would expect, two moderate dissertations do not count as one good one. He said that he would not advise you about economics and suggested that you should write to Marshall. Have you read Keynes'[1] book on the Scope and Method of Economics? I think that that perhaps might interest you. Frank tells me that McTaggart is rather horrified.

Your friend
Charles Percy Sanger

[1] The Keynes in question was the father of Lord Keynes.

Trinity College, Cambridge
Oct. 23, '94

Dear Russell

I'm very glad you're coming soon and it's all your eye to say you don't want to write a paper.

Your first letter to Sanger was most subversive, the effect on us can only be compared (in its humble way) to that produced on Europe by the Cabinet Council last month—Sanger came rushing round here to say you were quite mad, and finding me unprepared with an opinion offered me his. Not being entirely satisfied with my attitude he proceeded to spoil McTaggart's appetite by telling him the dreadful news as he was marching up to the Fellows' table. He's since been more or less pacified by Ward—I don't know anything about the rights and wrongs of the case, but I can't refrain from appealing to your better nature to consider what o'clock it is, to consider what a long way you've got to go before July, to consider anything—before embarking on a rash project.

I was awfully glad to get your letter (the day before I left Heidelberg) and hear you were happier in Paris; I don't know how often I've nearly answered it since—I seem to be working very hard this term, as I do nothing else in the day except perhaps a game of 5's, 30 pages of Zola, and of course meals, but these very moderate and un-Heidelberg. Life affords few distractions. I know lamentably few people, yet the temptation to call on freshers is one which is easy to resist. The fact is I'm getting old and posé, even rheumatic, and almost respectable; parts of this letter are in my new Mary Bennet style. Z.B., the idea of life affording few distractions, though not perhaps wholly new, strikes me as well expressed.

I saw Miss Pearsall Smith on Saturday at the Richter Concert, and we discussed the comparative fascination of space and economics. She looked very well—and had such a pretty green cloak with fur trimmings. Sanger said he was going to tell you what had been happening in the Society. Last Sat. was rather a failure, as I had discovered that my paper was all nonsense on Friday; besides wh. Sanger and I were so completely done by the Concert that we hadn't an idea in our heads. I had 'brain stoppage' every time I was asked a question. We are thinking of little Trevy,[1] but Moore who knows him better than anyone else has scruples. I'm rather hoping that a young Babe at King's may turn out embryonic—He's infinitely the cleverest and most fascinating of the family.

I've done a fabulous amount of work today so I'd better leave off, esp. as I shall see you so soon and talking is better than writing (esp. my writing wh. has gone rather funny on this page.)

Yrs. fraternally
E. M.
(*Edward Marsh*)

---

[1] George Trevelyan, Master of Trinity, OM, etc., etc.

Trinity College, Cambridge
Oct. 22nd, '94

Dear Russell

I am very glad that you can arrange to come up. I will see about the rooms. We should be very glad if you would read a paper as there are only four of us now.

Maggie Tulliver or Cleopatra sounds such a good subject that you had better read on it and thus don't trouble to send subjects for us to choose. Last week Marsh read an excellent paper on 'Do we like nature', but unfortunately the discussion was not so good as Marsh and I were quite stupid (we had heard the Choral Symphony in the afternoon) and there were only Moore and Dickinson besides. Dickinson was good and I expect that Moore was, but I couldn't understand him. In the letter that I wrote telling you what Ward had said, I don't know whether I sufficiently emphasized the fact that his great point was that you should work at what you like (in distinction I think to what you might think you ought to do). He was quite strong on the point that if Metageometry bored you, it was better that you should do something else. We are quite divided about George Trevey—that is to say Marsh and Wedgewood are in favour of him, and I am, on whole, neutral but Moore thinks that most of our discussions would not interest him. The spookical [psychical] society have got hold of a medium who does things that they can't explain. Myers is, of course, triumphant and Sidgwick is forced to admit that at the time he was convinced, but thinks that he isn't now.

Yours frat.
Charles Percy Sanger

Trinity College, Cambridge
Wednesday (1894)

Dear Russell

I'll send the paper off tomorrow; the end part is rather muddling to an uneducated person, but I'm glad I read it again.

I've just come back from a concert, I was next an old lady who was exactly like the leg of mutton in Alice; the features were almost identical and she had a becoming pink paper frill on her head, which a closer inspection revealed as a dyed feather. I don't think she can have known the picture.

MacT.'s paper on Sunday was very interesting. Mackenzie remarked afterwards that Hegel's theory of punishment was quite different, and MacT. simply continued to smile—I don't know wh. was in the right, but I never saw MacT. shut up so easily. It was very funny to see Trotter follow him in the room, humble and imitative—he had an air of being 'also stark mad, in white cotton' (do you remember the Confidante in the Critic?)

I had such a funny scene with my bedmaker the night you left. I was in my bedroom, and heard a timid voice calling me. 'Well', I said. 'Isn't this a sad affair, sir?' she began in her plaintive voice. 'What?' I asked (I thought Mrs Appleton must have had twins at least)—'about your table, sir'. 'Well?' 'Weren't you surprised to find the leaf still in?' 'Very much, why was it?'

'Didn't the gentleman tell you, sir?' 'What gentleman? What's happened?' It turned out she'd broken a bit of the wood, just as Tommy Booth came in with a pipe of mine. Wasn't it extraordinary how she couldn't tell me straight out? I hope when my wife dies, or anything like that, I shall always have someone to make my troubles ridiculous by their exaggerated concern. I never can mind when anything goes wrong in my room. I can't resist Mrs Roper's sympathy.

Oswald Sickert's book is out at last, he sent me a copy this morning. It is dedicated to me, which makes me very proud—it reads much better than it did in MS. I think it's splendid.

We're going to have another enormous meeting next Sat. Mayor, Trevy, Theo all coming to Moore's paper. I dare say I'll write to you about it. I think this is the end of my news for the present and it's near 12.

Goodnight
E. H. M. (*Marsh*)

Trinity College, Cambridge
Nov. 21st, '94

My dear Russell

I've just come back from such a funny concert—not that it was particularly funny, but I was put in a thoroughly unmusical frame of mind by the first performer who appeared—one of the wiry and businesslike kind (of monkeys, I mean—she is a monkey)—she played very much like a person, but not quite. Of course it was very creditable to the result of so recent an evolution to do it so well but it hindered one's appreciation of the music. The next person was a singer—one of those middle aged ladies who have an air of being caricatures of their former selves—she made one of those curious confessions which are only heard in Concert rooms about her behaviour once in a state of drink, when she embraced a gentleman in her arms—Te souviens-tu de notre ivresse quand nos bras étaient enlacés? Conybeare remarked that if she was in ivresse she was now in evening dress—her arch curtseys at the end were a sight to be seen.

When did I last write to you? Have you heard about Moore's paper on Friendship? There's not much to say about it, as it was a specification of one's own ideal more or less, without much practical bearing. Of course our poor old friend copulation came in for its usual slating, one wd. think from the way people talk about it in the Society that it was a kind of Home Rule Bill that has to be taken some notice of, but which everyone thinks a bore. The discussion was interesting. Trevy, Theo and Mayor were all up. Mayor gave Theo occasion to say he hadn't expected to find him such a middle aged phenomenon so soon. Mayor took wings—Wedd was there too, he and Theo talked well.[1] Last Sat. McT. read an old paper. Why are roseleaves crumpled?

1 Mayor and Theodore Davies were exact contemporaries, Mayor being the best and Theodore the second-best classical scholar of their year. To 'take wings' is to retire from habitual presence at meetings of The Society, which usually is done in the man's fifth or sixth year.

on the origin of evil.—It wasn't quite satisfactory, as on the one hand MacT. has changed his position since he wrote it, and on the other it was rather a nuisance no one except him knowing the dialectic—one felt like the audience at an extension-lecture. Sanger reads on What is education on Sat. Crompton will be up.

Lady Trevy was up today. I always like her very much, she has such an essential gaiety. I met a lovely person on Sunday, Miss Stawell, whom Dickinson was nice enough to ask me to meet. I think she's very superior indeed—she seems to have quite a rare feeling for beauty in art, I hope we shall see more of her. Mayor's sister was there too, she seemed rather common and flippant in comparison. It's great fun seeing so much of Verrall as I do now—(I go to him for composition again), the other day I asked him the meaning of something in the Shelley we had to translate—'I'm sure I can't tell you my little dear', he answered, 'you pays yr money and you takes your choice.' That kind of think makes me very cheerful.[1]

The day's coming very near now, isn't it? What a wonderful thought. Remember to tell me how your grandmother is when you write.

Yrs. fraternally
Edward M. (Marsh)

By the way thanks for the photograph, it's good on the whole, tho' you look rather bumptious.

Pembroke Lodge,
Richmond, Surrey
Sep. 16/'94

Dearest Bertie

I can't say I am much *disappointed* with your second letter—for 'I mean' to do so and so in yr first left little hope of yr considering any other course. Of course I am *very* sorry, as U.R. and Auntie will be—she writes as if she cd not think you wd. wish to be out of the country this winter—but that is nothing.[2] You must do what you think best, and I must remember

> As one by one thy hopes depart
> Be resolute and calm—

They *have* been departing in rapid succession of late—but when I turn my mind to good and happy Dunrozel, to human perfection in Agatha, to the goodness and unceasing affection of my *old* children and *their* children, to other relations and to many faithful friends, I feel how much beauty there still is in life for wch in my old age I have to thank God. And for you, my too dear boy, I can only try to hope, though the way is not easy to find. Have you called on the people to whom the Baronne gave you letters? She asked me yesterday. The Warburtons are gone, and Lotty,[3] dear wonderful Lotty, come. You know what it is to her and me to be together. I'm glad you like Mr Dodson

---

[1] Miss Stawell became a very distinguished classicist.
[2] On the ground that she was likely to die during the winter.
[3] Her sister, Lady Charlotte Portal.

(no J)—I think there must be everythg. to like in Mr Hardinge or Ld. Dufferin wd. not call him 'a great friend'—I did not imagine Ld. Terence to be very nice—Ld. D's children seem to be rather disappointments. Of course one cannot find everybody with whom one has intercourse having the same interests as oneself, but one can often be the better for entering into theirs—I do hope that as time goes on and you know more people, you will enjoy Paris thoroughly—there is so much to enjoy there. Very good accounts of Auntie you'll be glad to hear but this is horrid letterless Sunday. Rollo proposes to come to me the 20th when Lotty goes—brings Arthur and Lisa—for 10 days—such a joy in prospect.

Goodbye and God bless you my dearest Child.

Yr. ever loving
Granny

My letters are for you alone—Remember I am more than willing to believe that you will profit by yr German experience, as regards yr studies.

Pembroke Lodge
Richmond, Surrey
Oct. 9, '94

Dearest Bertie

I am glad you have had more Embassy work to do, I guessed it would be so, owing to the 'tension' I think that's the diplomatic word—between England and France—it must also have been more interesting work I shd think? I hope and trust that both countries will behave well, in wch case peace and goodwill will be preserved. I shd think the Govt of both likely to do so. I am also very glad Mr Austin Lee is back—he is a man well worth knowing. By this time, accordg to the D.E.'s (d'Estournelles), a good many of their friends are returning to Paris and I shall be anxious to hear how you get on with the scientific, the political, the musical and charming among them to whom you have letters. . . .

My dearest Child, you must not wish time to pass more quickly than it does! There is little enough of it for us to make the use of that we ought. Of course I understand as anybody would that you regret even this short separation—but perhaps you don't know how *very* much you would have suffered in the estimation of the many who wish you well in the highest sense and care for us and know what we had always thought and felt about, had you remained in England leading the life you were leading—indeed you had already suffered greatly and so had she and I felt that having work to do abroad was the only chance to prevent increasing blame and if you are to marry her, before you have learned to know anybody else, I do most earnestly wish that there may be as little unfavourable impression as possible. You wrote to me once, dear boy, that you dreamed of me constantly by night and thought of me by day and wondered how you cd make me happier about you—and I have sometimes thought of puttg down on paper what has made me and yr Uncle and Aunt so unhappy—in regular order of events and incidents—to help you, even now,

119

to make us happier. Shall I do so? There is nothing I wish more ardently than to have good reason to love dearly the person you marry if I live to see you married. I am going on pretty well—only a very slow downward progress of the disease—so that I am still able to do pretty much as usual, except breathing in bed—I have discomfort but nothg worth callg pain.

If you write to Auntie only say about me that you hear I am going on very well.

Yr most loving
Granny

Pembroke Lodge
Richmond, Surrey
Oct. 23/'94

Dearest Bertie

We were glad of your letter to Tat,[1] but sorry that no notice had yet been taken of your cards. The cycling in the Bois de Boulogne must be great fun. I suppose you go with the others? You don't mention Lord Dufferin having arrived; which according to newspapers ought I think to be the case. What a pity Frank's visit was no pleasure. I think he really went out of good nature to you on my telling him how lonely you felt, but we quite understand what you mean. I am better for the moment. I hope it may turn out for more than the moment—for Agatha's sake especially. She, poor darling, is far from well, and obliged to stay very late in bed. Dear good Isabel [Mrs Warburton] went yesterday—her visit has been touchingly delightful, in spite of or indeed partly because of my being very unwell most of the time—she is so simpatica, and we had much solemn conversation intermingled with pressing topics.—You have never answered my next to last letter, which I thought you would like but I will not enter upon the subject of you and Miss P. S.—writing is so unsatisfactory—except just to say her refusal to see me makes everything very difficult to me. It is the first time in my long life that such a thing has happened to me. I don't think it is doing her any good and tho' for her sake I put it as gently as I can. She was so good and thanked me when from my interest in her I several times told her where I thought she had been wrong—and on her various visits after that she was altogether nice, and I was growing happy and hopeful that we should find her deserving of the love we were more than ready to give. Then came the sudden and to us unaccountable change—and I cannot but be saddened by the thought that the person you love is one who refuses to see me and whom therefore I can never know any better even if I live longer than is likely. However nothing can pain me much longer here below, and in the meantime I try as a duty not to think about all this, as it seems that mental troubles are particularly bad for my kind of illness. God bless you, my boy, and her too, is my most earnest prayer.

Yr ever loving
Granny

[1] Aunt Agatha.

Pembroke Lodge
Richmond, Surrey
Oct. 30, 1894

Dearest Bertie

Granny is much less well again—bad nights, pains and weakness. She is quite kept to bed today—and yesterday. Of course she cannot see yr. letters. I have told her of them. She long ago saw Alys's letter to her and I think you will remember that in hers to Alys she said she wished *once* to say what she felt on that subject of yr proposed course—and never again. I suppose you will come here on yr way to Cambridge? *Let me know* at once. Granny I'm certain will be medically ordered never to touch on painful subjects and of course, I never shall, and she has once for all said what she felt and what was her duty to say if she cared for you and Alys. Dearest Bertie I cannot write more I am so disheartened seeing Granny suffer. It pains me beyond expression that you think I have been 'hard' and without sympathy. If my words have ever seemed so you must remember and will know some day that only love was in my heart and that nothing but love prevented absolute silence on my part for speaking was far more painful then you now understand

Your loving
Auntie

Pembroke Lodge
Richmond, Surrey
Nov. 19, 1894

My dear Alys

Rollo reminded us that Dec. 14th was the day of the death of Prince Albert and of Princess Alice—and considering our situation with regard to the Queen, we feel we could none of us like the Wedding being on that day. I am sure you will not mind our mentioning this. Would not the 15th do? We did not quite understand the reasons against that day. I hope you and Bertie had a pleasant visit to Dover Street.

Yours affectly.
Agatha Russell

Pembroke Lodge
Richmond, Surrey
Dec. 10, 1894

My dearest Child

As my voice fails me whenever I try to speak of what is coming, although it is an event so full of happiness to you, it is natural that I should write you a few farewell words. More especially on this anniversary of a day once among the gladdest and most beloved of the year[1]—now as sad as it is sacred for me. For the memories it brings me of my dear, my gentle, my noble and deeply loving and hardly tried Johnny, naturally turn my thoughts to you, in whom

[1] My father's birthday.

121

we have always felt that something was still left to us of him—My memories of him are memories of unutterable joy, mingled with sorrow and anguish hard to bear even now when *he* is past all sorrows.

When he and your mother, in the bloom of youth and health, asked me to look upon you as my own child in case of their death, I little thought that I should be called upon to fulfil the promise I gave them. But ere long the day came and your home was left empty. You came to us as an innocent, unconscious little comforter in our darkened home, and have been to us all three as our very own child. You were intertwined with our very being, our life was shaped and ordered with a view to your good; and as you grew in heart and mind you became our companion as well as our child. How thankfully I remember that all through your childhood and boyhood you would always cheerfully give up your own wishes for those of others, never attempt an excuse when you had done wrong, and never fail to receive warning or reproof as gratefully as praise. We trusted you, and you justified our trust, and all was happiness and affection.

Manhood came and brought with it fresh cause for thankfulness in your blameless and honourable University career. But manhood brings also severance and change. You are leaving us now for a new life, a new home, new ties and new affections. But your happiness and welfare must still be ours and our God will still be yours. May you take with you only that which has been best, and ask His forgiveness for what has been wrong, in the irrevocable past. May He inspire you to cherish holy thoughts and noble aims. May you remember that humble, loving hearts alone are dear to Him. May such a heart ever be yours, and hers who is to travel life's journey by your side.

God bless you both, and grant you light to find and to follow the heavenward path.

Ever, my dear, dear Child
Your most loving
Granny

The following letter was my last contact with Edward FitzGerald. He distinguished himself as a climber in New Zealand and the Andes, after escaping in this way from a period of despair brought about by his wife's death after only a few months of marriage. In the end he ran off with a married lady and made no attempt to keep up with old friends.

Colombo, Ceylon
Nov. 18th, '94

My dear Russell

Drop me a line occasionally to tell me how you are getting on and also when your marriage is coming off.

I have stopped here for a little while to look around. I went up country the other day to Anuradhapura and to Vauakarayankulam (don't try to pronounce that name, I find it worse than snakes) and got some big game shooting which I enjoyed. The country was however all under water and they said very feverish, but I did not feel that although I slept out several nights in the mists and got drenched through. I am off on a regular spree so to speak and am not coming home for three years at least. I have planned Japan and some climbing in South America before I return.

Drop me a line when you feel so inclined that I may know of your wandering. I will write occasionally when I feel so inclined, which you will say is not often. I suppose you have seen Austin's new apartment in the Avenue Hochell?

I will now draw this (letter?!) to a close.

Ever yours
Edw. A. Fitzgerald

CHAPTER V

FIRST MARRIAGE

ALYS AND I were married on December 13, 1894. Her family had been Philadelphia Quakers for over two hundred years, and she was still a believing member of the Society of Friends. So we were married in Quaker Meeting in St Martin's Lane. I seem to remember that one of the Quakers present was moved by the Spirit to preach about the miracle of Cana, which hurt Alys's teetotal feelings. During our engagement we had frequently had arguments about Christianity, but I did not succeed in changing her opinions until a few months after we were married.

There were other matters upon which her opinions changed after marriage. She had been brought up, as American women always were in those days, to think that sex was beastly, that all women hated it, and that men's brutal lusts were the chief obstacle to happiness in marriage. She therefore thought that intercourse should only take place when children were desired. As we had decided to have no children, she had to modify her position on this point, but she still supposed that she would desire intercourse to be very rare. I did not argue the matter, and I did not find it necessary to do so.

Neither she nor I had any previous experience of sexual intercourse when we married. We found, as such couples apparently usually do, a certain amount of difficulty at the start. I have heard many people say that this caused their honeymoon to be a difficult time, but we had no such experience. The difficulties appeared to us merely comic, and were soon overcome. I remember, however, a day after three weeks of marriage, when, under the influence of sexual fatigue, I hated her and could not imagine why I had wished to marry her. This state of mind lasted just as long as the journey from Amsterdam to Berlin, after which I never again experienced a similar mood.

We had decided that during the early years of our married life, we would see a good deal of foreign countries, and accordingly we spent the first three months of 1895 in Berlin. I went to the university, where I chiefly studied economics. I continued to work at my Fellowship dissertation. We went to concerts three times a week, and we began to know the Social Democrats, who were at that time considered very wicked. Lady Ermyntrude Malet, the wife of the Ambassador, was my cousin, so we were asked to dinner at the Embassy. Everybody was friendly, and the attachés all said they would call. However, none of them came, and when we called at the Embassy, nobody was at home. For a long time we hardly noticed all this, but at last we discovered that it was due to Alys having mentioned to the Ambassador that we had been to a socialist meeting. We learned this from a letter of Lady Ermyntrude's to my grandmother. In spite of my grandmother's prejudice against Alys, she completely sided with her on this matter. The issue was a public one, and on all public political issues, both she and my Aunt Agatha could always be relied upon not to be illiberal.

During this time my intellectual ambitions were taking shape. I resolved not to adopt a profession, but to devote myself to writing. I remember a cold, bright day in early spring when I walked by myself in the Tiergarten, and made projects of future work. I thought that I would write one series of books on the philosophy of the sciences from pure mathematics to physiology, and another series of books on social questions. I hoped that the two series might ultimately meet in a synthesis at once scientific and practical. My scheme was largely inspired by Hegelian ideas. Nevertheless, I have to some extent followed it in later years, as much at any rate as could have been expected. The moment was an important and formative one as regards my purposes.

When the spring came, we went to Fiesole and stayed with Alys's sister, who lived in a small villa, while Berenson lived next door in another small villa. After leaving her, we travelled down the Adriatic coast, staying at Pesaro, Urbino, Ravenna, Rimini, Ancona, and various other places. This remains in my memory as one of the happiest times of my life. Italy and the spring and first love all together should suffice to make the gloomiest person happy. We used to bathe naked in the sea, and lie on the sand to dry, but this was a somewhat perilous sport, as sooner or later a policeman would come along to see that no one got salt out of the sea in defiance of the salt tax. Fortunately we were never quite caught.

By this time, it was becoming necessary to think in earnest about my Fellowship dissertation, which had to be finished by August, so we settled down at Fernhurst, and I had my first experience of serious original work. There were days of hope alternating with days of despair, but at last, when my dissertation was finished, I fully believed that I had solved all philosophical questions connected with the foundations of geometry. I did not yet know that the hopes and despairs connected with original work are alike fallacious, that one's work is never so bad as it appears on bad days, nor so good as it appears on good days. My dissertation was read by Whitehead and James Ward, since it was in part mathematical and in part philosophical. Before the result was announced, Whitehead criticized it rather severely, though quite justly, and I came to the conclusion that it was worthless and that I would not wait for the result to be announced. However, as a matter of politeness I went to see James Ward, who said exactly the opposite, and praised it to the skies. Next day I learned that I had been elected a Fellow, and Whitehead informed me with a smile that he had thought it was the last chance anyone would get of finding serious fault with my work.

With my first marriage, I entered upon a period of great happiness and fruitful work. Having no emotional troubles, all my energy went in intellectual directions. Throughout the first years of my marriage, I read widely, both in mathematics and in philosophy. I achieved a certain amount of original work, and laid the foundations for other work later. I travelled abroad, and in my spare time I did a great deal of solid reading, chiefly history. After dinner, my wife and I used to read aloud in turns, and in this way we ploughed through large numbers of standard histories in many volumes. I think the last book that we read in this way was the *History of the City of Rome* by Gregorovius. This was intellectually the most fruitful period of my life, and I owe a debt of gratitude to my first wife for having made it possible. At first she disliked the idea of living quietly in the country, but I was determined to do so for the sake of my work. I derived sufficient happiness from her and my work to have no need of anything more, though as a matter of fact it was, as a rule, only about half the year that we spent quietly in the country. Even during that period, she would often be away making speeches on votes for women or total abstinence. I had become a pledged teetotaller in order to please her, and from habit I remained so after the original motive had ceased to move me. I did not take to drink until the King took the pledge during the first war. His motive was to facilitate the killing of Germans, and it therefore seemed as if there must be some connection between pacifism and alcohol.

In the autumn of 1895, after the Fellowship election, we went back to Berlin to study German Social Democracy. On this visit, we associated almost exclusively with socialists. We got to know Bebel and the elder Liebknecht. The younger Liebknecht, who was killed just after the first war, was at this time a boy. We must have met him when we dined at his father's house, although I have no recollection of him. In those days Social Democrats were fiery revolutionaries, and I was too young to realize what they would be like when they acquired power. At the beginning of 1896 I gave a course of lectures on them at the London School of Economics, which was at that time in John Street, Adelphi. I was, I believe, their first lecturer. There I got to know W. A. S. Hewins, who considerably influenced me from that time until 1901. He came of a Catholic family, and had substituted the British Empire for the Church as an object of veneration.

I was, in those days, much more high-strung than I became later on. While I was lecturing at the School of Economics, my wife and I lived in a flat at 90 Ashley Gardens, but I could not work there because the noise of the lift disturbed me, so I used to walk every day to her parents' house in Grosvenor Road, where I spent the time reading Georg Cantor, and copying out the gist of him into a notebook. At that time I falsely supposed all his arguments to be fallacious, but I nevertheless went through them all in the minutest detail. This stood me in good stead when later on I discovered that all the fallacies were mine.

When the spring came, we took a small labourer's cottage at Fernhurst, called 'The Millhanger', to which we added a fair-sized sitting-room and two bedrooms. In this cottage many of the happiest times of my life were passed. I acquired a great deal of knowledge that interested me, and my original work was praised by experts more highly than I expected. While I was an undergraduate I did not think my abilities so good as they afterwards turned out to be. I remember wondering, as an almost unattainable ideal, whether I should ever do work as good as McTaggart's. During the early years of my first marriage Whitehead passed gradually from a teacher into a friend. In 1890 as a Freshman at Cambridge, I had attended his lectures on statics. He told the class to study article 35 in the text-book. Then he turned to me and said, 'You needn't study it, because you know it already'. I had quoted it by number in the scholarship examination ten months earlier. He won my heart by remembering this fact.

In England, Whitehead was regarded only as a mathematician, and it was left to America to discover him as a philosopher. He and I disagreed in philosophy, so that collaboration was no longer possible, and after he went to America I naturally saw much less of him. We began to drift apart during the first world war when he completely disagreed with my pacifist position. In our differences on this subject he was more tolerant than I was, and it was much more my fault than his that these differences caused a diminution in the closeness of our friendship.

In the last months of the war his younger son, who was only just eighteen, was killed. This was an appalling grief to him, and it was only by an immense effort of moral discipline that he was able to go on with his work. The pain of this loss had a great deal to do with turning his thoughts to philosophy and with causing him to seek ways of escaping from belief in a merely mechanistic universe. His philosophy was very obscure, and there was much in it that I never succeeded in understanding. He had always had a leaning towards Kant, of whom I thought ill, and when he began to develop his own philosophy he was considerably influenced by Bergson. He was impressed by the aspect of unity in the universe, and considered that it is only through this aspect that scientific inferences can be justified. My temperament led me in the opposite direction, but I doubt whether pure reason could have decided which of us was more nearly in the right. Those who prefer his outlook might say that while he aimed at bringing comfort to plain people I aimed at bringing discomfort to philosophers; one who favoured my outlook might retort that while he pleased the philosophers, I amused the plain people. However that may be, we went our separate ways, though affection survived to the last.

Whitehead was a man of extraordinarily wide interests, and his knowledge of history used to amaze me. At one time I discovered by chance that he was using that very serious and rather out-of-the-way work Paolo Sarpi's *History of the Council of Trent*, as a bed book. Whatever historical subjects came up he could always supply some illuminating fact, such, for example, as the connection of Burke's political opinions with his interests in the City, and the relation of the Hussite heresy to the Bohemian silver mines. He had delightful humour and great gentleness. When I was an undergraduate he was given the nickname of 'the Cherub', which those who knew him in later life would think unduly disrespectful but which at the time suited him. His family came from Kent and had been clergymen ever since about the time of the landing of St Augustine in that county. He used to relate with amusement that my grandfather, who was much exercised by the spread of Roman Catholicism, adjured Whitehead's sister never to desert the Church of England. What amused him was that the contingency was so very improbable. Whitehead's theological opinions were not orthodox, but something of the vicarage atmosphere remained in his ways of feeling and came out in his later philosophical writings.

He was a very modest man, and his most extreme boast was that he did try to have the qualities of his defects. He never minded telling stories against himself. There were two old ladies in Cambridge who were sisters and whose manners suggested that they came straight out of *Cranford*. They were, in fact, advanced and even daring in their opinions, and were in the forefront of every movement of reform. Whitehead used to relate, somewhat ruefully, how when he first met them he was misled by their exterior and thought it would be fun to shock them a little. But when he advanced some slightly radical opinion they said, 'Oh, Mr Whitehead, we are so pleased to hear *you* say that', showing that they had hitherto viewed him as a pillar of reaction.

His capacity for concentration on work was quite extraordinary. One hot summer's day, when I was staying with him at Grantchester, our friend Crompton Davies arrived and I took him into the garden to say how-do-you-do to his host. Whitehead was sitting writing mathematics. Davies and I stood in front of him at a distance of no more than a yard and watched him covering page after page with symbols. He never saw us, and after a time we went away with a feeling of awe.

Those who knew Whitehead well became aware of many things in him which did not appear in more casual contacts. Socially he appeared kindly, rational and imperturbable, but he was not in fact imperturbable, and was certainly not that inhuman monster 'the rational man'. His devotion to his wife and his children was profound and passionate. He was at all times deeply aware of the importance of religion. As a young man, he was all but converted to Roman Catholicism by the influence of Cardinal Newman. His later philosophy gave him some part of what he wanted from religion. Like other men who lead extremely disciplined lives, he was liable to distressing soliloquies, and when he thought he was alone, he would mutter abuse of himself for his supposed shortcomings. The early years of his marriage were much clouded by financial anxieties, but, although he found this very difficult to bear, he never let it turn him aside from work that was important but not lucrative.

He had practical abilities which at the time when I knew him best did not find very much scope. He had a kind of shrewdness which was surprising and which enabled him to get his way on committees in a manner astonishing to those who thought of him as wholly abstract and unworldly. He might have been an able administrator but for one defect, which was a complete inability to answer letters. I once wrote a letter to him on a mathematical point, as to which I urgently needed an answer for an article I was writing against Poincaré. He did not answer, so I wrote again. He still did not answer, so I telegraphed. As he was still silent, I sent a reply-paid telegram. But in the end, I had to travel down to Broadstairs to get the answer. His friends gradually got to know this peculiarity, and on the rare occasions when any of them got a letter from him they would all assemble to congratulate the recipient. He justified himself by saying that if he answered letters, he would have no time for original work. I think the justification was complete and unanswerable.

Whitehead was extraordinarily perfect as a teacher. He took a personal interest in those with whom he had to deal and knew both their strong and their weak points. He would elicit from a pupil the best of which a pupil was capable. He was never repressive, or sarcastic, or superior, or any of the things that inferior teachers like to be. I think that in all the abler young men with whom he came in contact he inspired, as he did in me, a very real and lasting affection.

Whitehead and his wife used to stay with us in the country, and we used to stay with them in Cambridge. Once we stayed with the old Master, Montagu Butler, in the Lodge, and slept in Queen Anne's bed, but this experience fortunately was not repeated.

My lectures on German Socialism were published in 1896. This was my first book, but I took no great interest in it, as I had determined to devote myself to mathematical philosophy. I re-wrote my Fellowship dissertation, and got it accepted by the Cambridge University Press, who published it in 1897 under the title *An Essay on the Foundations of Geometry*. I subsequently came to think this book much too Kantian, but it was fortunate for my reputation that my first philosophical work did not challenge the orthodoxy of the time. It was the custom in academic circles to dismiss all critics of Kant as persons who had failed to understand him, and in rebutting this criticism it was an advantage to have once agreed with him. The book was highly praised, far more highly in fact than it deserved. Since that time, academic reviewers have generally said of each successive book of mine that it showed a falling-off.

In the autumn of 1896, Alys and I went to America for three months, largely in order that I might make the acquaintance of her relations.[1] The first thing we did was to visit Walt Whitman's house in Camden, N.J. From there we went to a small manufacturing town called Millville, where a cousin of hers, named Bond Thomas, was the manager of a glass factory which had, for a long time, been the family business. His wife, Edith, was a great friend of Alys's. According to the Census, the town had 10,002 inhabitants, and they used to say that they were the two. He was a simple soul, but she had literary aspirations. She wrote bad plays in the style of Scribe, and imagined that if only she could get away from Millville and establish contact with the literary lights of Europe, her talent would be recognized. He was humbly devoted to her, but she had various flirtations with men whom she imagined to be of finer clay. In those days the country round about consisted of empty woodland, and she used to take me long drives over dirt tracks in a buggy. She always carried a revolver, saying one could never know when it would come in handy. Subsequent events led me to suspect that she had been reading *Hedda Gabler*. Two years later, they both came to stay with us in a palace in Venice, and we introduced her to various writers. It turned out that the work she had produced with such labour

[1] With us we took Bonté Amos, the sister of Maurice Sheldon Amos; see pp. 141 ff.

during the ten years' isolation in Millville was completely worthless. She went back to America profoundly discouraged, and the next we heard was that, after placing her husband's love letters over her heart, she had shot herself through them with the revolver. He subsequently married another woman who was said to be exactly like her.

We went next to Bryn Mawr to stay with the President, Carey Thomas, sister of Bond Thomas. She was a lady who was treated almost with awe by all the family. She had immense energy, a belief in culture which she carried out with a business man's efficiency, and a profound contempt for the male sex. The first time I met her, which was at Friday's Hill, Logan said to me before her arrival: 'Prepare to meet thy Carey.' This expressed the family attitude. I was never able myself, however, to take her quite seriously, because she was so easily shocked. She had the wholly admirable view that a person who intends to write on an academic subject should first read up the literature, so I gravely informed her that all the advances in non-Euclidean geometry had been made in ignorance of the previous literature, and even because of that ignorance. This caused her ever afterwards to regard me as a mere *farceur*. Various incidents, however, confirmed me in my view of her. For instance, once in Paris we took her to see 'L'Aiglon', and I found from her remarks that she did not know there had been a Revolution in France in 1830. I gave her a little sketch of French history, and a few days later she told me that her secretary desired a handbook of French history, and asked me to recommend one. However, at Bryn Mawr she was Zeus, and everybody trembled before her. She lived with a friend, Miss Gwinn, who was in most respects the opposite of her. Miss Gwinn had very little will-power, was soft and lazy, but had a genuine though narrow feeling for literature. They had been friends from early youth, and had gone together to Germany to get the Ph.D degree, which, however, only Carey had succeeded in getting. At the time that we stayed with them, their friendship had become a little ragged. Miss Gwinn used to go home to her family for three days in every fortnight, and at the exact moment of her departure each fortnight, another lady, named Miss Garrett, used to arrive, to depart again at the exact moment of Miss Gwinn's return. Miss Gwinn, meantime, had fallen in love with a very brilliant young man, named Hodder, who was teaching at Bryn Mawr. This roused Carey to fury, and every night, as we were going to bed, we used to hear her angry voice scolding Miss Gwinn in the next room for hours together. Hodder had a wife and child, and was said to have affairs with the girls at the College. In spite of all these obstacles, however, Miss Gwinn finally married him. She insisted upon getting a very High

Church clergyman to perform the ceremony, thereby making it clear that the wife whom he had had at Bryn Mawr was not his legal wife, since the clergyman in question refused to marry divorced persons. Hodder had given out that there had been a divorce, but Miss Gwinn's action showed that this had not been the case. He died soon after their marriage, worn out with riotous living. He had a very brilliant mind, and in the absence of women could talk very interestingly.

While at Bryn Mawr, I gave lectures on non-Euclidean geometry, and Alys gave addresses in favour of endowment of motherhood, combined with private talks to women in favour of free love. This caused a scandal, and we were practically hounded out of the college. From there we went to Baltimore, where I lectured on the same subject at the Johns Hopkins University. There we stayed with her uncle, Dr Thomas, the father of Carey. The Thomases were a curious family. There was a son at Johns Hopkins who was very brilliant in brain surgery; there was a daughter, Helen, at Bryn Mawr, who had the misfortune to be deaf. She was gentle and kind, and had very lovely red hair. I was very fond of her for a number of years, culminating in 1900. Once or twice I asked her to kiss me, but she refused. Ultimately she married Simon Flexner, the Head of the Rockefeller Institute of Preventive Medicine. I remained very good friends with her, although in the last years of her life I saw her seldom. There was another daughter who had remained a pious and very orthodox Quaker. She always alluded to those who were not Quakers as 'the world's people'. They all of them used 'thee' in conversation, and so did Alys and I when we talked to each other. Some of the Quaker doctrines seemed a little curious to those not accustomed to them. I remember my mother-in-law explaining that she was taught to consider the Lord's Prayer 'gay'. At first this remark caused bewilderment, but she explained that everything done by non-Quakers but not by Quakers was called 'gay', and this included the use of all fixed formulas, since prayer ought to be inspired by the Holy Spirit. The Lord's Prayer, being a fixed formula, was therefore 'gay'. On another occasion she informed the dinner-table that she had been brought up to have no respect for the Ten Commandments. They also were 'gay'. I do not know whether any Quakers remain who take the doctrine of the guidance of the Spirit so seriously as to have no respect for the Ten Commandments. Certainly I have not met any in recent years. It must not, of course, be supposed that the virtuous people who had this attitude ever, in fact, infringed any of the Commandments; the Holy Spirit saw to it that this should not occur. Outside the ranks of the Quakers, similar doctrines some-times have more questionable consequences. I remember an account written by my mother-in-law of various cranks that she had known, in which there was one chapter entitled 'Divine Guidance'. On reading the chapter one discovered that this was a synonym for fornication.

My impression of the old families of Philadelphia Quakers was that they had all the effeteness of a small aristocracy. Old misers of ninety would sit brooding over their hoard while their children of sixty or seventy waited for their death with what patience they could command. Various forms of mental disorder appeared common. Those who must be accounted sane were apt to be very stupid. Alys had a maiden aunt in Philadelphia, a sister of her father, who was very rich and very absurd. She liked me well enough, but had a dark suspicion that I thought it was not *literally* the blood of Jesus that brought salvation. I do not know how she got this notion, as I never said anything to encourage it. We dined with her on Thanksgiving Day. She was a very greedy old lady, and had supplied a feast which required a gargantuan stomach. Just as we were about to eat the first mouthful, she said: 'Let us pause and think of the poor.' Apparently she found this thought an appetizer. She had two nephews who lived in her neighbourhood and came to see her every evening. They felt it would be unfair if the nephew and nieces in Europe got an equal share at her death. She, however, liked to boast about them, and respected them more than those whom she could bully as she chose. Consequently they lost nothing by their absence.

America in those days was a curiously innocent country. Numbers of men asked me to explain what it was that Oscar Wilde had done. In Boston we stayed in a boarding-house kept by two old Quaker ladies, and one of them at breakfast said to me in a loud voice across the table: 'Oscar Wilde has not been much before the public lately. What has he been doing?' 'He is in prison', I replied. Fortunately on this occasion I was not asked what he had done. I viewed America in those days with the conceited superiority of the insular Briton. Nevertheless, contact with academic Americans, especially mathematicians, led me to realize the superiority of Germany to England in almost all academic matters. Against my will, in the course of my travels, the belief that everything worth knowing was known at Cambridge gradually wore off. In this respect my travels were very useful to me.

Of the year 1897 I remember very little except that my *Foundations of Geometry* was published in that year. I remember also very great pleasure in receiving a letter of praise of this book from Louis Couturat, whom at that time I had never met, though I had reviewed his book *The Mathematical Infinite*. I had dreamed of receiving letters of praise from unknown foreigners, but this was the first time it had happened to me. He related how he had worked his way through my book 'armé d'un dictionnaire', for he knew no English. At a slightly later date I went to Caen to visit him, as he was at that time a professor there. He was surprised to find me so young, but in spite of that a friendship began which lasted until he was killed by a lorry during the mobilization of 1914. In the last years I had lost contact with him, because he became absorbed in the question of an international language. He advocated Ido rather than Esperanto. According to his conversation, no human beings in the whole previous history of the human race had ever been quite so depraved as the Esperantists. He lamented that the word Ido did not lend itself to the formation of a word similar to Esperantist. I suggested 'idiot', but he was not quite pleased. I remember lunching with him in Paris in July 1900, when the heat was very oppressive. Mrs Whitehead, who had a weak heart, fainted, and while he was gone to fetch the *sal volatile* somebody opened the window. When he returned, he firmly shut it again, saying: 'De l'air, oui, mais pas de courant d'air.' I remember too his coming to see me in a hotel in Paris in 1905, while Mr Davies and his daughter Margaret (the father and sister of Crompton and Theodore) listened to his conversation. He talked without a moment's intermission for half an hour, and then remarked that 'the wise are those who hold their tongues'. At this point, Mr Davies, in spite of his eighty years, rushed from the room, and I could just hear the sound of his laughter as he disappeared. Couturat was for a time a very ardent advocate of my ideas on mathematical logic, but he was not always very prudent, and in my long duel with Poincaré I found it sometimes something of a burden to have to defend Couturat as well as myself. His most valuable work was on Leibniz's logic. Leibniz wished to be thought well of, so he published only his second-rate work. All his best work remained in manuscript. Subsequent editors, publishing only what *they* thought best, continued to leave his best work unprinted. Couturat was the first man who unearthed it. I was naturally pleased, as it afforded documentary evidence for the interpretation of Leibniz which I had adopted in my book about him on grounds that, without Couturat's work, would have remained inadequate. The first time I met Couturat he explained to me that he did not practise any branch of 'le sport'. When shortly afterwards I asked him if he rode a bicycle, he replied: 'But no, since I am not a sportsman.' I corresponded with him for many years, and during the early stages of the Boer War wrote him imperialistic letters which I now consider very regrettable.

In the year 1898 Alys and I began a practice, which we continued till 1902, of spending part of each year at Cambridge. I was at this time beginning to emerge from the bath of German idealism in which I had been plunged by McTaggart and Stout. I was very much assisted in this process by Moore, of whom at that time I saw a great deal. It was an intense excitement, after having supposed the sensible world unreal, to be able to believe again that there really were such things as tables and chairs. But the most interesting aspect of the matter to me was the logical aspect. I was glad to think that relations are real, and I was interested to discover the dire effect upon metaphysics of the belief that all propositions are of the subject-predicate form. Accident led me to read Leibniz, because he had to be lectured upon, and McTaggart wanted to go to New Zealand, so that the College asked me to take his place so far as this one course was concerned. In the study and criticism of Leibniz I found occasion to exemplify the new views on logic to which, largely under Moore's guidance, I had been led.

We spent two successive autumns in Venice, and I got to know almost every stone in the place. From the date of my first marriage down to the outbreak of the first war, I do not think any year passed without my going to Italy. Sometimes I went on foot, sometimes on a bicycle; once in a tramp steamer calling at every little port from Venice to Genoa. I loved especially the smaller and more out-of-the-way towns, and the mountain landscapes in the Apennines. After the outbreak of the war, I did not go back to Italy till 1949. I had the intention of going there to a Congress in the year 1922, but Mussolini, who had not yet accomplished his *coup d'état*, sent word to the organizers of the Congress that, while no harm should be done to me, any Italian who spoke to me should be assassinated. Having no wish to leave a trail of blood behind me, I avoided the country which he defiled, dearly as I loved it.

I remember the summer of 1899 as the last time that I saw Sally Fairchild until one afternoon in 1940, when we met as old people and wondered what we had seen in each other. She was an aristocratic Bostonian of somewhat diminished fortunes, whom I had first come to know in 1896 when we were staying in Boston. In the face she was not strikingly beautiful, but her movements were the most graceful that I have ever seen. Innumerable people fell in love with her. She used to say that you could always tell when an Englishman was going to propose, because he began: 'The governor's a rum sort of chap, but I think you'd get on with him.' The next time that I met her, she was staying with her mother at Rushmore, the country house of my Uncle, General Pitt-Rivers. With the exception of the General, most of the family were more or less mad. Mrs Pitt-Rivers, who was a Stanley, had become a miser, and if visitors left any of their bacon and egg she would put it back in the dish. The eldest son was a Guardsman, very smart and very correct. He always came down late for breakfast and rang the bell for fresh food. When he ordered it, my Aunt would scream at the footman, saying that there was no need of it as there was plenty left from the scrapings from the visitors' plates. The footman, however, paid no attention to her, but quietly obeyed the Guardsman. Then there was another son, who was a painter, mad and bad, but not sad. There was a third son who was a nice fellow, but incompetent. He had the good luck to marry Elspeth Phelps, the dressmaker, and thus escaped destitution. Then there was St George, the most interesting of the family. He was one of the first inventors of electric light, but he threw up all such things for esoteric Buddhism and spent his time travelling in Tibet to visit Mahatmas. When he returned, he found that Edison and Swan were making electric lights which he considered an infringement of his patent. He therefore entered upon a long series of lawsuits, which he always lost and which finally left him bankrupt. This confirmed him in the Buddhist faith that one should overcome mundane desires. My grandmother Stanley used to make him play whist, and when it came to his turn to deal, she used to say: 'I am glad it is your turn to deal, as it will take away your air of saintliness.' He combined saintliness and Company promoting in about equal proportions. He was in love with Sally Fairchild and had on that account invited her mother and her to Rushmore. There was as usual not enough food, and on one occasion at lunch there was a tug-of-war between Sally and the artist for the last plate of rice pudding, which I regret to say the artist won. On the day of her departure she wished to catch a certain train but Mrs Pitt-Rivers insisted that she should visit a certain ruin on the way to the station, and therefore catch a later train. She appealed to St George to support her, and at first he said he would, but when it came to the crisis, he preached instead the vanity of human wishes. This caused her to reject his proposal. (His subsequent marriage was annulled on the ground of his impotence.[1]) In the summer of 1899 she paid a long visit to Friday's Hill, and I became very fond of her. I did not consider myself in love with her, and I never so much as kissed her hand, but as years went by I realized that she had made a deep impression on me, and I remember as if it were yesterday our evening walks in the summer twilight while we were restrained by the strict code of those days from giving any expression whatever to our feelings.

In the autumn of 1899 the Boer War broke out. I was at that time a Liberal Imperialist, and at first by no means a pro-Boer. British defeats caused me much anxiety, and I could think of nothing else but the war news. We were living at The Millhanger, and I used most afternoons to walk the four miles to the station in order to get an evening paper. Alys, being American, did not have the same feelings in the matter, and was rather annoyed by my absorption in it. When the Boers began to be defeated, my interest grew less, and early in 1901 I became a pro-Boer.

[1] He married Lady Edith Douglas, sister of Lord Alfred

In the year 1900, my book on the *Philosophy of Leibniz* was published. In July of that year I went to Paris, where a new chapter of my life began.

LETTERS

Pembroke Lodge
Richmond, Surrey
May 30, '95

Dearest Bertie

I hope yr Cambridge days have been useful though I don't exactly know in what way—I have asked you before, but forget yr answer, what yr dissertation is called—how do you think you are succeeding with it? How vividly I remember the first tidings of yr first success, before you went to Cambridge—when you rushed upstairs to tell Auntie and me—the dear dear Bertie of that day —and then the last—oh the happy tears that start to eyes, at such moments in the old withered life to wch the young fresh life is bringing joy—Yet how I always felt 'these things wd not give me one moment's happiness if he were not loving and good and true'.

I came upon something of that kind yesty in a chance book I was reading— and am always comg upon passages in all kinds of books which seem written on purpose to answer to some experiences of my life—I suppose this is natural when life has been long. By the bye you have not yet said a word to Auntie about her little birthday letter—*she* has not said so, and she told me it was only a few lines, but such as they were she made an effort over illness to write them—the fact is that you take only the fag-end of the fragment of the shred of a minute or two for yr letters to us—and though it is pleasant now and then to look back to the full and talky ones you wrote in past days, they are not exactly substitutes for what those of the present might be! However as long as you have no *wish* for talkings on paper, wch at best is a poor affair, go on with yr scraps—I don't forget how very busy you are, but the very busy people are those who find most time for everything somehow—don't you think so? (What an ugly smudge!) As for talking off paper, you didn't intend as far as I cd make out when you went away, ever, within measurable distance to make that possible—Oh dear how many things I meant to say and have not said—about Quakers, of whose peculiar creed or rules we have been hearing things true or false—and about much besides. But it must all wait. What lovely skies and earth! and how glad you must have been to get back. Love and thanks to Alys.

Yr ever loving
Granny

I hope you found my untidy pencilled glossaries wch were loose inside the book—I thought they wd help to more pleasure in the book when you do read it. How I wish we cd have read it together!

Pembroke Lodge
Richmond, Surrey
(1896)

Dearest Bertie

You say you have 'settled' yr plans—please mention them in case P.L. [Pembroke Lodge] comes into them—Gertrude[1] and bairns are to be here Sep. 1 to 16, I'm happy to say. U.R. in Scotland and elsewhere—so, that time wd not do—I can imagine the 'deeper Philosophy' and even 'L'Infini Mathematique' to be most interesting. It is rather painful dear Bertie, that knowing our love for Miss Walker, you still leave the death unmentioned. Nor do you say a word of dear Lady Tennyson's although so near you—Sir Henry Taylor called her 'very woman of very woman'—no length of words could add to the praise of those five. I have sent for Green for Alys—a delightful history but not quite what I shd have liked as a gift to her.

Yr loving
Granny

Auntie has a *beautiful* note from poor Hallam.

Pembroke Lodge
Richmond, Surrey
Aug. 11, 1896

Dearest Alys

We are delighted with the Bertie photo—It is perfect, such a natural, not photographic smile. As for you, we don't like you, and I hope Bertie doesn't, neither pose, nor dusky face, nor white humpy tippet—this is perhaps ungrateful of Agatha but she can't help it, nor can I. When is or was your birthday? I forget and only remember that I said I would give you a book. I will try to think of one and then ask you if you have it, but not Green I think—something less solid and instructive—have you Henriette Renan's letters? Agatha has just read them and says they are beautiful. Of course, my dear child, I should never think of giving my health or want of it as an objection to your going to America. I felt it was for yourselves alone to decide whether 'to go or not to go'. I trust it may turn out for Bertie's good. It is sad that the last of the eminent group of authors, Holmes and Lowell, are gone—but no doubt there must be men well worth his knowing, whether authors or not. It is quite true that I have earnestly wished him to be thrown into a wider and more various set of men and women than has been the case—but this is most to be desired in his own country. Harold and Vita[2] came down—did I tell you? last week, such a nice natural pleasant girl. Thanks for your nice note. What a pity about your cold! Is it any fault in the cottage? What a horrible season for crossing and returning! Will sea air be good for your indigestion?

Your always affectionate
Granny

---

[1] Rollo's second wife.   [2] My cousin Harold Russell and his wife.

Pembroke Lodge
Richmond, Surrey
May 17, '98

My dearest Bertie

I shall think of you very much tomorrow and of happy birthdays long ago when she was with us[1] to guide counsel and inspire to all good and when you were still the child brightening our home and filling us with hope of what you might some day become dear dear Bertie has it been an upward growth since those days? Have the joys of life which are now yours helped you to be not less but more loving, more helpful, more thoughtful, for those whose lives may be full of sorrow illness pain and loneliness. All of us who have known what it was to have Granny's love and prayers and wishes—and who have the blessed memory of her wonderful example must feel, at times almost despairingly, how terribly terribly far away we are from her ideal and her standard of life—but we must strive on and hope for more of her spirit. You cannot think how very lovely everything is here just now and though the aching longing for her is awful, yet I love to look upon it all and remember how she loved it.

Uncle Rollo is very unwell and has been for a long time. I was very anxious long ago about him when he was doing far too much, now he is ordered complete rest;—Perhaps you have been to Dunrozel. There has been an immense deal to do here and I have been quite overdone several times. Gwennie [Gwendoline Villiers] has saved me from a breakdown by working incessantly and helping in every possible way—It has been most painful to see the beautiful pictures go away and the house more and more dismantled and I shall be thankful when it is over. I am *most* glad that Uncle Rollo has several of the good pictures. They ought to be his and also I am grateful to Herbrand[2] for giving the Grant picture of your grandfather to the National Portrait Gallery. I am sorry I have no present for you just yet but it has been simply impossible during this unceasing business. Give Alys very best love.

God bless you dearest Bertie.

Your very loving
Auntie

To Graham Wallas

The Deanery
Bryn Mawr, Pa.
Nov. 13, 1896

Dear Wallas

I have been meaning to write to you ever since the Presidential election, on account of a specimen ballot paper wh. I am sending you by book post. This document, I am told, is more complicated than in any other state: certainly it is a triumph. It seems to me to contain within it the whole 18th century theory of the free and intelligent demos, or the whole 19th century practice of bossism. Imagine using such a phrase as 'straight ticket' on a ballot-paper, and imagine the stupendous intellect of a man who votes anything else on such a ballot-

---

[1] My grandmother had lately died.   [2] The Duke of Bedford.

paper. I have never seen a document more replete with theory of politics, or illustrating more neatly the short road from bad metaphysics to political corruption. The whole interest, in Philadelphia, centred about the election of the sheriff—Crow, the independent Republican, was making a stand against bossism, and strange to say, he got in, tho' by a very narrow majority.

I am sending you also some rather transparent boss's devices for allowing fictitious voters to vote. You will see that the vouchers I enclose enable a man to vote without being on the register. I was taken to a polling-booth in Philadelphia, and there stood, just outside, a sub-deputy boss, named Flanagan, instructing the ignorant how to vote, illegally watching them mark their ballot-paper, and when necessary vouching for the right to vote. A Republican and a Democrat got inside to see that all was fair, it being supposed they would counteract each other; as a matter of fact, they make a deal, and agree to keep up their common friends the bosses, even if they have to admit fraudulent votes for the opposite party. Americans seem too fatalistic and pessimistic to do much against them: I was taken by a man appointed as official watcher by the Prohibitionists, but tho' he observed and pointed out the irregularities, he merely shrugged his shoulders when I asked why he did not interfere and make a row. The fact is, Americans are unspeakably lazy about everything but their business: to cover their laziness, they invent a pessimism, and say things can't be improved: tho' when I confront them, and ask for any single reform movement wh. has not succeeded, they are stumped, except one who mentioned the Consular service—naturally not a very soul-stirring cry. One of them, who prides himself on his virtue, frankly told me he found he could make more money in business than he could save in rates by fighting corruption—it never seemed to enter his head that one might think that a rather lame excuse. However, everything seems to be improving very fast, tho' nothing makes the lazy hypocritical Puritans so furious as to say so. They take a sort of pride in being the most corrupt place in the Union: everywhere you go they brag of the peculiar hopelessness of their own locality. The fall of Altgeld and the defeat of Tammany seem to irritate them: it might so easily have been otherwise, they say, and will be otherwise next election. Altogether I don't see that they deserve any better than they get. The Quakers and Puritans, so far as I have come across them, are the greatest liars and hypocrites I have ever seen and are as a rule totally destitute of vigour. Here's a Philadelphia story. Wanamaker is the local Whitely, enormously rich and religious. The protective tariff is dear to his soul. In the election of 1888, when New York was the critical State, it was telegraphed to the Phila. Republican Committee that 80,000 dollars would win the election. Wanamaker planked down the sum, New York State was won by a majority of 500, and Wanamaker became Postmaster General. Here is a New York tale. Jay Gould, in 1884, offered a huge sum to the Republicans. This became known to the Democrats, who next day had a procession of several hours past his house shouting as they marched: 'Blood! Blood! Jay Gould's Blood!' He turned pale, and telegraphed any sum desired to the Democrats. Cleveland was elected.— However, individual Americans are delightful: but whether from lack of courage or from decentralization, they do not form a society of frank people, and all in turn complain that they would be universally cut if they ever spoke their minds. I think this is largely due to the absence of a capital. A similar cause I think accounts for the religiosity and timidity of the universities. Professor Ely was dismissed from the Johns Hopkins for being a Xtian Socialist! There are possibilities tho': everybody is far more anxious to be educated than in England, the level of intelligence is high, and thoughtful people admit— though only within the last few years, I am told, apparently since Bryce— that their form of government is not perfect. I think you will have, as we have, a very good time here. We probably sail December 30th, and strongly urge you to arrive before then. We shall be in New York, and want very much to see you, as also to introduce you to several nice people who will be there. If you have not yet written about the date of your arrival, please write soon.— This College is a fine place, immeasurably superior to Girton and Newnham; the Professor of Pol. Econ. oddly enough is a Socialist and a Free Silver man and has carried all his class with him tho' many of them are rich New Yorkers. Those I have met are intelligent and generous in their views of social questions.

> *Yours*
> *Bertrand Russell*

Maurice Sheldon Amos (afterwards Sir) was my only link between Cambridge and Friday's Hill. His father, who died in the '80's, was a theoretical lawyer of some eminence, and was the principal author of the Egyptian Constitution imposed by the English after their occupation of Egypt in 1881. His mother, as a widow, was devoted to Good Works, especially Purity. She was popularly supposed to have said: 'Since my dear husband's death I have devoted my life to prostitution.' It was also said that her husband, though a very hairy man, became as bald as an egg within six weeks of his marriage: but I cannot vouch for these stories. Mrs Amos, through her work, became a friend of Mrs Pearsall Smith. Accordingly Logan, when visiting me at Cambridge, took me to call on Maurice, then a freshman just beginning the study of moral science. He was an attractive youth, tall, enthusiastic, and awkward. He used to say: 'The world is an odd place: whenever I move about in it I bump into something.'

He became a barrister and went to Egypt, where his father was remembered. There he prospered, and after being a Judge for a long time retired, and stood for Cambridge as a Liberal. He was the only man I ever knew who read mathematics for pleasure, as other people read detective stories.

He had a sister named Bonté, with whom Alys and I were equally friends. Bonté suffered greatly from her mother's fanatical religiosity. She became a doctor, but a few weeks before her final examination her mother developed the habit of waking her up in the night to pray for her, so we had to send her money to enable her to live away from home. Alys and I took her with us to America in 1896.

Bonté also went to Egypt, where she was at one time quarantine medical officer at Suez, whose duty (inter alia) it was to catch rats on ships declared by their captains to be free from such animals. She finally married an army officer who was at the head of the police force of Egypt. He had endured shipwrecks and mutinies and all kinds of 'hair-breadth 'scapes', but when I remarked to him, 'you seem to have had a very adventurous life', he replied, 'Oh no, of course I never missed my morning tea'.

Both brother and sister refused to continue to know me when I ceased to be respectable, but the brother relented in the end. The sister remained adamant.

c/o Miss Frigell
Cairo
November 6th, 1898

My dear Bertie

It is a great pleasure to hear from you and to be reminded that the right sort of people exist. Do you know that *Brunyate* has come out here to a law berth of £1200 a year? He is amiable, but a savage. He thinks apparently that no subject but mathematics can be of any difficulty to a really great mind. He sneered at Political Economy, in the person of Sanger, at Metaphysics in the person of McT.—and I fear did not spare yourself, telling me that Forsythe did not believe in your theories. I questioned Forsythe's competence; he said that F. was capable of judging any *logical* proposition. So I could only say that it took six months or a year to state any metaphysical proposition to a person who knew nothing about it. The beast seems to think that Trinity has fallen into the hands of mugs who give fellowships to political economists and metaphysicians for corrupt motives. However one ought to remember that some are predestined to damnation, and that instead of worrying oneself to set them right, one had better spend one's time lauding the G.A. for his inscrutable decrees, especially in the matter of one's own election. Sometimes I confess I have qualms that I also am a reprobate. What for instance Moore means by saying that the world consists of concepts alone, I do not know.

I should much like to discuss my own and your affairs with you. It seems to me that I at any rate fall further away as time goes on from the state of having definite and respectable ambitions. The worst of all is to feel flamboyant—as one does occasionally—and to see no opening for drilling—or even for being tried on.

I shall not really know what to think of this place till you and Alys and Bonté come and report on it to me from a dispassionate point of view. Meanwhile I think I am learning various useful things. I am only occupied at the Ministry in the mornings; and I have just arranged to spend my afternoons in the office of the leading lawyer here, a Belgian, where I think I shall pick up a lot. Meanwhile it is night, getting fairly cool, cheerful, and I have about enough to live on and come home in the summer. I also have plenty to do.

The plan of your book sounds splendid. Perhaps I shall be able to understand it when it comes out, but probably not. I think it possible that I may take up my mathematics again out here because—I wish I had said this to that b.f. Brunyate, there is no doubt that Mathematics is a less strain on the attention than any other branch of knowledge: you are borne up and carried along by the notation as by the Gulf Stream. On the other hand it is shiftless work, getting up a subject without any definite aim.

I am glad to hear that you are Jingo. But I think it is a good thing that we should win diplomatically, if possible, without a war—although the old Adam wants the latter.

This we now seem to have done, in the most triumphant manner. The Fashoda incident gives us a new position in Egypt: we now have it by right of Conquest, having offered fight to the French, which they have refused.

I very much wish I was doing anything of the same kind of work as you, so as to be able to write to you about it. I wonder if there is such a thing as mental paralysis, or if one is bound to emerge after all.

Your affectionate friend
M. S. Amos

Cairo
May 5, 1899

Dear Bertie

I have just got leave for three months and a half from the 9th of June. I shall be home about the 10th, and I am looking forward very much to seeing you and Alys. I shall unfortunately have to go to Paris during July for an examination, but I think I shall have long enough in England altogether to bore my friends. I hope you will give me a fair chance of doing so to you.

I was much struck by your lyrical letter about Moore. I have made it the text of more than one disquisition for the benefit of Frenchmen and other Barbarians, on the *real* state of spirits in England. I explain that our colonial and commercial activity is a mere pale reflection of the intense blaze of quint-essential flame that consumes literary and philosophical circles. In fact that the true character of the present time in England is that of a Great Age, in which, under a perfect political system, administered by a liberal, respected and unenvied aristocracy teeming millions of a prosperous working class vie with the cultured and affluent orders of the middle rank in Imperial enthusiasm, loyalty to the Throne, and respect for learning—the same generous and stimulating atmosphere which has lent new life to trade, has had an even more stupendous and unprecedented effect on the intellectual life of the nation: this is especially seen in the Great Universities, which are not only, as heretofore, the nurseries of proconsuls of statesmen and of a territorial gentry of unrivalled liberality and elegance, but have within the last generation equalled and far surpassed all other seats of learning in Europe and America as centres of pure and abstract scientific inquiry. You should see the Frenchmen squirm. They can stand Spithead Reviews: they can just bear Fashoda, because they doubt where it is. But when it comes to new systems of Platonic philosophy, they tear their hair.

This is inexcusable frivolity. But it will be very nice to see you and Alys again and talk about all sorts of matters in all sorts of moods. Have you read *Les Déracinés* of Barrés?

Yours affectionately
M. Sheldon Amos

CHAPTER VI

'PRINCIPIA MATHEMATICA'

IN JULY 1900, there was an International Congress of Philosophy in Paris in connection with the Exhibition of that year. Whitehead and I decided to go to this Congress, and I accepted an invitation to read a paper at it. Our arrival in Paris was signalized by a somewhat ferocious encounter with the eminent mathematician Borel. Carey Thomas had asked Alys to bring from England twelve empty trunks which she had left behind. Borel had asked the Whiteheads to bring his niece, who had a teaching post in England. There was a great crowd at the Gare du Nord, and we had only one luggage ticket for the whole party. Borel's niece's luggage turned up at once, our luggage turned up fairly soon, but of Carey's empty trunks only eleven appeared. While we were waiting for the twelfth, Borel lost patience, snatched the luggage ticket out of my hands, and went off with his niece and her one valise, leaving us unable to claim either Carey's trunks or our personal baggage. Whitehead and I seized the pieces one at a time, and used them as battering-rams to penetrate through the ring of officials. So surprised were they that the manœuvre was successful.

The Congress was a turning point in my intellectual life, because I there met Peano. I already knew him by name and had seen some of his work, but had not taken the trouble to master his notation. In discussions at the Congress I observed that he was always more precise than anyone else, and that he invariably got the better of any argument upon which he embarked. As the days went by, I decided that this must be owing to his mathematical logic. I therefore got him to give me all his works, and as soon as the Congress was over I retired to Fernhurst to study quietly every word written by him and his disciples. It became clear to me that his notation afforded an instrument of logical analysis such as I had been seeking for years, and that by studying him I was acquiring a new and powerful technique for the work that I had long wanted to do. By the end of August I had become completely familiar with all the work of his school. I spent September in extending his methods to the logic of relations. It seems to me in retrospect that, through that month, every day was warm and sunny. The Whiteheads stayed with us at Fernhurst, and I explained my new ideas to him. Every evening the discussion ended with some difficulty, and every morning I found that the difficulty of the previous evening had solved itself while I slept. The time was one of intellectual intoxication. My sensations resembled those one has after climbing a mountain in a mist, when, on reaching the summit, the mist suddenly clears, and the country becomes visible for forty miles in every direction. For years I had been endeavouring to analyse the fundamental notions of mathematics, such as order and cardinal numbers. Suddenly, in the space of a few weeks, I discovered what appeared to be definitive answers to the problems which had baffled me for years. And in the course of discovering these answers, I was introducing a new mathematical technique, by which regions formerly abandoned to the vaguenesses of philosophers were conquered for the precision of exact formulae. Intellectually, the month of September 1900 was the highest point of my life. I went about saying to myself that now at last I had done something worth doing, and I had the feeling that I must be careful not to be run over in the street before I had written it down. I sent a paper to Peano for his journal, embodying my new ideas. With the beginning of October I sat down to write *The Principles of Mathematics*, at which I had already made a number of unsuccessful attempts. Parts III, IV, V, and VI of the book as published were written that autumn. I wrote also Parts I, II, and VII at that time, but had to rewrite them later, so that the book was not finished in its final form until May 1902. Every day throughout October, November and December, I wrote my ten pages, and finished the MS on the last day of the century, in time to write a boastful letter to Helen Thomas about the 200,000 words that I had just completed.

Oddly enough, the end of the century marked the end of this sense of triumph, and from that moment onwards I began to be assailed simultaneously by intellectual and emotional problems which plunged me into the darkest despair that I have ever known.

During the Lent Term of 1901, we joined with the Whiteheads in taking Professor Maitland's house in Downing College. Professor Maitland had had to go to Madeira for his health. His housekeeper informed us that he had 'dried hisself up eating dry toast', but I imagine this was not the medical diagnosis. Mrs Whitehead was at this time becoming more and more of an invalid, and used to have intense pain owing to heart trouble. Whitehead and Alys and I were all filled with anxiety about her. He was not only deeply devoted to her but also very dependent upon her, and it seemed doubtful whether he would ever achieve any more good work if she were to die. One day, Gilbert Murray came to Newnham to read part of his translation of *The*

Hippolytus, then unpublished. Alys and I went to hear him, and I was profoundly stirred by the beauty of the poetry.[1] When we came home, we found Mrs Whitehead undergoing an unusually severe bout of pain. She seemed cut off from everyone and everything by walls of agony, and the sense of the solitude of each human soul suddenly overwhelmed me. Ever since my marriage, my emotional life had been calm and superficial. I had forgotten all the deeper issues, and had been content with flippant cleverness. Suddenly the ground seemed to give way beneath me, and I found myself in quite another region. Within five minutes I went through some such reflections as the following: the loneliness of the human soul is unendurable; nothing can penetrate it except the highest intensity of the sort of love that religious teachers have preached; whatever does not spring from this motive is harmful, or at best useless; it follows that war is wrong, that a public school education is abominable, that the use of force is to be deprecated, and that in human relations one should penetrate to the core of loneliness in each person and speak to that. The Whitehead's youngest boy, aged three, was in the room. I had previously taken no notice of him, nor he of me. He had to be prevented from troubling his mother in the middle of her paroxysms of pain. I took his hand and led him away. He came willingly, and felt at home with me. From that day to his death in the War in 1918, we were close friends.

At the end of those five minutes, I had become a completely different person. For a time, a sort of mystic illumination possessed me. I felt that I knew the inmost thoughts of everybody that I met in the street, and though this was, no doubt, a delusion, I did in actual fact find myself in far closer touch than previously with all my friends, and many of my acquaintances. Having been an Imperialist, I became during those five minutes a pro-Boer and a Pacifist. Having for years cared only for exactness and analysis, I found myself filled with semi-mystical feelings about beauty, with an intense interest in children, and with a desire almost as profound as that of the Buddha to find some philosophy which should make human life endurable. A strange excitement possessed me, containing intense pain but also some element of triumph through the fact that I could dominate pain, and make it, as I thought, a gateway to wisdom. The mystic insight which I then imagined myself to possess has largely faded, and the habit of analysis has reasserted itself. But something of what I thought I saw in that moment has remained always with me, causing my attitude during the first war, my interest in children, my indifference to minor misfortunes, and a certain emotional tone in all my human relations.

[1] See letter to Gilbert Murray and his reply, p. 156. Also the subsequent letters relating to the *Bacchae*.

At the end of the Lent Term, Alys and I went back to Fernhurst, where I set to work to write out the logical deduction of mathematics which afterwards became *Principia Mathematica.* I thought the work was nearly finished, but in the month of May I had an intellectual set-back almost as severe as the emotional set-back which I had had in February. Cantor had a proof that there is no greatest number, and it seemed to me that the number of all the things in the world ought to be the greatest possible. Accordingly, I examined his proof with some minuteness, and endeavoured to apply it to the class of all the things there are. This led me to consider those classes which are not members of themselves, and to ask whether the class of such classes is or is not a member of itself. I found that either answer implies its contradictory. At first I supposed that I should be able to overcome the contradiction quite easily, and that probably there was some trivial error in the reasoning. Gradually, however, it became clear that this was not the case. Burali-Forti had already discovered a similar contradiction, and it turned out on logical analysis that there was an affinity with the ancient Greek contradiction about Epimenides the Cretan, who said that all Cretans are liars. A contradiction essentially similar to that of Epimenides can be created by giving a person a piece of paper on which is written: 'The statement on the other side of this paper is false.' The person turns the paper over, and finds on the other side: 'The statement on the other side of this paper is false.' It seemed unworthy of a grown man to spend his time on such trivialities, but what was I to do? There was something wrong, since such contradictions were unavoidable on ordinary premisses. Trivial or not, the matter was a challenge. Throughout the latter half of 1901 I supposed the solution would be easy, but by the end of that time I had concluded that it was a big job. I therefore decided to finish *The Principles of Mathematics,* leaving the solution in abeyance. In the autumn Alys and I went back to Cambridge, as I had been invited to give two terms' lectures on mathematical logic. These lectures contained the outline of *Principia Mathematica,* but without any method of dealing with the contradictions.

About the time that these lectures finished, when we were living with the Whiteheads at the Mill House in Grantchester, a more serious blow fell than those that had preceded it. I went out bicycling one afternoon, and suddenly, as I was riding along a country road, I realized that I no longer loved Alys. I had had no idea until this moment that my love for her was even lessening. The problem presented by this discovery was very grave. We had lived ever since our marriage in the closest possible intimacy. We always shared a bed, and neither of us ever had a separate dressing-room. We talked over together everything that ever happened to either of us. She was five years older than I was, and I had been accustomed to regarding her as far more practical and far more full of worldly wisdom than myself, so that in many matters of daily life I left the initiative to her. I knew that she was still devoted to me. I had no wish to be unkind, but I believed in those days (what experience has taught me to think possibly open to doubt) that in intimate relations one should speak the truth. I did not see in any case how I could for any length of time successfully pretend to love her when I did not. I had no longer any instinctive impulse towards sex relations with her, and this alone would have been an insuperable barrier to concealment of my feelings. At this crisis my father's priggery came out in me, and I began to justify myself with moral criticisms of Alys. I did not at once tell her that I no longer loved her, but of course she perceived that something was amiss. She retired to a rest-cure for some months, and when she emerged from it I told her that I no longer wished to share a room, and in the end I confessed that my love was dead. I justified this attitude to her, as well as to myself, by criticisms of her character.

Although my self-righteousness at that time seems to me in retrospect repulsive, there were substantial grounds for my criticisms. She tried to be more impeccably virtuous than is possible to human beings, and was thus led into insincerity. Like her brother Logan, she was malicious, and liked to make people think ill of each other, but she was not aware of this, and was instinctively subtle in her methods. She would praise people in such a way as to cause others to admire her generosity, and think worse of the people praised than if she had criticized them. Often malice made her untruthful. She told Mrs Whitehead that I couldn't bear children, and that the Whitehead children must be kept out of my way as much as possible. At the same time she told me that Mrs Whitehead was a bad mother because she saw so little of her children. During my bicycle ride a host of such things occurred to me, and I became aware that she was not the saint I had always supposed her to be. But in the revulsion I went too far, and forgot the great virtues that she did in fact possess.

My change of feeling towards Alys was partly the result of perceiving, though in a milder form, traits in her which I disliked in her mother and brother. Alys had an unbounded admiration of her mother, whom she regarded as both a saint and a sage. This was a fairly common view; it was held, for example, by William James. I, on the contrary, came gradually to think her one of the wickedest people I had ever known. Her treatment of her husband, whom she despised, was humiliating in the highest degree. She never spoke to him or of him except in a tone that made her contempt obvious. It cannot be denied that he was a silly old man, but he did not deserve what she gave him, and no one capable of mercy could have given it. He had a mistress, and fondly supposed that his wife did not know of her. He used to tear up this woman's letters and throw the pieces into the waste-paper basket. His wife would fit the bits together, and read out the letters to Alys and Logan amid fits of laughter. When the old man died, she sold his false teeth and refused to carry out his death-bed request to give a present of £5 to the gardener. (The rest of us made up the sum without any contribution from her.) This was the only time that Logan felt critical of her: he was in tears because of her hardheartedness. But he soon reverted to his usual reverential attitude. In a letter written when he was 3½ months old, she writes:

Logan and I had our first regular battle today, and he came off conqueror, though I don't think he knew it. I whipped him until he was actually black and blue, and until I really *could not* whip him any more, and he never gave up one single inch. However, I hope it was a lesson to him.[1]

It was. She never had to whip him black and blue again. She taught her family that men are brutes and fools, but women are saints and hate sex. So Logan, as might have been expected, became homosexual. She carried feminism to such lengths that she found it hard to keep her respect for the Deity, since He was male. In passing a public house she would remark: 'Thy housekeeping, O Lord.' If the Creator had been female, there would have been no such thing as alcohol.

I found Alys's support of her mother difficult to bear. Once, when Friday's Hill was to be let, the prospective tenants wrote to inquire whether the drains had been passed by a sanitary inspector. She explained to us all at the tea-table that they had not, but she was going to say that they had. I protested, but both Logan and Alys said 'hush' as if I had been a naughty child who had interrupted Teacher. Sometimes I tried to discuss her mother with Alys, but this proved impossible. In the end, some of my horror of the old lady spread to all who admired her, not excluding Alys.

The most unhappy moments of my life were spent at Grantchester. My bedroom looked out upon the mill, and the noise of the millstream mingled inextricably with my despair. I lay awake through long nights, hearing first the nightingale, and then the chorus of birds at dawn, looking out upon sunrise and trying to find consolation in external beauty. I suffered in a very intense form the loneliness which I had perceived a year before to be the essential lot of man. I walked alone in the fields about Grantchester, feeling dimly that the whitening

---

[1] *A Religious Rebel*, by Logan Pearsall Smith, p. 8.

willows in the wind had some message from a land of peace. I read religious books, such as Taylor's *Holy Dying*, in the hope that there might be something independent of dogma in the comfort which their authors derived from their beliefs. I tried to take refuge in pure contemplation; I began to write *The Free Man's Worship*. The construction of prose rhythms was the only thing in which I found any real consolation.

Throughout the whole time of the writing of *Principia Mathematica* my relations with the Whiteheads were difficult and complex. Whitehead appeared to the world calm, reasonable, and judicious, but when one came to know him well one discovered that this was only a façade. Like many people possessed of great self-control, he suffered from impulses which were scarcely sane. Before he met Mrs Whitehead he had made up his mind to join the Catholic Church, and was only turned aside at the last minute by falling in love with her. He was obsessed by fear of lack of money, and he did not meet this fear in a reasonable way, but by spending recklessly in the hope of persuading himself that he could afford to do so. He used to frighten Mrs Whitehead and her servants by mutterings in which he addressed injurious objurgations to himself. At times he would be completely silent for some days, saying nothing whatever to anybody in the house. Mrs Whitehead was in perpetual fear that he would go mad. I think, in retrospect, that she exaggerated the danger, for she tended to be melodramatic in her outlook. But the danger was certainly real, even if not as great as she believed. She spoke of him to me with the utmost frankness, and I found myself in an alliance with her to keep him sane. Whatever happened his work never flagged, but one felt that he was exerting more self-control than a human being could be expected to stand and that at any moment a break-down was possible. Mrs Whitehead was always discovering that he had run up large bills with Cambridge tradesmen, and she did not dare to tell him that there was no money to pay them for fear of driving him over the edge. I used to supply the wherewithal surreptitiously. It was hateful to deceive Whitehead, who would have found the humiliation unbearable if he had known of it. But there was his family to be supported and *Principia Mathematica* to be written, and there seemed no other way by which these objects could be achieved. I contributed all that I could realize in the way of capital, and even that partly by borrowing. I hope the end justified the means. Until 1952 I have never mentioned this to anyone.

Meanwhile Alys was more unhappy than I was, and her unhappiness was a great part of the cause of my own. We had in the past spent a great deal of time with her family, but I told her I could no longer endure her mother, and that we must therefore leave Fernhurst. We spent the summer near Broadway in Worcestershire. Pain made me sentimental, and I used to construct phrases such as 'Our hearts build precious shrines for the ashes of dead hopes'. I even descended to reading Maeterlinck. Before this time, at Grantchester, at the very height and crisis of misery, I finished *The Principles of Mathematics*. The day on which I finished the manuscript was May 23rd. At Broadway I devoted myself to the mathematical elaboration which was to become *Principia Mathematica*. By this time I had secured Whitehead's co-operation in this task, but the unreal, insincere, and sentimental frame of mind into which I had allowed myself to fall affected even my mathematical work. I remember sending Whitehead a draft of the beginning, and his reply: 'Everything, even the object of the book, has been sacrificed to making proofs look short and neat.' This defect in my work was due to a moral defect in my state of mind.

When the autumn came we took a house for six months in Cheyne Walk, and life began to become more bearable. We saw a great many people, many of them amusing or agreeable, and we both gradually began to live a more external life, but this was always breaking down. So long as I lived in the same house with Alys she would every now and then come down to me in her dressing-gown after she had gone to bed, and beseech me to spend the night with her. Sometimes I did so, but the result was utterly unsatisfactory. For nine years this state of affairs continued. During all this time she hoped to win me back, and never became interested in any other man. During all this time I had no other sex relations. About twice a year I would attempt sex relations with her, in the hope of alleviating her misery, but she no longer attracted me, and the attempt was futile. Looking back over this stretch of years, I feel that I ought to have ceased much sooner to live in the same house with her, but she wished me to stay, and even threatened suicide if I left her. There was no other woman to whom I wished to go, and there seemed therefore no good reason for not doing as she wished.

The summers of 1903 and 1904 we spent at Churt and Tilford. I made a practice of wandering about the common every night from eleven till one, by which means I came to know the three different noises made by night-jars. (Most people only know one.) I was trying hard to solve the contradictions mentioned above. Every morning I would sit down before a blank sheet of paper. Throughout the day, with a brief interval for lunch, I would stare at the blank sheet. Often when evening came it was still empty. We spent our winters in London, and during the winters I did not attempt to work, but the two summers of 1903 and 1904 remain in my mind as a period of complete intellectual deadlock. It was clear to me that I could not get on without solving the contradictions, and I was determined that no difficulty should turn me aside from the completion of *Principia Mathematica*, but it seemed quite likely that the whole of the rest of my life might be consumed in looking at that blank sheet of paper. What made it the more annoying was that the contradictions were trivial, and that my time was spent in considering matters that seemed unworthy of serious attention.

It must not be supposed that all my time was consumed in despair and intellectual effort. I remember, for instance, the occasion mentioned earlier when Maynard Keynes came to spend Saturday to Monday with us at Tilford.

In 1905 things began to improve. Alys and I decided to live near Oxford, and built ourselves a house in Bagley Wood. (At that time there was no other house there.) We went to live there in the spring of 1905, and very shortly after we had moved in I discovered my Theory of Descriptions, which was the first step towards overcoming the difficulties which had baffled me for so long. Immediately after this came the death of Theodore Davies, of which I have spoken in an earlier chapter. In 1906 I discovered the Theory of Types. After this it only remained to write the book out. Whitehead's teaching work left him not enough leisure for this mechanical job. I worked at it from ten to twelve hours a day for about eight months in the year, from 1907 to 1910. The manuscript became more and more vast, and every time that I went out for a walk I used to be afraid that the house would catch fire and the manuscript get burnt up. It was not, of course, the sort of manuscript that could be typed, or even copied. When we finally took it to the University Press, it was so large that we had to hire an old four-wheeler for the purpose. Even then our difficulties were not at an end. The University Press estimated that there would be a loss of £600 on the book, and while the syndics were willing to bear a loss of £300, they did not feel that they could go above this figure. The Royal Society very generously contributed £200, and the remaining £100 we had to find ourselves. We thus earned minus £50 each by ten years' work. This beats the record of *Paradise Lost*.

The strain of unhappiness combined with very severe intellectual work, in the years from 1902 till 1910, was very great.[1] At the time I often wondered whether I should ever come out at the other end of the tunnel in which I seemed to be. I used to stand on the footbridge at Kennington, near Oxford, watching the trains go by, and determining that tomorrow I would place myself under one of them. But when the morrow came I always found myself hoping that perhaps *Principia Mathematica* would be finished some day. Moreover the difficulties appeared to me in the nature of a challenge, which it would be pusil-

[1] See my letters to Lucy on pp. 163 ff.

lanimous not to meet and overcome. So I persisted, and in the end the work was finished, but my intellect never quite recovered from the strain. I have been ever since definitely less capable of dealing with difficult abstractions than I was before. This is part, though by no means the whole, of the reason for the change in the nature of my work.

Throughout this period my winters were largely occupied with political questions. When Joseph Chamberlain began to advocate Protection, I found myself to be a passionate Free Trader. The influence which Hewins had exerted upon me in the direction of Imperialism and Imperialistic Zollverein had evaporated during the moments of crisis in 1901 which turned me into a Pacifist. Nevertheless in 1902 I became a member of a small dining club called 'The Coefficients', got up by Sidney Webb for the purpose of considering political questions from a more or less Imperialist point of view. It was in this club that I first became acquainted with H. G. Wells, of whom I had never heard until then. His point of view was more sympathetic to me than that of any other member. Most of the members, in fact, shocked me profoundly. I remember Amery's eyes gleaming with blood-lust at the thought of a war with America, in which, as he said with exultation, we should have to arm the whole adult male population. One evening Sir Edward Grey (not then in office) made a speech advocating the policy of the Entente, which had not yet been adopted by the Government. I stated my objections to the policy very forcibly, and pointed out the likelihood of its leading to war, but no one agreed with me, so I resigned from the club. It will be seen that I began my opposition to the first war at the earliest possible moment. After this I took to speaking in defence of Free Trade on behalf of the Free Trade Union. I had never before attempted public speaking, and was shy and nervous to such a degree as to make me at first wholly ineffective. Gradually, however, my nervousness got less. After the Election of 1906, when Protection ceased for the moment to be a burning question, I took to working for women's suffrage. On pacifist grounds I disliked the Militants, and worked always with the Constitutional party. In 1907 I even stood for Parliament at a by-election, on behalf of votes for women. The Wimbledon Campaign was short and arduous. It must be quite impossible for younger people to imagine the bitterness of the opposition to women's equality. When, in later years, I campaigned against the first world war, the popular opposition that I encountered was not comparable to that which the suffragists met in 1907. The whole subject was treated, by a great majority of the population, as one for mere hilarity. The crowd would shout derisive remarks: to women, 'Go home and mind the baby'; to men, 'Does your mother know you're out?' no matter what the man's age. Rotten eggs were aimed at me and hit my wife. At my first meeting rats were let loose to frighten the ladies, and ladies who were in the plot screamed in pretended terror with a view to disgracing their sex. An account of this is given in the following newspaper report:

Election Uproar
Rats let loose to scare women suffragists.
Wimbledon fight

The Hon. Bertrand Russell, the suffragist candidate for the Wimbledon division, opened his campaign on Saturday night, when he addressed a crowded and rather noisy meeting in Worple Hall. A mixed reception was given to the chairman, Mr O. H. Beatty, a member of the local Liberal Association executive council, and the platform party, which included the candidate, Mrs Russell, Mr St George Lane Fox-Pitt, the unsuccessful Liberal candidate at the General Election, Mrs Philip Snowden, Miss Alison Garland, and many others connected with the National Union of Women's Suffrage Societies.

From the outset it was apparent that a section of the audience—about 2,000—was hostile to the promoters. The chairman often appealed in vain for silence. Within ten minutes of the start a free fight took place in one corner of the hall, and five minutes elapsed before peace was restored. People jumped on to the forms and chairs and encouraged the squabblers.

At another stage two large rats were let loose from a bag, and ran about the floor of the hall among a number of ladies sitting in the front seats. For a moment there was great commotion, the ladies jumping on the chairs, whilst a number of men hunted the rats about the seats, and at last managed to kill them. After the meeting one of the dead rats was taken to Victoria Crescent and flung into the candidate's committee room.

The rowdyism of the meeting, however, was confined to a large crowd of irresponsible young men and youths, who ought never to have been admitted, and it would therefore be unfair to blame the general body of Wimbledon electors for the blackguardly conduct of the political rabble.

Mr Russell was greeted with loud applause and general interruptions, and, the latter being persisted in, the chairman remarked: 'Surely this is not the way that Wimbledon men and women greet a stranger.' (A Voice: 'Are we down-hearted?' and cries of 'No'.) A minute or so later the chairman again made an appeal to the rowdy section, and by asking them not to disgrace the name of Wimbledon he secured quietness for a time.

Mr Russell declared that he stood first and foremost for the suffrage for women on the same terms as men, and on the terms on which hereafter it might be granted to men. (A Voice: 'Do we want petti-coats?' and cries of 'No'.)

Proceeding, the candidate said he supported the present Government. (Cheers and uproar.) The most important of all the questions that divided the Liberal and Conservative parties was Free Trade, and a question closely associated with Free Trade was taxation of land values.

Mr Fox-Pitt rose, with a broad smile on his face. He wanted to tell them something about Mr Chaplin's history, but the meeting would have none of it, and he too gave up the task as hopeless.

Mrs Philip Snowden showed greater determination, and although at the start she was howled and jeered at, she was given a fairly good hearing. Mrs Arthur Webb, Miss Alison Garland, and Mr Walter MacLaren also spoke, and a resolution in support of Mr Russell was carried by an overwhelming majority.

The savagery of the males who were threatened with loss of supremacy was intelligible. But the determination of large numbers of women to prolong the contempt of the female sex was odd. I cannot recall any violent agitation of negroes or Russian serfs against emancipation. The most prominent opponent of political rights for women was Queen Victoria.

I had been a passionate advocate of equality for women ever since in adolescence I read Mill on the subject. This was some years before I became aware of the fact that my mother used to campaign in favour of women's suffrage in the 'sixties. Few things are more surprising than the rapid and complete victory of this cause throughout the civilized world. I am glad to have had a part in anything so successful.

Gradually, however, I became convinced that the limited enfranchise-ment of women which was being demanded would be more difficult to obtain than a wider measure, since the latter would be more advan-tageous to the Liberals, who were in power. The professional suffragists objected to the wider measure, because, although it would enfranchise more women, it would not enfranchise them on exactly the same terms as men, and would therefore not, in their opinion, concede the principle of women's equality with men. On this point I finally left the orthodox suffragists, and joined a body which advocated adult suffrage. This body was got up by Margaret Davies (the sister of Crompton and Theodore), and had Arthur Henderson as its chairman. In those days I was still a Liberal, and tried to suppose that Arthur Henderson was somewhat of a fire-brand. In this effort, however, I was not very successful.

In spite of amusing and pleasant interludes, the years from 1902 to

1910 were very painful to me. They were, it is true, extremely fruitful in the way of work, but the pleasure to be derived from the writing of *Principia Mathematica* was all crammed into the latter months of 1900. After that time the difficulty and the labour were too great for any pleasure to be possible. The last years were better than the earlier ones because they were more fruitful, but the only really vivid delight connected with the whole matter was that which I felt in handing over the manuscript to the Cambridge University Press.

LETTERS

To and from Gilbert Murray:

Downing College
Cambridge
February 26, 1901

Dear Gilbert

I have now read the *Hippolytus*, and feel impelled to tell you how much it has affected me. Those of us who love poetry read the great masterpieces of modern literature before we have any experience of the passions they deal with. To come across a new masterpiece with a more mature mind is a wonderful experience, and one which I have found almost overwhelming.

It had not happened to me before, and I could not have believed how much it would affect me. Your tragedy fulfils perfectly—so it seems to me—the purpose of bringing out whatever is noble and beautiful in sorrow; and to those of us who are without a religion, this is the only consolation of which the spectacle of the world cannot deprive us.

The play itself was entirely new to me, and I have felt its power most keenly. But I feel that your poetry is completely worthy of its theme, and is to be placed in the very small list of truly great English poems. I like best of all the lyric with which you ended your reading at Newnham. I learnt it by heart immediately, and it has been in my head ever since. There is only one word in it which I do not wholly like, and that is the word *bird-droves*. Metrically it is excellent, but a drove seems to me to be something driven, which spoils the peacefulness of the idea to my mind.

Yours ever
Bertrand Russell

Barford, Churt,
Farnham, Surrey
March 2, 1901

My dear Bertie

I will not say that I feel pleased or delighted by your great enjoyment of my *Hippolytus*, because my feelings are quite different from that. It is rather that your strong praise makes a sort of epoch in my life and in my way of regarding my work. Of course I have felt great emotion in working at the *Hippolytus*; I have been entranced by it. And then the thought has always come to me, that there were dozens of translations of the Greek Tragedians in all the second-hand shops; and that I could not read any of them with the least interest; and that probably the authors of nearly all of them had felt exactly as I was feeling about the extraordinary beauty and power of the matter they were writing down. A translator, if he takes pains, naturally gets nearer to understanding his author than an ordinary reader does; and every now and again the poem means to him something approaching that which it meant to the poet.

Of course all authors—in different degrees, but all enormously—fail to convey their meaning. And translators, being less good writers and having a harder task, fail even more deplorably. That is the normal state of the case. But what seems to have happened in our case is that you have somehow or other understood and felt the whole of what I meant to convey.

I do not mean that I had anything mysterious or extraordinary to say; but merely that, even in the case of a bad poet or the Man-in-the-Street when in certain moods, if you could really understand what was in his mind it would be something astonishingly beautiful compared with what one ordinarily gets from reading a very good poem. When I am bored with poetry, I constantly have the feeling that I am simply not understanding the man or he is not expressing himself, and that probably something very fine indeed is going on inside him. And in some moment of special insight one might see inside him and get the fine thing.

I see what you mean about 'Bird-droves'. I will try to change it, but I can not think of anything better so far. The MS arrived all right.

> *Yours ever*
> *Gilbert Murray*

> Friday's Hill
> April 3, 1902

Dear Gilbert

In all our discussions on ethical subjects, I observe a difference as to pre-misses, a real divergence as to moral axioms. As I am very anxious to be clear on the subject of immediate moral intuitions (upon which, as is evident, all morality must be based), and as a divergence upon fundamentals raises doubts, I should like to make an attempt to discover precisely what our differences are, and whether either of us holds at the same time mutually incompatible axioms.

Our differences seem to spring from the fact that you are a utilitarian, whereas I judge pleasure and pain to be of small importance compared to knowledge, the appreciation and contemplation of beauty, and a certain intrinsic excellence of mind which, apart from its practical effects, appears to me to deserve the name of virtue. What I want to discover is, whether you too do not hold moral principles not deducible from utilitarianism, and there-fore inconsistent with it. (It is important to observe that the method of Sidgwick's *Ethics*, in which a number of commonly received moral axioms are shown to be roughly such as Utilitarianism would deduce as *middle* axioms', is fallacious if, with Sidgwick, we accept the general basis of Intuitionism— i.e. the doctrine that immediate intuitions are the only source (for us) of moral premisses. For, if such axioms are immediate deliverances of moral consciousness, they are to be accepted even in those exceptional cases in which they are inconsistent with Utilitarianism; and thus any axiom not rigidly deducible from Utilitarianism is inconsistent with it.)

I may as well begin by confessing that for many years it seemed to me perfectly self-evident that pleasure is the only good and pain the only evil. Now, however, the opposite seems to me self-evident. This change has been brought about by what I may call moral experience. The ordinary *a priori* philosopher will tell you that experience has nothing to do with morals, since it tells us only what is, not what ought to be. This view seems to me philosophically and practically erroneous; it depends upon the sensational theory of knowledge, which, alas, is held in some form by many would be *a priori* philosophers. Having recognized that, in perception, our knowledge is not caused by the object perceived, it is plain that, if perception is experience, so is any other genesis in time, due to whatever cause, of knowledge not obtained by inference from other knowledge. Now circumstances are apt to generate perfectly concrete moral convictions: this or that, now present to me, is good or bad; and from a defect of imagination, it is often impossible to judge beforehand what our moral opinion of a fact will be. It seems to me that the genuine moral intuitions are of this very concrete kind; in fact that we see goodness or badness in things as we see their colours and shapes. The notion that general maxims are to be found in conscience seems to me to be a mistake fostered by the Decalogue. I should rather regard the true method of Ethics as inference from empirically ascertained facts, to be obtained in that moral laboratory which life offers to those whose eyes are open to it. Thus the principles I should now advocate are all inferences from such immediate concrete moral experiences.

What first turned me away from utilitarianism was the persuasion that I myself ought to pursue philosophy, although I had (and have still) no doubt that by doing economics and the theory of politics I could add more to human happiness. It appeared to me that the dignity of which human existence is capable is not attainable by devotion to the mechanism of life, and that unless the contemplation of eternal things is preserved, mankind will become no better than well-fed pigs. But I do not believe that such contemplation on the whole tends to happiness. It gives moments of delight, but these are outweighed by years of effort and depression. Also I reflected that the value of a work of art has no relation whatever to the pleasure it gives; indeed, the more I have dwelt upon the subject, the more I have come to prize austerity rather than luxuriance. It seems to me now that mathematics is capable of an artistic excellence as great as that of any music, perhaps greater; not because the pleasure it gives (although very pure) is comparable, either in intensity or in the number of people who feel it, to that of music, but because it gives in absolute perfection that combination, characteristic of great art, of godlike freedom, with the sense of inevitable destiny; because, in fact, it constructs an ideal world where everything is perfect and yet true. Again, in regard to actual human existence, I have found myself giving honour to those who feel its tragedy, who think truly about Death, who are oppressed by ignoble things even when they are inevitable; yet these qualities appear to me to militate against happiness, not only to the possessors, but to all whom they affect. And, generally, the best life seems to me one which thinks truly and feels greatly about human things, and which, in addition, contemplates the world of beauty and of abstract truths. This last is, perhaps, my most anti-utilitarian opinion: I hold all knowledge that is concerned with things that actually exist—all that is commonly called Science—to be of very slight value compared to the knowledge which, like philosophy and mathematics, is concerned with ideal and eternal objects, and is freed from this miserable world which God has made.

My point, in all this, is to suggest that my opinions would be shared by most moral people who are not biassed by a theory. Archimedes, I believe, was despised by contemporary geometers because he used geometry to make useful inventions. And utilitarians have been strangely anxious to prove that the life of the pig is not happier than that of the philosopher—a most dubious proposition, which, if they had considered the matter frankly, could hardly have been decided in the same way by all of them. In the matter of Art, too, I certainly have educated common sense on my side: anyone would hold it a paradox to regard Home Sweet Home as better than Bach. In this connection, too, it is necessary for the Utilitarian to hold that a beautiful object is not good *per se*, but only as a means; thus it becomes difficult to see why the contemplation of beauty should be specially good, since it is scarcely deniable that the same emotion which a person of taste obtains from a beautiful object may be obtained by another person from an ugly object. And a person of taste can only be defined as one who gets the emotion in question from beauty, not from ugliness. Yet all of us judge a person to be the better for the possession of taste, though only a blind theorist could maintain that taste increases happiness. Here is a hard nut for the Utilitarian!

All these arguments are at least as old as Plato; but I should like to know, when you have leisure, what answer a Utilitarian can make to them. The books contain only sophistries and lies—opinions possible, perhaps, to men who live only in the study, and have no knowledge of life whatever, but quite untenable by anyone who faces this ghastly world of ignoble degradation, in which only virtue is punished and vice lives and dies happy and respected.

Yours ever
Bertrand Russell

14 Cheyne Walk
Chelsea, S.W.
November 27, 1902

Dear Gilbert

I have been reading the *Bacchae* over again, and it seems to me now a much greater play than the *Hippolytus*, more marvellous, indeed, than any play I have ever read, unless perhaps *Hamlet* and *Lear*. It has been growing on me gradually ever since I read it first; like all great things, it is impossible to see the whole of it, but new points perpetually strike one.

The strange mystic exaltation of the chorus is very haunting, and the way that their world of frenzy and beauty supports itself till just the end against the everyday world is extraordinarily powerful. As a whole, I confess, the play does not strike me as at all puzzling: it is surely intelligible enough how those to whom such divine intoxication comes are filled with fury against the sceptics who try to drag them back to common life. And it is a commonplace that the worship of beauty makes for anarchy. It would have been absurd to make Pentheus a sympathetic character; I suppose he represents the British Public and Middle Class Respectability, and the respectable, though they are undoubtedly morally superior to the worshippers of Bacchus, are yet obviously unloveable in the conflict which they stir up.

I think your metres, now that I have mastered them, are exceedingly fine and wonderfully suited to the emotions they are meant to express: although there is perhaps no single chorus as good as some in the *Hippolytus*, I think you have shown more skill than you showed there; and altogether you are very much to be congratulated. Do you not think you would do well to make more translations? The two you have done have both been to me a really great help in trying times, helping me to support faith in the world of beauty, and in the ultimate dignity of life, when I was in danger of losing it: without them I should have often found the day much harder to get through. Surely there would be many who would feel the same, and as you have the power you have also the duty, have you not? Each of us is an Atlas to the world of his own ideals, and the poet, more than anyone else, lightens the burden for weary shoulders.

I wish I knew how to reconcile the world of beauty and the world of morals: some virtues, it is true, are beautiful, but many do not seem so.

I have been reading the *Republic*, and I agree with Plato that tragic poets ought to make us feel virtue to be beautiful, and ought (on the whole) to avoid the praises of vice. His austerity in matters of Art pleases me, for it does not seem to be the easy condemnation that comes from the Philistine.

> *Yours gratefully*
> *Bertrand Russell*

14 Cheyne Walk
Chelsea, S.W.
December 4, 1902

Dear Gilbert

I am glad my appreciation of your work is encouraging to you. Yes, an 'elegant leisure devoted to translating the classics' doesn't sound very nice as an epitaph! But one must choose more inspiring phrases to describe one's activity to oneself.

I have looked up again the chorus beginning 'O hounds raging and blind', and I still fail to find any difficulty in it. It seems very probable that the 'old bottles' is, as a matter of fact, the explanation of the savagery; but it is easy enough, if one wants such things, to find a psychological explanation. Have you never, when you were admiring the sunset, suddenly been jarred into 'Hell and Damnation, there are the so-and-so's come to call'? A country neighbour, under such circumstances, may easily be felt as a 'spy upon God's possessed'. And do you not know, when a Philistine breaks in upon a delicate imaginary world, the oscillation backwards and forwards between the exquisite mood one is loath to lose and rage against the wretch who is desecrating one's Holy of Holies? Do you know Blake's Defiled Sanctuary, beginning 'I saw a chapel all of gold', and ending 'So I turned into a sty, And laid me down among the swine'? This is from a worshipper of Bacchus who had been unable to combat his Pentheus. It was on account of the rapid alternation that I instanced Levine as a parallel. But I feel no doubt that it is the work of clarification that you have put into your translation that has made the *Bacchae* seem plain to me.

Yes, I know who the Storrs are and I can imagine that it is very hard for you to get away at present; it must make more of a burden on Mary when you are away. I am sorry you are sleepless and bedevilled. Sometimes sleepless nights are a time for thoughts that remain with one as a comfort through the day: I find darkness a help to isolating the essentials of things and fixing one's whole attention upon them. But I gather you do not find that compensation.

Alys is keeping well. The river shines like burnished bronze under the frosty sun, and the barges float dimly through the brightness like dream-memories of childhood.

Give my love to Mary, and write again when you can find time. I like to hear how domestic matters go—how Rosalind is, and so on.

Yours ever
Bertrand Russell

14 Cheyne Walk
Chelsea, S.W.
December 12, 1902

Dear Gilbert

It will suit us very well indeed to see you on Monday for luncheon and as early before it as you can manage to arrive. I shall expect you about 11-45. But it seems Miss Harrison will be gone; we have been urging her to stay, but she asserts (at present) that it is impossible. She begs you instead to go on to see her later, as soon after luncheon as you can manage, at an address which I do not know, but which she will no doubt divulge in due course. It will be perfectly delightful to see you, and I look forward to it very much; but I am sorry you will not find Miss Harrison. She has turned the tables on me by producing your poem in print; do bring me a copy on Monday. Could you not spend Monday night here? We shall be delighted to put you up, in case my Aunt Rosalind does not come to town; but we shall be dining out. London is a weary place, where it is quite impossible to think or feel anything worthy of a human being—I feel horribly lost here. Only the river and the gulls are my friends; they are not making money or acquiring power. Last night we made the acquaintance of the MacCails, which we were very glad of. How beautiful she is! I had heard so much about his balance and judgment that I was surprised to find him a fanatic. But he is too democratic for me—he said his charwoman was more in contact with real things than anybody else he knew. But what can a charwoman know of the spirits of great men or the records of fallen empires or the haunting visions of art and reason? All this and much more I wished to say; but the words stuck in my throat. Let us not delude ourselves with the hope that the best is within the reach of all, or that emotion uninformed by thought can ever attain the highest level. All such optimisms seem to me dangerous to civilization, and the outcome of a heart not yet sufficiently mortified. 'Die to Self' is an old maxim; 'Love thy neighbour as thyself' is new in this connexion, but also has an element of truth. From heaven we may return to our fellow-creatures, not try to make our heaven here among them; we ought to love our neighbour through the love of God, or else our love is too mundane. At least so it seems to me. But the coldness of my own doctrine is repellent to me; except at moments when the love of God glows brightly.

Modern life is very difficult; I wish I lived in a cloister wearing a hair shirt and sleeping on a crucifix. But now-a-days every impulse has to be kept within the bounds of black-coated Respectability, the living God.

Yours ever
Bertrand Russell

I Tatti, Settignano
Florence
December 28th, 1902

Dear Gilbert

Our crossing and journey were uneventful and prosperous, and the beauty here is overwhelming. I do wish you had been able to come. We have had day after day of brilliant sunshine—hoar frosts in the morning, warmth that made sitting out agreeable in the day. Just behind the house is a hill-side covered with cypress and pine and little oaks that still have autumn leaves, and the air is full of deep-toned Italian bells. The house has been furnished by Berenson with exquisite taste; it has some very good pictures, and a most absorbing library. But the business of existing beautifully, except when it is hereditary, always slightly shocks my Puritan soul—thoughts of the East End, of intelligent women whose lives are sacrificed to the saving of pence, of young men driven to journalism or schoolmastering when they ought to do research, come up perpetually in my mind; but I do not justify the feeling, as someone ought to keep up the ideal of beautiful houses. But I think one makes great demands on the mental furniture where the outside is so elaborate, and one is shocked at lapses that one would otherwise tolerate. . . . I am glad you abandoned your plan of reading a mathematical book, for any book on the Calculus would have told you lies, and also my book is (I fear) not worth while for you to read, except a few bits. What general value it may have is so buried in technicalities and controversies that it is really only fit for those whose special business it is to go in for such things. The later mathematical volume, which will not be ready for two years or so, will I hope be a work of art; but that will be only for mathematicians. And this volume disgusts me on the whole. Although I denied it when Leonard Hobhouse said so, philosophy seems to me on the whole a rather hopeless business. I do not know how to state the value that at moments I am inclined to give it. If only one had lived in the days of Spinoza, when systems were still possible. . . .

Yours ever
Bertrand Russell

14 Cheyne Walk
Chelsea, S.W.
March 21st, 1903

Dear Gilbert

Your doctrine on beauty does not repel me in the least, indeed I agree with it strongly, except the slight sneer at specialists. Specializing is necessary to efficiency, which is a form of altruism, and however narrow the specialist becomes, we ought to pardon him if he does good work. This I feel strongly, because the temptation to be interesting rather than technically effective is a dangerous one.

I shall be more glad than I can say when you come back; though I shall have nothing to give you in the conversational way. I have been merely oppressed by the weariness and tedium and vanity of things lately: nothing stirs me, nothing seems worth doing or worth having done: the only thing that I strongly *feel* worth while would be to murder as many people as possible so as to diminish the amount of consciousness in the world. These times have to be lived through: there is nothing to be done with them.

Yours ever
B. Russell

To Lucy Martin Donnelly:

The Mill House
Grantchester, Cambridge
Telegrams, Trumpington
May 23, 1902

Dear Lucy

. . . You will wonder at my writing to you: the fact is, I finished today my magnum opus on the principles of Mathematics, on which I have been engaged since 1897. This has left me with leisure and liberty to remember that there are human beings in the world, which I have been strenuously striving to forget. I wonder whether you realize the degree of self-sacrifice (and too often sacrifice of others), of sheer effort of will, of stern austerity in repressing even what is intrinsically best, that goes into writing a book of any magnitude. Year after year, I found mistakes in what I had done, and had to re-write the

163

whole from beginning to end: for in a logical system, one mistake will usually vitiate everything. The hardest part I left to the end: last summer I undertook it gaily, hoping to finish soon, when suddenly I came upon a greater difficulty than any I had known of before. So difficult it was, that to think of it at all required an all but superhuman effort. And long ago I got sick to nausea of the whole subject, so that I longed to think of anything else under the sun; and sheer fatigue has become almost incapacitating. But now at last all is finished, and as you may imagine, I feel a new man; for I had given up hope of ever coming to an end of the labour. Abstract work, if one wishes to do it well, must be allowed to destroy one's humanity; one raises a monument which is at the same time a tomb, in which, voluntarily, one slowly inters oneself. But the thankless muse will not share her favours—she is a jealous mistress.— Do not believe, if you wish to write, that the current doctrine of experience has any truth; there is a thousand times more experience in pain than in pleasure. Artists must have strong passions, but they deceive themselves in fancying it good to indulge their desires. The whole doctrine, too, that writing comes from technique, is quite mistaken; writing is the outlet to feelings which are all but overmastering, and are yet mastered. Two things are to be cultivated: loftiness of feeling, and control of feeling and everything else by the will. Neither of these are understood in America as in the old countries; indeed, loftiness of feeling seems to depend essentially upon a brooding consciousness of the past and its terrible power, a deep sense of the difference between the great eternal facts and the transient dross of merely personal feeling. If you tell these things to your fine-writing class, they will know less than if you hold your tongue.

Give my love to Helen. My advice to anyone who wishes to write is to know all the *very* best literature by heart, and ignore the rest as completely as possible.

Yours ever
Bertrand Russell

N.B.—This letter is not for Carey!

Trinity College, Cambridge
July 6, 1902

Dear Lucy

Many thanks for your very interesting letter, and for the excellent account of Harvard and Barrett Wendell. What a monstrous thing that a University should teach journalism! I thought that was only done at Oxford. This respect for the filthy multitude is ruining civilization. A certain man had the impudence to maintain in my presence that every student ought to be made to expound his views to popular audiences, so I lifted up my voice and testified for a quarter of an hour, after which he treated me with the kind of respect accorded to wild beasts.—I suppose Wendell is better than his books: I was disappointed in his American literature. For, though I agree with him that America, like the Australian marsupials, is an interesting relic of a bygone age, I care little for the great truth that American writers have all been of good family, and that Harvard is vastly superior to Yale. And his failure to appreciate Walt Whitman to my mind is very damaging. He talks of Brooklyn ferry and so on, and quite forgets 'out of the cradle endlessly rocking', and 'when lilacs last in the dooryard bloomed'. This seems to me to show a deplorable conventionality, both in taste generally, and in judgment of Whitman specially.

When my book was finished, I took ten days' holiday. Since then I have been working as usual, except during four days that I spent with my Aunt Agatha at Pembroke Lodge. A strange, melancholy, weird time it was: we talked of merriment long since turned to sadness, of tragedies in which all the actors are gone, of sorrows which have left nothing but a fading memory. All the life of the present grew to me dreamy and unreal, while the majestic Past, weighed down by age and filled with unspeakable wisdom, rose before me and dominated my whole being. The Past is an awful God, though he gives Life almost the whole of its haunting beauty. I believe those whose childhood has been spent in America can scarcely conceive the hold which the Past has on us of the Old World: the continuity of life, the weight of tradition, the great eternal procession of youth and age and death, seem to be lost in the bustling approach of the future which dominates American life. And that is one reason why great literature is not produced by your compatriots.

At present, I am staying in College by myself: none of my friends are up, and when work is over, I have a great deal of leisure left for meditation. I have been reading Maeterlinck's works straight through: alas, I have nearly come to the end of them. *Le Temple Enseveli* seems to me very admirable, both as literature and as morality. I am simple-minded enough, in spite of Miss Gwinn and Mr Hodder's grave man's world (being I suppose, not a grave man) to think it unnecessary for literature to have an immoral purpose. I hate this notion of being true to life! Life, thank God, is very largely what we choose to make of it, and ideals are unreal only to those who do not wish them to be otherwise. Tell Miss Gwinn, with my compliments, that every word of St Augustine's Confessions is true to life, and that Dante's love for Beatrice is a piece of unadulterated realism. If people will not realize this, they are sure to lose out of life its finest, rarest, most precious experiences. But this is too large a theme! ...

> *Yours very sincerely*
> *Bertrand Russell*

Friday's Hill
Haslemere
September 1, 1902

Dear Lucy

Vanity in regard to letter writing is not an emotion to encourage! One's friends are sure to be glad of one's news, even if it is not told in the most gorgeous diction. But as a matter of fact I found your letter very interesting. Yes, one's people are very trying: they are a living caricature of oneself, and have the same humiliating effect that is produced by the monkeys in the Zoo: one feels that here is the unvarnished truth at last. To most people, their family is real in a higher sense than any later acquaintance, husband or wife even. You may notice that with Carlyle—his people in Annandale existed for him in a way in which his wife never existed till she was dead. People are less cased in Self as children, and those associated with childhood have a vividness that becomes impossible later—they live in one's instinctive past. This is a frequent source of trouble in marriage.—I haven't read the Elizabethans since I was an undergraduate; as I remember them, their chief merit is a very rich and splendid diction. The old drama is not a gospel to regenerate you, its world is too hopelessly unreal. Your own life, naturally, is a paper life, as you say, a life in which experience comes through books, not directly. For this disease, more books are *not* the remedy. Only real life is the remedy—but that is hard to get. Real life means a life in some kind of intimate relation to other human beings—Hodder's life of passion has no reality at all. Or again, real life means the experience in one's own person of the emotions which make the material of religion and poetry. The road to it is the same as that recommended to the man who wanted to found a new religion: Be crucified, and rise again on the third day.

If you are prepared for both parts of this process, by all means take to real life. But in the modern world, the cross is usually self-inflicted and voluntary, and the rising again, to the hopes of new crucifixions, requires a considerable effort of will. It seems to me that your difficulty comes from the fact that there are no real people to speak of in your world. The young are never real, the unmarried very seldom. Also, if I may say so, the scale of emotion in America seems to me more frivolous, more superficial, more pusillanimous, than in Europe; there is a triviality of feeling which makes real people very rare—I find in England, that most women of 50 and upwards have gone through the experience of many years' voluntary endurance of torture, which has given a depth and a richness to their natures that your easy-going pleasure-loving women cannot imagine. On the whole, real life does not consist, as Hodder would have you believe, in intrigues with those who are already married. If one wants uncommon experiences, a little renunciation, a little performance of duty, will give one far more unusual sensations than all the fine free passion in the universe. But a life in books has great calm and peace—it is true that a terrible hunger for something less thin comes over one, but one is spared from remorse and horror and torture and the maddening poison of regret. For my part, I am constructing a mental cloister, in which my inner soul is to dwell in peace, while an outer simulacrum goes forth to meet the world. In this inner sanctuary I sit and think spectral thoughts. Yesterday, talking on the terrace, the ghosts of all former occasions there rose and walked before me in solemn procession—all dead, with their hopes and fears, their joys and sorrows, their aspirations and their golden youth—gone, gone into the great limbo of human folly. And as I talked, I felt myself and the others already faded into the Past and all seemed very small—struggles, pains, everything, mere fatuity, noise and fury signifying nothing. And so calm is achieved, and Fate's thunders become mere nursery-tales to frighten children. --Life here is always, in the summer, a strange phantasmagory: we had yesterday Grace, the Amos's, Miss Creighton, the Kinsellas, the Robinsons and J. M. Robertson, the man on whom Bradlaugh's mantle has fallen. Miss Creighton had to be rescued, because Robertson began to discuss whether God was made of green cheese or had whiskers—infinite for choice.

We have all been reading with great pleasure James on Religious Experience—everything good about the book except the conclusions. I have been re-reading the most exquisite of all bits of history, Carlyle's *Diamond Necklace*. He is the only author who knows the place of History among the Fine Arts.

Love to Helen.

Yours very sincerely
Bertrand Russell

14 Cheyne Walk
Chelsea, S.W.
November 25, 1902

Dear Lucy

Many thanks for your letter. I am grateful to you for writing about yourself: after all, people can tell one nothing more interesting than their own feeling towards life. It is a great comfort that you are so much better, and able to enjoy life again. All that you write about the little most people get out of experience is most true: but I was not thinking when I wrote, of 'experiences', but of the inward knowledge of emotions. This, if one is rightly constituted, requires an absolute minimum of outward circumstances as its occasion; and this it is that is required for the development of character and for certain sorts of writing. But there is no profit in feeling unless one learns to dominate it and impersonalize it.—For people like you and me, whose main business is necessarily with books, I rather think experience of life should be as far as possible vicarious. If one has instinctive sympathy, one comes to know the true history of a certain number of people and from that one can more or less create one's world. But to plunge into life oneself takes a great deal of time and energy, and is, for most people, incompatible with preserving the attitude of a spectator. One needs, as the key to interpret alien experience, a personal knowledge of great unhappiness; but that is a thing which one need hardly set forth to seek, for it comes unasked. When once one possesses this key, the strange, tragic phantasmagoria of people hoping, suffering, and then dying, begins to suffice without one's desiring to take part, except occasionally to speak a word of encouragement where it is possible.

I have not been reading much lately: Fitzgerald's letters have interested me, also the new Cambridge Modern History, where one gets a connected view of things one has read before in a very fragmentary fashion. Gilbert Murray's translations of Euripides are out, and I recommend them to you (published by George Allen). I have been trying to be interested in Politics, but in vain: the British Empire is unreal to me, I visualize the Mother Country and the Colonies as an old hen clucking to her chickens, and the whole thing strikes me as laughable. I know that grave men take it seriously, but it all seems to me so unimportant compared to the great eternal facts. And London people, to whom the Eternal is represented by the Monthlies, to which they rise with difficulty from the daily papers, strike me as all puppets, blind embodiments of the forces of nature, never achieving the liberation that comes to man when he ceases to desire and learns at last to contemplate. Only in thought is man a God; in action and desire we are the slaves of circumstance.

> *Yours very sincerely*
> *Bertrand Russell*

Lucy Donnelly's life had for many years centred about her friendship for Helen Thomas. When Helen became engaged to Dr Simon Flexner, Lucy suffered profoundly. The following letter was an attempt to comfort her.

> 14 Cheyne Walk
> Chelsea, S.W.
> 7th February, 1903

Dear Lucy

I have just heard of Helen's engagement and for her sake I am glad—it has always seemed to me that she ought to marry and that College life was distinctly a second-best for her. But for you, I know, it must be hard, very hard. It is a dangerous thing to allow one's affections to centre too much in one person; for affection is always liable to be thwarted, and life itself is frail. One learns many things as year by year adds to the burden of one's life; and I think the chief of all is the power of making all one's loves purely contemplative. Do you know Walt Whitman's 'Out of the rolling ocean the crowd'? One learns to love all that is good with the same love—a love that knows of its existence, and feels warmed to the world by that knowledge, but asks for no possession, for no private gain except the contemplation itself. And there is no doubt that there are real advantages in loss: affection grows wider, and one learns insight into the lives of others. Everyone who realizes at all what human life is must feel at some time the strange loneliness of every separate soul; loneliness makes a new strange tie, and a growth of pity so warm as to be almost a compensation for what is lost.

Phrases, I know, do not mend matters; but it makes unhappiness far more bearable to think that some good will come of it; and indeed the facing of the world alone, without one's familiar refuge, is the beginning of wisdom and courage.

Forgive my writing so intimately; but the world is too serious a place, at times, for the barriers of reserve and good manners.

We shall hope to see a great deal of you when you come to England, as I hope you will do. And I shall be very glad to hear from you whenever you feel inclined to write.

> *Yours very sincerely*
> *Bertrand Russell*

Churt, Farnham
April 13, '03

Dear Lucy

It is impossible to tell you how like sunshine it was to me to hear that my letter had been a comfort. But alas! it is easier to see what is good than to practise it; and old as this observation is, I have not yet got used to it, or made up my mind that it really is true. Yet I have seen and known, at times, a life at a far higher level than my present one; and my precepts are very greatly superior to anything that I succeed in achieving.

Yes, the logic of life is a wonderful thing: sometimes I think of making up a set of aphorisms, to be called 'Satan's joys'; such as: Giving causes affection, receiving causes tedium; the reward of service is unrequited love. (This is the biography of all virtuous mothers, and of many wives.) Passions are smirched by indulgence and killed by restraint: the loss in either case is inevitable. And so on. But these bitter truths, though they deserve to be recognized so far as they are true, are not good to dwell upon. Wherever one finds oneself inclined to bitterness, it is a sign of emotional failure; a larger heart and a greater self-restraint, would put a calm autumnal sadness in the place of the instinctive outcry of pain. One of the things that make literature so consoling is, that its tragedies are all in the past, and have the completeness and repose that comes of being beyond the reach of our endeavours. It is a most wholesome thing, when one's sorrow grows acute, to view it as having all happened long, long ago: to join in imagination, the mournful company of dim souls whose lives were sacrificed to the great machine that still grinds on. I see the past, like a sunny landscape, where the world's mourners mourn no longer. On the banks of the river of Time, the sad procession of human generations is marching slowly to the grave; but in the quiet country of the past, the tired wanderers rest, and all their weeping is hushed.

But as for me, I have felt no emotions of any kind, except on rare occasions, for some time now; and that is a state of things most convenient for work, though very dull. We are living a quiet country life: Alys is well, except now and then for a day or two. We read Montaigne aloud: he is pleasant and soothing, but very unexciting. To myself I am reading the history of Rome in the middle ages, by Gregorovius, a delightful book. Gilbert Murray, who is our near neighbour, has been telling me about Orphic tablets, and their directions to the soul after death: 'Thou wilt find a cypress, and by the cypress a spring, and by the spring two guardians, who will say to thee: who art thou? whence comest thou? And thou wilt reply: I am the child of earth and of the starry heaven; I am parched with thirst, I perish.' Then they tell him to drink of the fountain; sometimes the fountain itself speaks. Certainly a beautiful mysticism.

Yours very sincerely
Bertrand Russell

Friday's Hill
Haslemere
July 29, 1903

Dear Lucy

It is impossible to tell you how glad I am that our letters have been a help to you. It is *the* great reward of losing youth that one finds oneself able to be of use; and I cannot, without seeming to cant, say how great a reward I feel it. You need not mind bringing a budget of problems; I look forward to hearing them, and to thinking about them. . . .

Yes, the way people regard intimacy as a great opportunity for destroying happiness is most horrible. It is ghastly to watch, in most marriages, the competition as to which is to be torturer, which tortured; a few years, at most, settle it, and after it is settled, one has happiness and the other has virtue. And the torturer smirks and speaks of matrimonial bliss; and the victim, for fear of worse, smiles a ghastly assent. Marriage, and all such close relations, have quite infinite possibilities of pain; nevertheless, I believe it is good to be brought into close contact with people. Otherwise, one remains ignorant of much that it is good to know, merely because it increases human comradeship to suffer what others suffer. But it is hard not to long, in weak moments, for a simple life, a life with books and things, away from human sorrow. I am amazed at the number of people who are wretched almost beyond endurance. 'Truly the food man feeds upon is Pain.' One has to learn to regard happiness, for others as well as for oneself, as more or less unimportant—but though I keep on telling myself this, I do not yet fully and instinctively believe it.

I am glad to hear that Helen is getting rested. It has been no surprise not hearing from her; but tell her not to forget me, and to write again when she is able. Seeing Grace just before her departure, the other day, seemed to bring America nearer. Usually, when I write to you or Helen, I feel almost as if I were writing to dead people whom I have read about in books—the whole place seems so remote, so plunged in memories of an utterly different person who occupied my body seven years ago, that I can hardly believe it to be real or inhabited by real people. But when you come over in the autumn, I shall doubt whether you have really been in America all this time.

The last four months, I have been working like a horse, and have achieved almost nothing. I discovered in succession seven brand-new difficulties, of which I solved the first six. When the seventh turned up, I became discouraged, and decided to take a holiday before going on. Each in turn required a reconstruction of my whole edifice. Now I am staying with Dickinson; in a few days I shall go to town and plunge into the Free Trade question (as a student only). We are all wildly excited about Free Trade; it is to me the last piece of sane internationalism left, and if it went I should feel inclined to cut my throat. But there seems no chance whatever of Chamberlain's succeeding—all the brains are against him, in every class of society. . . .

Yours very sincerely
B. Russell

14 Cheyne Walk, Chelsea S.W.
February 28, 1904

My dear Lucy

... Really the feeling of the worthlessness of one's work, where it is not justified, is the last refuge of self-love. It comes partly of too high an ideal of what one might hope to achieve, which is a form of pride; and partly of rebellion against one's private sufferings, which, one feels, can only be outweighed by some immense public good. But I know it is intolerably hard to drive self-love from this entrenchment, and I certainly have not yet succeeded. I do wish I could be with you, not only for the beauty of Sicily, but because it would be a great pleasure to see you, and because it would be so much easier to say just the things to build up in you the self-respect you deserve to have. You are really too modest altogether; but your friends' affection ought to persuade you that you have things to give which people value. I have not found myself, though, any way of banishing self except work; and while you are unable to work, it is very difficult for you.

I am glad Helen writes you nice letters. But I gather from what you say that her happiness is not great enough to exclude pains. That is a pity; yet perhaps it is a safeguard against greater pains in the future. This sounds a commonplace reflection, and I confess I think it better to have both pain and pleasure in an extreme degree than to have both soberly. But consolations are not to be rejected, even if they are commonplace....

There is not much news here. I have been very busy, but now my labours are practically ended. We go to Cambridge for two days this week, and Alys goes to visit Logan and look for sites at Oxford. I have been reading novels: *Diana*, and *Beauchamp's Career*, are the two I have read last. Meredith's psychology seems to me very good as a rule, though I didn't think Diana's betrayal was made credible. I fell in love with her at the Ball, and remained so through all her vagaries.

Last night I went to a remote part of London, to lecture to the local Branch of the Amalgamated Society of Engineers. They meet in a Public House, but permit no drinks during their meeting. They seemed excellent people, *very* respectable—indeed I shouldn't have guessed they were working men. They were of all shades of opinion, from Tory to Socialist. The Chairman, when I had finished, begged them not to follow their usual practice of flattering the lecturer; but even so I got not much criticism. The Secretary explained this to me on the way home by saying my arguments had 'bottled them up'. I liked them all, and felt an increased respect for the skilled workman, who seems usually an admirable person.

In a fortnight I shall have done with fiscal things, and then I shall go a walking-tour in Devonshire and Cornwall before settling down to Philosophy. MacCarthy will go with me.

Write again as soon as you can. I feel there is much more to be said in answer to your letter, but Politics has rather scattered my thoughts. Try to keep up your spirits; and *please* don't imagine your life a useless one.

Yours affectionately
Bertrand Russell

St Catherine's House
First-Class Private Hotel
Fowey, Cornwall
March 29, 1904

My dear Lucy

... As for work, I have not thought at all, either with satisfaction or the reverse, about my fiscal career, now happily closed—that whole episode seems to have just faded away. Also I have not thought much about philosophy; though when I do think of it, the thought is rather pleasant. MacCarthy, who was an ideal companion, left me about 5 days ago. Since then I have been alone, and have found the time most valuable. A great sense of peace comes over me as I walk over green hills by the sea, with nobody to consult, and nobody to be careful of. In a quiet instinctive way (very uncommon with me) I think through practical difficulties that had seemed insoluble, and lay up a store of peace of mind to last through the agitations and fatigues of ordinary life. When I am not thinking of the way, or the scenery, I am mostly thinking about people's affairs; trying to get the facts straight, and to decide how much I can do to better the facts. It takes a good deal of time and thought to imagine oneself in a certain situation, and decide whether one could be sufficiently impressive to effect a great result. My Self comes in in being flattered by my knowledge of people's affairs, and anxious to have their confidence; but I try hard to make Self in this form subservient to good ends.

Then, when I reach an Inn, the people are all interesting owing to the solitude of my walks; I observe their little ways, compare landladies, and listen to the local gossip and the trials of innkeepers' lives. I could write at length on this subject; but it would be rather Pickwickian. In this Hotel, we are a happy family party, and all dine together. As I came downstairs, a middle-aged woman was giving herself some final touches before the Hall looking-glass; she looked round quickly, and when she saw I was not the man for whom she was doing it, she went on as before. Another middle-aged woman, with an earnest manner and a very small waist, was in great form, because *the* young man had given her a bunch of white violets, which she was wearing. Then there was the inevitable old lady who dined at a table apart, and only joined the conversation occasionally, throwing in a remark about how sweet the spring flowers are; and there was the pompous man, who was saying, 'Well, my opinion is that the directors have just thrown away £12,000 of the shareholders' money'. Then there was myself, much ashamed of having no change of clothes among all these respectable people, and much despised by them for the same reason; and like the man at the helm in the *Snark*, I spoke to no one and no one spoke to me; but I was well amused. Yesterday I stayed at a place called Mevagissey, where there was a Parish Council Election going on. The landlady's daughter was laying my dinner, when I asked her if it was a contest of Liberal and Tory.

'Oh no, Sir, it's only some of them wanted to put up a Doctor, and others said he wasn't a Mevagissey man, and had only lived 6 or 7 years in the place.'

'Disgraceful', I said.

'Yes it is, Sir, ain't it? And they had a show of hands and he got the worst of it, but he demanded a poll and now the fisherman hope he'll be turned out.'

'Well,' I said, 'he doesn't seem to have much chance.'

'You see, Sir, the people who are backing him are powerful people, they're fish-buyers, and some of the fishermen get their nets from them. Then he's backed up by what they call the Christians, the people who are against us poor innkeepers.'

Oho, I thought, now I'm getting it. 'Is he a Nonconformist?' I asked.

'Oh yes, Sir, he's not a churchman'—in a tone of great contempt.

Then I found his backers were also Nonconformists, that they had made their own money, were very kind to sober men, but very hard on drunkards; and that several pubs had been annoyed by them. I was interested to find that, in the common parlance of church-people 'Christian' is the antithesis to 'Churchman'. I found further from the Landlady that these monsters in human shape actually proposed a new drainage scheme and a new water supply, although the rates were already dreadfully high.

'How high?' I asked.

'I couldn't say, Sir, but I know they're dreadfully high.'

The Doctor was not elected; but I was consoled to learn that the parson had also been turned out.—These little distractions keep me from having a moment's boredom. . . .

> *Yours affectionately*
> *Bertrand Russell*

Castle Howard
York
August 15, 1904

My dear Lucy

. . . This place is a large 18th century house, embodying family pride and the worship of reason in equal measure. It is a family party—the Murrays, whom you know; Cecilia and Roberts—she, devoted to all her family, especially her mother, placid usually, but capable of violent sudden rage, in which she utters magnificent invective, though at all other times she is a fat good-humoured saint and (oddly enough) a Christian; Roberts (her husband) tall, thin, nervous, quivering like a poplar in the wind, an idealist disillusioned and turned opportunist; Oliver Howard, lately back from Nigeria, where he administered brilliantly a lately-conquered district, containing a town of 500,000 inhabitants, in which he was almost the only white man. He is smart, thin, delicate, conventional, with a soft manner concealing an oriental cruelty and power of fury, of which his mother is the occasion and his wife the victim—at least probably in the future. He is very beautiful and his wife is very pretty: both are Christians; she too is very smart and very conventional, but she has real good nature, and is on the whole likeable. They are very openly affectionate; in him, one dimly feels in the background the kind of jealousy that would lead to murder if it saw cause. Being very like his mother in character, he differs from her in every opinion, and relations are painfully strained.—Then there is Dorothy, who seems to me just like my grandmother Stanley—crude, sometimes cruel, plucky, very honourable, and full of instinctive vitality and healthy animalism, oddly overlaid with her mother's principles. Last there is Leif Jones,[1] Lady Carlisle's private secretary, an infinitely lovable man: he does everything for everybody, has sunk his own career, his own desires, the hope of a private life of any personal kind: and all the family take him as a matter of course, and no more expect him to make demands than they expect the stones to call out for food.

Lady Carlisle conducts conversation in a way which makes it a game of skill played for high stakes. It is always argument, in which, with consummate art, she ignores relevancy and changes the issue until she has the advantage, and then she charges down and scatters the enemy like chaff before the wind. A large proportion of her remarks are designed to cause pain to someone who has shown independence or given ground for one of the thousand forms of jealousy. She has the faults of Napoleonic women, with less mendacity and more deliberate cruelty than in the case you know best, but with a desire to cause quarrels and part friends which is really terrible. On the other hand, she has really great public spirit, and devotes time and money to really important objects. She has a just sense of values, and a kind of high-mindedness—a most mixed and interesting character. . . .

> *Yours affectionately*
> *Bertrand Russell*

Audierne, Finistère
October 3, 1904

My dear Lucy

This is not a real letter, but only a counter-irritant to my last. As soon as I got away I began to see things in their true proportions, and to be no longer oppressed by the complication of things. But on the whole, I think I shall have to avoid growing intimate with people I don't respect, or trying to help them: it seems to be a job for which I am not fitted.

Brittany is quite wonderful—it has a great deal of purely rural beauty, woods and streams and endless orchards of big red apples, scenting all the air; and besides all this, it has a combination of the beauties of Devonshire and Cornwall. We have been walking lately round the S.W. coast, places where the Atlantic rules as God. Every tiny village has a huge Gothic church, usually very beautiful; many churches stand quite by themselves, facing the sea as relics of ancient courage. At first I wondered how anyone could believe in God in the presence of something so much greater and more powerful as the sea; but very soon, the inhumanity and cruelty of the sea became so oppressive that I saw how God belongs to the human world, and is, in their minds, the Captain of an army in which they are the soldiers: God is the most vigorous assertion that the world is not all omnipotent Matter. And so the fishermen became and have remained the most religious population in the world. It is a strange, desolate, wind-swept region, where long ago great

[1] Later Lord Rhayader.

towns flourished, where Iseult of Brittany lived in a castle over the sea, and where ancient legends seem far more real than anything in the life of the present. The very children are old: they do not play or shout, like other children: they sit still, with folded hands and faces of weary resignation, waiting for the sorrows that time is sure to bring. The men are filled with melancholy; but they escape from it by drink. I have never imagined a population so utterly drunken; in every village we have seen men reeling into the gutter. Ordinary days here are as bad as Bank Holiday with us—except that I don't think the women drink much.

A very curious contrast to the Bretons was the proprietor of the last Inn we stayed at, at a place called St Guénolé, near the Pointe de Penmarc'h. He was tall and very erect, with a magnificent black beard, and quick, vigorous dramatic movements. We were wet, so we sat in the kitchen, where he was cooking the dinner with an energy and delight in his work which I have never seen surpassed. We soon found that he was a Parisian, that he had a sister married to a hotel-keeper in Lancaster, & another in the service of Lord Gerard (!) in Egypt; that he had been cook on a Far-Eastern liner, & that he had now at last saved up enough capital to start on a venture of his own. He told us that he was *really* a sculptor, not a cook, & that in winter, when no guests come, he devotes his time to statuary. He had a voice that would easily have filled the Albert Hall, & he used it as a dinner-gong. Indeed, at all sorts of times, from sheer good spirits, he would bellow some joke or some command through the Hotel, so that all the walls resounded. His cooking, needless to say, was perfect. We saw a poor fisherman come in & sell sardines to him for our dinner; a vast number were purchased for threepence, which, as far as I could discover, the miserable wretch immediately spent in the bar.

> *Yours affectionately*
> *Bertrand Russell*

4 Ralston Street
Tite Street, S.W.
February 8, 1905

My dear Lucy

... Now that we are back in Chelsea, I often wish you too were here again, and when I walk the Battersea Park round, I miss you very much. There is much too much of the Atlantic. This year, when I go walks, it is usually with MacCarthy, whom I find wonderfully soothing and restful, full of kindly humour, which makes the world seem gay. George Trevelyan also I walk with; but he, though he maintains that the world is better than I think, maintains it with an air of settled gloom, by comparison with which my jokes against optimism seem full of the joy of life! His wife, by the way, is one of the most simply lovable people I have ever met. She has not much to say, and I often find the talk flagging when I am with her; but she is filled full of generous loves and friendships, and honest and sincere in a very rare degree. She is ignorant of the world, as everyone is who has met with nothing but kindness and good fortune: she instinctively expects that everybody she meets will be nice. This gives her the pathos of very young people, and makes one long to keep sorrows away from her, well as one may know that that is impossible. I have liked and respected other people more, with almost no desire to shield them from pain; but towards her I feel as one does towards a child.

We see a great many people now that we are in town. Last night we dined at the Sidney Webbs, to meet

Lion Phillimore

Mackinder, whom you doubtless remember—the head Beast of the School of Economics.

Granville Barker, the young and beautiful actor, who has been producing Shaw's and Murray's plays

Sir Oliver Lodge, Scientist and Spiritualist

Arthur Balfour; and, greatest of all,

Werner, of Werner Beit and Co, the chief of all the South African million-aires; a fat, good-natured, eupeptic German with an equally fat gold watch-chain and a strong German accent (characteristic of all the finest types of British Imperialists), bearing very lightly the load of blood, of nations destroyed and hatreds generated, of Chinese slavery and English corruption, which, by all the old rules, ought to weigh upon him like a cope of lead. It was an amusing occasion. When everyone had come except Balfour and Werner, Mrs Webb observed that we should see which of them thought himself the bigger swell, by which came last. Sure enough, Werner came last; for though Balfour governs the Empire, Werner governs Balfour. Balfour was most agreeable, absolutely free from the slightest sign of feeling himself a personage, sympathetic, anxious to listen rather than to talk. He puts his finger in his mouth, with the air of a small child deep in thought. He is quite obviously weak, obviously without strong feelings, apparently kindly, and not apparently able; at least I saw nothing I should have recognized as showing ability, except his tact, which probably is the main cause of his success. He professed not to know whether the Government would last another fortnight; said he could not arrange to see Shaw's play, for fear of a General Election intervening. All this I took to be blarney. He drew me out about Moore's philosophy, and then listened to a lecture from Mrs Webb on 'the first principles of Government, for beginners'; at least that would have been an appropriate title for her dinner-table discourse.

Sir Oliver Lodge, though I had a prejudice against him on account of theological differences, struck me as delightful: calm, philosophic, and dis-interested. Poor Mackinder made a bee-line for Balfour, but got landed with me, much to my amusement. It was a sore trial to his politeness, from which he extricated himself indifferently.[1]

I am not working now, but merely seeing people and enjoying myself. I have fits of depression at times, but they don't last long. I have had a fair share of other people's tragedies lately; some in which intimate friends have behaved badly, which is always painful. Others, which vex me almost more, I only suspect and have to watch their disastrous effects in total impotence. Who

[1] This dinner is also described by Mrs Webb in *Our Partnership*, p. 300.

was the heartless fool who said that loving other people made one happy? Still, with all its pains, it does help to make life tolerable. . . .

Yours affectionately
Bertrand Russell

Lower Copse
Bagley Wood, Oxford
June 13, 1905

My dear Lucy

. . . I did not remember (if I ever knew) that the *Spectator* had spoken of my writing; your allusion makes me curious to know what it said. I have not done any more of that sort of writing, but I have been getting on very well with my work. For a long time I have been at intervals debating this conundrum: If two names or descriptions apply to the same object, whatever is true of the one is true of the other. Now George the Fourth wished to know whether Scott was the author of *Waverley*; and Scott was as a matter of fact the same person as the author of *Waverley*. Hence, putting 'Scott' in the place of 'the author of *Waverley*', we find that George the Fourth wished to know whether Scott was Scott, which implies more interest in the Laws of Thought than was possible for the First Gentleman of Europe. This little puzzle was quite hard to solve; the solution, which I have now found, throws a flood of light on the foundations of mathematics and on the whole problem of the relation of thought to things. It is a great thing to find a puzzle; because, so long as it is puzzling, one knows one has not got to the bottom of things. I have hopes that I shall never again as long as I live have such difficult work as I had last year, and the year before; certainly this year, so far, my work has not been nearly so hard, and I have been reaping the harvest of previous work.

This place is a very great success. The house is pretty and comfortable, my study is so palatial that I am almost ashamed of it, and the country round has the typical English charm of fields and meadows and broad open views, with Oxford and the river besides. Alys seems to like the place thoroughly, and has been on the whole much better than in town. I find it a great advantage being in touch with Oxford people—it is easier to keep alive my interest in work when I can bring it into some relation with human interests. I have had to take myself in hand rather severely, and being here has made it much more feasible. . . .

Do write to me again as soon as you can, and tell me about yourself and also about Helen. Your letters are always a great pleasure to me. Just now I am in the middle of a fit of work; but though I shall do my best, it is likely to stop soon. Life would be delightfully simple if one could enjoy all one's duties, as some people do; it would be simpler than it is if one always did the duties one doesn't enjoy. Failing both, it is complicated to a frightful extent. But I live in hopes of becoming middle-aged, which, they tell me, makes everything easy.

Yours affectionately
Bertrand Russell

1 Barton Street
Westminster
August 3, 1905

My dear Lucy

You will probably have heard, by the time this reaches you, of the disaster which has befallen us all. Theodore Davies, bathing alone in a pool near Kirkby Lonsdale, was drowned; presumably by hitting his head against a rock in diving, and so getting stunned. It is a loss, to very many, which we shall feel as long as we live; and the loss to the public is beyond anything one can possibly estimate. But all other losses seem as nothing compared to Crompton's. They had been always together, they shared everything, and Theodore was as careful of Crompton and as tender with him as any mother could have been. Crompton bears it with wonderful courage; his mind endures it, but I doubt whether his body will. I am here to do what I can for him— there is little enough except to sit in silence with him and suffer as he suffers. As soon as he can get away, I am going abroad with him. This is Miss Sheep-shanks's house; she and the other inmates are all away, and she has kindly lent it to me. Alys was very much upset by the news. When we got it, we were just starting for Ireland, to stay with the Monteagles. It seemed best for her not to be alone, so I went over with her, and then came back here. She will be there another 10 days or more. They are kind good people, who will take care of her. Crompton's sorrow is crushing, and I hardly know how to bear it. But it is a comfort to feel able to be of some help to him. Theodore had very many devoted friends, and all have done everything they could; their sympathy has pulled Crompton through the first shock, but there is a long anxious time to come.

... I have written an article[1] on George IV for '*Mind*', which will appear in due course; there you will find the 'answer' ...

I am too tired to write more now. I wanted to write to you about Theodore, but I have no thoughts for other things.

Yours affectionately
Bertrand Russell

Rozeldene, Grayshott
Haslemere, Surrey
September 3, 1905

My dear Lucy

Thank you very much for your kind letter. Crompton and I went to France for a fortnight, which was all the holiday he could get. I think it did him good. We stayed first with the Frys and then with the Whiteheads. I have not seen him since we got home 10 days ago. But I feel good hopes that he will avoid a complete collapse.

It has been, in a less degree, a rather terrible time for me too. It made everything seem uncertain and subject to chance, so that it was hard to keep any calm about all the goods whose loss one fears. And it brought up, as mis-

[1] The title was 'On Denoting'.

fortunes do, all the memories of buried griefs which one had resolved to be done with. One after another, they burst their tombs, and wailed in the desert spaces of one's mind. And the case was one which admitted of no philosophy at all—I could not see that there was anything to be said in mitigation of the disaster. But I have got myself in hand now, and tomorrow I go back to work, after a week's tour by myself. This Sunday I am with my Aunt Agatha. We talk of long-ago things, of people who are dead and old-world memories—it is very soothing. It is odd how family feeling is stirred by anything that makes one feel the universe one's enemy. . . .

Yours affectionately
Bertrand Russell

Lower Copse
Bagley Wood, Oxford
November 10, 1905

My dear Lucy

It was a great pleasure to hear from you again. I think letters *are* more important than one is apt to realize. If one doesn't write, one's doings and one's general state of mind cease to be known, and when a time comes for explaining, there are so many preliminaries that the task seems impossible in writing. So I do hope you will not be deterred by the fear of many words— it really doesn't do to wait till you are *in extremis*. What you say about Alys and my 'right living' rather makes me feel that there is something wrong— too much profession and talk about virtue; for I certainly know many people who live better lives than I do, and are more able to accomplish long and difficult duties without any moments of weakness. Only they make less fuss about it, and people do not know how difficult the duties are that they perform in silence.

I am grateful to you for writing about Helen. I understand very well the renewal of pain that comes when you see her, and the dread of entering the real life, with its tortures, after the numbness of routine. I am very sorry that it is still so bad. I wonder, though, whether any but trivial people could really find it otherwise. Life *is* a burden if those one loves best have others who come first, if there is no corner in the world where one's loneliness is at an end. I hardly know how it can be otherwise. Your problem is to face this with courage, and yet retain as much as possible of what is important to you. It would be easier to renounce everything once for all, and kill one's chief affection. But that leads to hardness, and in the long run to cruelty, the cruelty of the ascetic. The other course has its disadvantages too: it is physically and mentally exhausting, it destroys peace of mind, it keeps one's thoughts absorbed with the question of how much that one values one can hope to rescue without undue encroachment on the territory of others. It is horribly difficult. There is a temptation to let one's real life become wholly one of memory and imagination, where duty and facts do not fetter one, and to let one's present intercourse be a mere shadow and unreality; this has the advantage that it keeps the past unsmirched.

But to come to more practical things. I believe when one is not first in a person's life, it is necessary, however difficult, to make one's feelings towards that person purely receptive and passive. I mean, that one should not have an opinion about what such a person should do, unless one is asked; that one should watch their moods, and make oneself an echo, responding with affection in the measure in which it is given, repressing whatever goes further, ready to feel that one has no rights, and that whatever one gets is so much to the good. This must be, for example, the attitude of a good mother to a married son. Difficult as it is, it is a situation which is normal in the life of the affections, and a duty which one has to learn to perform without spiritual death. . . .

I have been seeing a good deal of Crompton Davies. . . . He is and will remain very profoundly unhappy, and I do not think that marriage or anything will heal the wound. But he is brave, and to the world he makes a good show. To his friends he is lovable in a very rare degree.

The Japanese alliance seems to me excellent—I am glad England should be ready to recognize the yellow man as a civilized being, and not wholly sorry at the quarrel with Australia which this recognition entails. Balfour's government has ceased to do any harm, having grown impotent. The general opinion is that Balfour will resign in February, trying to force the Liberals to take office before dissolving. Whatever happens, the Liberals are almost certain of an overwhelming majority in the next Parliament.

I am interested to hear that I have a disciple at Bryn Mawr. Two young men, Huntington at Harvard and Veblen at Princeton, have written works in which they make pleasing references to me. The latter, at least, is brilliantly able. . . .

Alys told me to say she has not time to write by this Saturday's mail—she is occupied with alternations of visitors and meetings, and rather tired. On the whole, however, she has been very well lately. She asked me also to tell you about Forster's 'Where Angels fear to tread'—it seems to me a clever story, with a good deal of real merit, but too farcical in parts, and too sentimental at the end. He is one of our Cambridge set; his age, I suppose, about 26. He seems certainly to have talent.

Dickinson's new book is out, *A Modern Symposium*. It is quite excellent. He does the Tories with more sympathy than the Liberals, but all except Gladstone and the biologist are done with much sympathy. Besides Gladstone, there are Disraeli, Henry Sidgwick, and various private friends—Bob Trevelyan, Ferdinand Schiller (Audubon), a compound of Berenson and Santayana, Sidney Webb, and some characters who are nobody in particular. You must certainly read it.

My work has gone very well this summer, in spite of a long interruption caused by Theodore's death. I have made more solid and permanent progress than I usually do. But the end of Volume II is as far off as ever—the task grows and grows. For the rest, I have been much occupied with other people's tragedies—some unusually painful ones have come in my way lately. What rather adds to the oppression is the impossibility of speaking of them—Still, I could hardly endure life if I were not on those terms with people that make me necessarily share their sorrows; and if the sorrows exist, I would always rather know them than not. Only I feel increasingly helpless before misfortune; I used to be able to speak encouraging words, but now I feel too weary, and have too little faith in any remedy except endurance.

Yours affectionately
Bertrand Russell

Lower Copse
Bagley Wood, Oxford
January 1, 1906

My dear Lucy

I am very glad your sense of values prevailed over your Puritan instinct, and I am sure your sense of values was right. Letters are important; I care about getting letters from you, and it is the only way not to meet as strangers when people only meet at intervals of some years. And generally, I am sure you are right not to give all your best hours to routine; people who do that infallibly become engrossed in routine, by which they both lose personally and do the routine less well. In this, at least, I practise what I preach: I spent the first hour and a half of the new year in an argument about ethics, with young Arthur Dakyns, who is supposed to be my only disciple up here, but is a very restive disciple, always going after the false gods of the Hegelians. (We were staying with his people at Haslemere.) His father is a delightful man, with a gift of friendliness and of generous admirations that I have seldom seen equalled; and Arthur has inherited a great deal of his father's charm. He is the only person up here (except the Murrays) that I feel as a real friend—the rest are rather alien, so far as I know them. . . .

I am looking forward very much indeed to your visit, and I do hope nothing will happen to prevent it. I shall not be very busy at that time, as I shall have been working continuously all the spring. I am afraid you will find me grown more middle-aged, and with less power of throwing off the point of view of the daily round. The efforts of life and of work are great, and in the long run they tend to subdue one's spirit through sheer weariness. I get more and more into the way of filling my mind with the thoughts of what I have to do day by day, to the exclusion of things that have more real importance. It is perhaps inevitable, but it is a pity, and I feel it makes one a duller person. However, it suits work amazingly well. My work during 1905 was certainly better in quality and quantity than any I have done in a year before, unless perhaps in 1900. The difficulty which I came upon in 1901, and was worrying over all the time you were in Europe, has come out at last, completely and finally, so far as I can judge. It all came from considering whether the King of France is bald—a question which I decided in the same article in which I proved that George IV was interested in the Law of Identity. The result of this is that Whitehead and I expect to have a comparatively easy time from now to the publication of our book, which we may hope will happen within four or five years. Lately I have been working 10 hours a day, living in a dream, realizing the actual world only dimly through a mist. Having to go first to my Aunt Agatha on Hindhead, then to the Dakyns's, I woke up suddenly from the dream; but now I must go back into it, until we go abroad with old Mr Ll. Davies and his daughter (on the 25th January). . . .

I found your kind present to Alys on my return today, but she has not had it yet, as she has gone to West Ham to canvass for Masterman. He is not the man I should have chosen, but she promised long ago, that she would help him when the election came on. The political outlook is good on the whole. The Liberals have done wisely, as well as rightly, in stopping the S. African Slave Trade in Chinamen. Campbell-Bannerman caused a flutter by declaring more or less for Home Rule; but today Redmond and the Duke of Devonshire both advise electors to vote Liberal, so Campbell-Bannerman has caught the Home Rule vote without losing the Free Trade Unionist vote. Exactly the opposite might just as well have happened, so it is a stroke of luck. But by the time you get this letter, the results will be coming in. The Cabinet is excellent. I am very glad John Burns is in it. But it may go to pieces later on the Irish question. However, I hope not. I breathe more freely every moment owing to those scoundrels being no longer in office; but I wish I knew what majority we shall get. The question is: Will the Liberals be independent of the Irish? It is bound to be a near thing one way or other.

I hope you will enjoy Dickinson's *Modern Symposium.* You will recognize Bob Trevelyan and Sidney Webb. I like the book immensely.

Do write again soon. Your letters are a great pleasure to me.

Yours affectionately
Bertrand Russell

14 Barton Street
Westminster
February 18, 1906

My dear Lucy

. . . I have myself been horribly depressed lately. Margaret Davies is still in the depths of unhappiness, and needs a great deal of silent sympathy, which is much more tiring than the sort one can express. And I am as usual oppressed by a good many anxieties that I cannot speak about. I am looking forward to work, which is a refuge. But I tired myself out before starting for abroad, and I feel still rather slack, so I may find I need more holiday. Sometimes I think I should like never to stop work, if only I had the strength of body. Mathematics is a haven of peace without which I don't know how I should get on. So I am hardly the person to tell you how to avoid depression; because I can only give advice which I do not myself find effective. I have, however, two things which really make me happier—one is the result of the general election, which does mean that for the next few years at least public affairs in England will be more or less what one could wish; the other, more personal, is that my work has prospered amazingly, and that I have solved the most difficult problems I had to deal with, so that I have a prospect of some years of easy and rapid progress. I stayed a few days in Paris, and they got up a dinner of philosophers and mathematicians for me, which I found most agreeable—it was interesting to meet the people, and was sweet incense to my self-esteem. I was interested to observe, on a review of noses, that they were mostly Jews. They seemed most civilized people, with great public spirit and intense devotion to learning. One of them said he had read an English poem called 'le vieux matelot'; I couldn't think who had written anything called 'the old sailor' and began to think there might be something by Hood of that name, when the truth flashed upon me. I also saw Miss Minturn and Santayana in Paris, which I enjoyed.—I go back to Oxford the end of this week. Alys has been very well, not at all exhausted by her labours in West Ham. I shall hope for another letter from you soon.

> *Yours affectionately*
> *Bertrand Russell*

> Providence House
> Clovelly, near Bideford
> April 22, 1906

My dear Lucy

... I am down here in absolute solitude for the best part of 2 months, and find it so far a very great success. The country is beautiful, beyond belief—tangled sleeping-beauty sort of woods, sloping steep down to the sea, and little valleys full of ferns and mosses and wild flowers of innumerable kinds. I take a long walk every afternoon, and all the rest of the day and evening I work, except at meals, when I re-read *War and Peace*, which I expect will last me most of my time. On my walks I stop and read little bits of Walton's *Lives*, or something else that is exquisite. My work goes ahead at a tremendous pace, and I get intense delight from it.[1] Being alone, I escape oppression of more things to think out, and more complicated decisions to make, than I have energy to accomplish; and so I am contented, and find enough to occupy me in work, and enough vigour to make work a pleasure instead of a torment.

As for fame, which you speak of, I have no consciousness of possessing it—certainly at Oxford they regard me as a conceited and soulless formalist. But I do not now care greatly what other people think of my work. I did care, until I had enough confidence that it was worth doing to be independent of praise. Now it gives me rather less pleasure than a fine day. I feel better able than anyone else to judge what my work is worth; besides, praise from the learned public is necessarily for things written some time ago, which probably now seem to me so full of imperfections that I hardly like to remember them. Work, when it goes well, is in itself a great delight; and after any considerable achievement I look back at it with the sort of placid satisfaction one has after climbing a mountain. What is absolutely vital to me is the self-respect I get from work—when (as often) I have done something for which I feel remorse, work restores me to a belief that it is better I should exist than not exist. And another thing I greatly value is the kind of communion with past and future discoverers. I often have imaginary conversations with Leibniz, in which I tell him how fruitful his ideas have proved, and how much more beautiful the result is than he could have foreseen; and in moments of self-

[1] It turned out to be all nonsense.

confidence, I imagine students hereafter having similar thoughts about me. There is a 'communion of philosophers' as well as a 'communion of saints', and it is largely that that keeps me from feeling lonely.

Well, this disquisition shows how self-absorbed one grows when one is alone! . . .

I am glad your country girl has married the painter. All's well that ends well; which is the epitaph I should put on my tombstone if I were the last man left alive.

I am on the whole satisfied with Birrell. The Government have made some bad mistakes, but seem satisfactory in the main.

Write again when you can, and address here.

Yours affectionately
Bertrand Russell

To Lowes Dickinson:

Little Buckland
Nr. Broadway, Wors.
Aug. 2, '02

Dear Goldie
. . . This neighbourhood, which I didn't know before, is very charming; all the villages are built of a very good stone, and most of the houses are Jacobean or older. There is a great plain full of willows, into which the sun sets, and on the other side high hills. Our lodgings are in an old and very picturesque farm house. The place is bracing, and I have been getting through eight or nine hours of work a day, which has left me stupid at the end of it. My book, and Moore's too probably, will be out some time in the winter. The proofs come occasionally, and seem to me very worthless; I have a poor opinion of the stuff when I think of what it ought to be. Whitehead turned up in College, but I got little of his society, as he was terribly busy with exam-papers. It is a funny arrangement, by which the remuneration of dons is inversely proportional to the value of their work. I wish something better could be devised.—It would be most agreeable to live in Cambridge, and I daresay I shall do so some day; but at present it is out of the question. However, we shall be in town after September 15 for six months; I hope you will visit us during your weekly excursions to that haunt of purposeless activity and foolish locomotion. When I see people who desire money or fame or power, I find it hard to imagine what must be the emotional emptiness of their lives, that can leave room for such trivial things.

Yours ever
Bertrand Russell

Address: Friday's Hill
   Haslemere

Little Buckland
Nr. Broadway, Wors.
26 August, 1902

Dear Goldie

I was very glad of your letter, and I agreed with all you said about the *Paradiso*, though it is many years since I read it. I feel also very strongly what you say about Italy and the North, though at bottom I disagree with you. I do not think, to begin with, that Dante can count as an Italian; Italy begins with the Renaissance, and the mediaeval mind is international. But there is to me about Italy a quality which the rest of Europe had in the 18th century, a complete lack of mystery. Sunshine is very agreeable, but fogs and mists have effects which sunshine can never attain to. Seriously, the unmystical, rationalistic view of life seems to me to omit all that is most important and most beautiful. It is true that among unmystical people there is no truth unperceived, which the mystic might reveal; but mysticism creates the truth it believes in, by the way in which it feels the fundamental facts—the helplessness of man before Time and Death, and the strange depths of feeling which lie dormant until some one of the Gods of life calls for our worship. Religion and art both, it seems to me, are attempts to humanize the universe—beginning, no doubt, with the humanizing of man. If some of the stubborn facts refuse to leave one's consciousness, a religion or an art cannot appeal to one fully unless it takes account of those facts. And so all religion becomes an achievement, a victory, an assurance that although man may be powerless, his ideals are not so. The more facts a religion takes account of, the greater is its victory, and that is why thin religions appeal to Puritan temperaments. I should myself value a religion in proportion to its austerity—if it is not austere, it seems a mere childish toy, which the first touch of the real Gods would dispel. But I fear that, however austere, any religion must be less austere than the truth. And yet I could not bear to lose from the world a certain awed solemnity, a certain stern seriousness—for the mere fact of life and death, of desire and hope and aspiration and love in a world of matter which knows nothing of good and bad, which destroys carelessly the things it has produced by accident, in spite of all the passionate devotion that we may give—all this is not sunshine, or any peaceful landscapes seen through limpid air; yet life has the power to brand these things into one's soul so that all else seems triviality and vain babble. To have endowed only one minute portion of the universe with the knowledge and love of good, and to have made that portion the plaything of vast irresistible irrational forces, is a cruel jest on the part of God or Fate. The best Gospel, I suppose, is the Stoic one; yet even that is too optimistic, for matter can at any moment destroy our love of virtue.

After all this moping, you will be confirmed in your love of the South; and indeed I feel it too, but as a longing to have done with the burden of a serious life. 'Ye know, my friends, with what a gay carouse'—and no doubt there is much to be said for the Daughter of the Vine, as for any other of Satan's many forms. To Hell with unity, and artistic serenity, and the insight that perceives the good in other people's Pain—it sickens me. (And yet I know there is truth in it.)

Yes, one must learn to live in the Past, and so to dominate it that it is not a disquieting ghost or a horrible gibbering spectre stalking through the vast bare halls that once were full of life, but a gentle soothing companion, reminding one of the possibility of good things, and rebuking cynicism and cruelty— but those are temptations which I imagine you do not suffer from. For my part, I do not even wish to live rather with eternal things, though I often give them lip-service; but in my heart I believe that the best things are those that are fragile and temporary, and I find a magic in the Past which eternity cannot possess. Besides, nothing is more eternal than the Past—the present and future are still subject to Time, but the Past has escaped into immortality —Time has done his worst, and it yet lives.

I don't wonder you hate taking up your routine again. After one has had liberty of mind, and allowed one's thoughts and emotions to grow and expand, it is horrible to go back to prison, and enclose all feelings within the miserable compass of the prudent and desirable and practically useful—Pah!—But all good things must be left to the wicked—even virtue, which only remains spotless if it is kept under a glass case, for ornament and not for use.

I have been working nine hours a day until yesterday, living in a dream, thinking only of space; today I begin to realize the things that are in it, and on the whole they do not seem to me an improvement. But I hope we shall see you in town.

Yours ever
Bertrand Russell

Churt, Farnham
July 16, 1903

Dear Goldie

I enclose the translation, but I rather wish you would get someone with a better knowledge of French to look it over, as my French is not at all correct. And by the way, I expect *mémoire* would be better than *article*, but I am not sure.

I am glad you are writing on Religion. It is quite time to have things said that all of us know, but that are not generally known. It seems to me that our attitude on religious subjects is one which we ought as far as possible to preach, and which is not the same as that of any of the well-known opponents of Christianity. There is the Voltaire tradition, which makes fun of the whole thing from a common-sense, semi-historical, semi-literary point of view; this, of course, is hopelessly inadequate, because it only gets hold of the accidents and excrescences of historical systems. Then there is the scientific, Darwin– Huxley attitude, which seems to me perfectly true, and quite fatal, if rightly carried out, to all the usual arguments for religion. But it is too external, too coldly critical, too remote from the emotions; moreover, it cannot get to the root of the matter without the help of philosophy. Then there are the philosophers, like Bradley, who keep a shadow of religion, too little for comfort, but quite enough to ruin their systems intellectually. But what we have to do, and what privately we do do, is to treat the religious instinct with profound respect, but to insist that there is no shred or particle of truth in any of the metaphysics it has suggested: to palliate this by trying to bring out the beauty of the world and of life, so far as it exists, and above all to insist upon pre-serving the seriousness of the religious attitude and its habit of asking ultimate questions. And if good lives are the best thing we know, the loss of religion gives new scope for courage and fortitude, and so may make good lives better than any that there was room for while religion afforded a drug in mis-fortune.

And often I feel that religion, like the sun, has extinguished the stars of less brilliancy but not less beauty, which shine upon us out of the darkness of a godless universe. The splendour of human life, I feel sure, is greater to those who are not dazzled by the divine radiance; and human comradeship seems to grow more intimate and more tender from the sense that we are all exiles on an inhospitable shore.

Yours ever
B. Russell

Churt, Farnham
July 19, 1903

Dear Goldie

Many thanks for sending me the three articles on Religion: they strike me as exceedingly good, and as saying things that much need saying. All your eloquent passages seem to me very successful; and the parable at the end I like quite immensely. I enclose a few remarks on some quite tiny points that struck me in reading—mostly verbal points.

The attack on Ecclesiasticism is, I think, much needed; you if anything underestimate, I should say, the danger of Ecclesiasticism in this country. Whenever I happen to meet Beatrice Creighton I feel the danger profoundly; and she illustrates one of the worst points from a practical point of view, that even when a man belonging to an ecclesiastical system happens to be broad-minded and liberal himself, he takes care to avoid such a state of mind in others whom he can influence.

Why should you suppose I think it foolish to wish to see the people one is fond of? What else is there to make life tolerable? We stand on the shore of an ocean, crying to the night and the emptiness; sometimes a voice answers out of the darkness. But it is a voice of one drowning; and in a moment the silence returns. The world seems to me quite dreadful; the unhappiness of most people is very great, and I often wonder how they all endure it. To know people well is to know their tragedy: it is usually the central thing about which their lives are built. And I suppose if they did not live most of the time in the things of the moment, they would not be able to go on.

Yours ever
B. Russell

Ivy Lodge
Tilford, Farnham
July 20, 1904

Dear Goldie

Yes, I think you would do well to republish your articles on Religion in a book. It is hard to say what one gathers from them in a constructive way, yet there certainly is something. I think it is chiefly, in the end, that one becomes persuaded of the truth of the passage you quote from Maeterlinck, i.e. that the emotion with which we contemplate the world may be religious, even if we have no definite theological beliefs. (Note that if Maeterlinck were not in French, he would be saying the same as In Memoriam, 'there lives more faith, etc.' This remark is linguistic.) You are likely to convince a certain number of people that the absence of a creed is no reason for not thinking in a religious way; and this is useful both to the person who insists on a creed in order to save his religious life, and to the person who ceases to think seriously because he has lost his creed.

Schiller, in his article, struck me as a pathetic fool, who had seized on Pragmatism as the drowning man's straw. I agree with you wholly that Philosophy cannot give religion, or indeed anything of more than intellectual interest. It seems to me increasingly that what gives one the beliefs by which one lives is of the nature of experience: it is a sudden realization, or perhaps a gradual one, of ethical values which one had formerly doubted or taken on trust; and this realization seems to be caused, as a rule, by a situation containing the things one realizes to be good or bad. But although I do not think philosophy itself will give anything of human interest, I think a philosophical training enables one to get richer experiences, and to make more use of those that one does get. And I do not altogether wish mankind to become too firmly persuaded that there is no road from philosophy to religion, because I think the endeavour to find one is very useful, if only it does not destroy candour.

What is valuable in Tolstoi, to my mind, is his power of right ethical judgments, and his perception of concrete facts; his theorizings are of course worthless. It is the greatest misfortune to the human race that he has so little power of reasoning.

I have never read Lady Welby's writings, but she sent me some remarks on my book, from which I judged that she is interested in a good many questions that interest me. I doubt very much, all the same, how much she understood my book. I know too little of her to know whether I should understand her or not.

I think Shaw, on the whole, is more bounder than genius; and though of course I admit him to be 'forcible', I don't admit him to be 'moral'. I think envy plays a part in his philosophy in this sense, that if he allowed himself to admit the goodness of things which he lacks and others possess, he would feel such intolerable envy that he would find life unendurable. Also he hates self-control, and makes up theories with a view to proving that self-control is pernicious. I couldn't get on with Man and Superman: it disgusted me. I don't think he is a soul in Hell dancing on red-hot iron. I think his Hell is merely diseased vanity and a morbid fear of being laughed at.

Berenson is here. I shall be very curious to see what you say on Music. I have never made up my mind whether, if I were founding the Republic, I should admit Wagner or even Beethoven; but not because I do *not* like them.

I am working hard at Vol. II. When it goes well, it is an intense delight, when I get stuck, it is equally intense torture.

Yours always
Bertrand Russell

Ivy Lodge
Tilford, Farnham
Sep. 22, 1904

Dear Goldie

Thanks for sending me the enclosed, which I have read with interest. I, think you state your position clearly and very well. It is not a position that I can myself agree with. I agree that 'faith in some form or other seems to be an almost necessary condition, if not of life, yet of the most fruitful and noble life'. But I do not agree that faith 'can be legitimate so long as it occupies a region not yet conquered by knowledge'. You admit that it is wrong to say: 'I believe, though truth testify against me.' I should go further, and hold it is wrong to say: 'I believe, though truth do not testify in my favour.' To my mind, truthfulness demands as imperatively that we should doubt what is doubtful as that we should disbelieve what is false. But here and in all arguments about beliefs for which there is no evidence, it is necessary to distinguish propositions which may be fairly allowed to be self-evident, and which therefore afford the basis of indirect evidence, from such as ought to have proofs if they are to be accepted. This is a difficult business, and probably can't be done exactly. As for faith, I hold (a) that there are certain propositions, an honest belief in which, apart from the badness of believing what is false, greatly improves the believer, (b) that many of these very propositions are false. But I think that faith has a legitimate sphere in the realm of ethical judgments, since these are of the sort that ought to be self-evident, and ought not to require proof. For practice, it seems to me that a very high degree of the utility of faith can be got by believing passionately in the goodness of certain things which are good, and which, in a greater or less degree, our actions are capable of creating. I admit that the love of God, if there were a God, would make it possible for human beings to be better than is possible in a Godless world. But I think the ethical faith which *is* warranted yields *most* of what is necessary to the highest life conceivable, and all that is necessary to the highest life that is possible. Like every religion, it contains ethical judgments and judgments of fact, the latter asserting that our actions make a difference, though perhaps a small one, to the ethical value of the universe. I find this enough faith to live by, and I consider it warranted by knowledge; but anything more seems to me more or less *untruthful*, though not demonstrably *untrue*.

Let me know what you would reply. Address here, though I shall be away. I am going tomorrow to Brittany with Theodore for a fortnight. I hope your sciatica is better.

> Yours ever
> B. Russell

> I Tatti,
> Settignano, Florence
> March 22, 1903

Dear Bertie

I have read your essay three times, and liked it better and better. Perhaps the most flattering appreciation to be given of it is that the whole is neither out of tune with nor unworthy of the two splendid passages you wrote here— I see no objection to this essay form. I have no wish of my own with regard to the shape your writing is to take. I am eager that you shall express yourself sooner or later, and meanwhile you must write and write until you begin to feel that you are saying what you want to say, in the way that you wish others to understand it.

The really great event of the last few weeks has been Gilbert Murray. I fear I should fall into school-girlishness if I ventured to tell you how much I liked him. You will judge when I say that no woman in my earlier years made me talk more about myself than he has now. Conversation spread before us like an infinite thing, or rather like something opening out higher and greater with every talk. I found him so gentle, so sweetly reasonable—almost the ideal companion. Even I could forgive his liking Dickens, and Tennyson.—He has been responsible for the delay of this scrawl, for he absorbed my energies. What little was left went to my proofs. Happily they are nearly done.

I am so glad that Alys is coming out. It is very good of her. I shall enjoy her visit, and be much the better for it. Dickinson will I fear suffer from the contrast with Murray.

I am in the middle of the *Gespräche mit Goethe* all interesting.—What have you done with your paper on mathematics?

> Yours ever
> B. B. (*Berenson*)

> Grayshott
> Haslemere, Surrey
> Ja. 10, 1904

My dearest Bertie

I was so very, very sorry to hear that you were not at Dora's[1] funeral. I felt quite sure you would be present and can only think that something very definite must have prevented you.—I know you *may* feel that this last token of respect means little and is of no avail—but I am *quite* sure after all she did for you in old days and all the love she gave you that her sister and friends will have felt pained at your absence—if you could have gone.—Many thanks to Alys for

---

[1] 'Dora' was my former Swiss governess, Miss Bühler.

her letter and the little Memorial Book she forwarded—I conclude you have one.—Perhaps you have never heard it at the grave of one you loved—but the Burial Service is about the most impressive and solemn—and especially with music is sometimes a real help in hours of awful sorrow in lifting one up above and beyond it.—I have had a third letter from Dora's sister to whom I wrote as I feel most deeply for her—it is a terrible loss—she is alone and had hoped some day Dora would live with her.—I hope you wrote to her.

Miss Sedgfield[1] is probably going on Tuesday to Highgate for a week and very much hopes to be at your lecture next Friday.—Perhaps you will see her but anyhow please ask Alys if she will look out for her. She has written for tickets. She asks me to tell you that she particularly hopes you are going to make it comprehensible to the feeblest intelligence—no angles and squares and triangles no metaphysics or mathematics to be admitted!

Thank Alys very much for the enclosures which I was delighted to see they are very interesting and I should like some to send to a few who might be interested. But I don't like the sentence about Retaliation. The word alone is distasteful and I have just looked it out in Johnson—To 'retaliate' (even when successful so-called) is not a Tolstoyan or better a Christian maxim.—I hope your lectures will contain some sentiment and some ideals!—even from the low point of success they will be more effective if they do!—*How* I wish I could come and hear you—I will read you in the *Edinburgh* but it would be more interesting to hear and I never have heard you or Alys once!

With much love to you both and best wishes for your work in the good cause,[2]

> *Your loving*
> *Auntie*

> Ivy Lodge
> Tilford, Farnham
> May 17, 1904

My dearest Bertie

I hope thee will not mind my writing thee a real letter on thy birthday. I try very hard always to keep on the surface, as thee wishes, but I am sure thee will remember how some feelings long for expression.

I only want to tell thee again how very much I love thee, and how glad I am of thy existence. When I could share thy life and think myself of use to thee, it was the greatest happiness anyone has ever known. I am thankful for the memory of it, and thankful that I can still be near thee and watch thy development. When thee is well and happy and doing good work, I feel quite contented, and only wish that I were a better person and able to do more work and be more worthy of thee. I never wake in the night or think of thee in the daytime without wishing for blessings on my darling, and I shall always love thee, and I hope it will grow more and more unselfish.

> *Thine ever devotedly*
> *Alys*

[1] My aunt's companion.

[2] The cause of Free Trade.

191

Cambo
Northumberland
(July, 1904)

Dear Bertie

I want to tell you how very fine the last part of your article is. If I could now and then write like that I should feel more certainly justified than I do in adopting writing as a business.

When I get south again at the beginning of August I should much like to talk to you. I have much to ask you now. Tolstoi's letter in *Times* has set me thinking very uncomfortably—or *feeling* rather. It fills me with (i) a new sense of doubt and responsibility as to my own manner of life (ii) as to this of war. I feel as if we were all living in the City of Destruction but I am not certain as to whether I ought to flee—or whither.

It may all come to nothing definite, but it ought at least to leave a different spirit.

I have for long been too happy and contented with everything including my work. Then the intense moral superiority of Tolstoi's recusant conscripts knocks all the breath out of one's fatuous Whig bladder of self contentment.

1. In ½ a sheet do you agree with Tolstoi about war?
2. Where will you be in August?

Yours
George Trevelyan

Cambo
Northumberland
July 17, 1904

Dear Bertie

I am deeply grateful to you for having written me so long and carefully considered a letter. But it was not a waste of time. I am deeply interested in it and I think I agree with it altogether.

On the other hand I hold that though you are right in supposing the preparation of war to be a necessary function of modern states, in the spirit and under the restrictions you name,—*still* one of the principal means by which war will eventually be abolished is the passive resistance of conscripts in the conscription nations (to whose number we may be joined if things go badly). It will take hundreds of years to abolish war, and there will be a 'fiery roll of martyrdom', opening with these recusant convicts of Tolstoi's. It is these people, who will become an ever increasing number all over Europe, who will finally shame the peoples of Europe into viewing war and international hatred as you do, instead of viewing it as they do now. Great changes are generally effected in this way, but by a double process—gradual change in the general sentiment and practice, led and really inspired by the extreme opinion and action of people condemned by the mass of mankind, whom nevertheless they affect.

Three cheers for Tolstoi's letter all the same. Also I think that any proposal to introduce conscription into England must be resisted on this ground (among others) that govt. has not the right to coerce a person's conscience into fighting or training for war if he thinks it wrong.

I think I also agree with you as to the duty of living and working in the City of Destruction, rather than fleeing from it. But a duty that is also a pleasure, though it is none the less still a duty, brings dangers in the course of its performance. It is very difficult, in retaining the bulk of one's property and leisure at the disposal of one's own will, to live in the spirit of this maxim: 'One has only a right to that amount of property which will conduce most to the welfare of others in the long run.'

I enclose a letter and circular. Will you join? I have done so, and I think we are probably going to elect Goldie Dickinson who expressed a willingness to join. There will certainly be perfectly free discussion and the people will be worth getting to know. There is no obligation, as of reading papers, incumbent on any member. I think the various points of view of the really religious who are also really free seekers after truth (a meagre band) is worth while our getting to know. They have expressed great hopes that you will join.

> *Yours ever*
> *George Trevelyan*

> 8 Cheyne Gardens
> Tuesday
> Oct. 11, '04

My dear Russell

It did me much good to see you again. I had a tale of woe and desperation to pour out—vague enough and yet not enough so it seemed while I was revolving it this morning; but when I had been with you a little while I did not feel—well, magnificently wretched enough to use desperate language. I was reminded of so many things I had well worth having. And my trouble seemed nothing that rational fortitude and very ordinary precepts properly obeyed could not surmount.

I look to you to help me more than anybody else just now. I feel that all those refinements which you suspect often are half weaknesses and I too, help me. It is everything to me to feel that you have no cut and dried rules of what one man ought and ought not to say to another, yet I know how you hate a spiritual indelicacy.

Do not answer this letter unless you want to or unless you have anything you want to say. We can talk of so many things right to the bottom which is the blessing of blessings.

I want to stop in London for a fortnight or so and get some work done. Then I shall be better able to tell you how it is with [*sic*]. I must begin to hope a little before I can talk about my despair.

> *Your affectionate*
> *Desmond MacCarthy*

41 Grosvenor Road
Westminster Embankment
Oct. 16, 1904

My dear Bertie

It was kind of you to write to me your opinion of L. H. [Leonard Hobhouse] pamphlet and I am glad that it coincides so exactly with my own. I quite agree with you in thinking that the fact that a 'mood' (such, for instance, as the instinctive faith in a 'Law of Righteousness', and my instinctive faith in prayer) is felt to be 'compelling and recurrent' has no relevance, as Proof of its correspondence 'with our order of things.'

I make an absolute distinction between the realm of proof (Knowledge of Processes) and the realm of aspiration or Faith—(the choice of Purposes.) All I ask for this latter World, is tolerance—a 'Let live' policy. In my interpretation of this 'Let live' policy, I should probably differ with you and L. H.— since I would permit each local community to teach its particular form of 'aspiration' or 'Faith' out of common funds. I should even myself desire this for my own children—since I have found that my own existence would have been more degraded without it—and as I 'desire' what we call nobility of Purpose, I wish for the means to bring it about. I know no other way of discovering these means but actual experience or experiment, and so far my own experience and experiment leads me to the working Hypothesis of persistent Prayer. I do not in the least wish to force this practice on other people and should be equally glad to pay for a school in which the experiment of complete secularization (viz. nothing but the knowledge of Processes) was tried or for an Anglican or Catholic or Christian Science Establishment. All I desire is that each section or locality should, as far as possible, be free to teach its own kind of aspirations or absence of Aspirations.

Can you and Alys come to lunch on *Thursday 10th* and meet Mr Balfour? I am taking him to Bernard Shaw's play. Could you not take tickets for that afternoon? It will be well for you to know Mr Balfour—in case of Regius Professorships and the like!

Ever
B. *Webb*

Private

Rozeldene, Grayshott
Haslemere, Surrey
March 20, 1905

My dearest Bertie

I am only writing today on one subject which I wish now to tell you about. —I have had and kept carefully ever since his death, your Grandfather's gold watch and chain—I need not tell you how *very very* precious it is to me as of course I so well remember his always wearing it.

But I should like very much now to give it to you—only with one condition that you will leave it to Arthur,—or failing Arthur to Johnny—as I am anxious it should remain a Russell possession. I do not remember whether you have and wear now any watch which has any past association—if so of course do not hesitate to tell me and I will keep this, for Arthur later on. But if not you could of course give (or keep if you prefer) your present watch away—as I should like to feel you will wear and use this one—not put it away.—However this you will tell me about.

Dear dear Bertie I should like to feel that you will always try to be worthy —you *will* try I know—of being his grandson for he was indeed one of the very best men the world has known—courageous—gentle—true—and with a most beautiful childlike simplicity and straightforwardness of nature which is most rare—I like to think that you remember him—and that his last words to you 'Good little boy', spoken from his deathbed with loving gentleness, —can remain with you as an inspiration to goodness through life;—but of course you cannot remember and cannot know all that he was.—But if you will have it I should like you to wear and treasure this watch in memory of him—and of the long ago days in the dear home of our childhood.[1]

God bless you.

> *Your loving*
> *Auntie*

I have just had the watch seen to in London—it is in perfect condition. I could give it you on the 28th.—Thanks for your welcome letter last week.

> Vicarage
> Kirkby Lonsdale
> 27 July, 1905

Bertie

Theodore is dead, drowned while bathing alone on Tuesday in a pool in the Fells, stunned as I have no doubt by striking his head in taking a header and then drowned.

I shall be back in London on Monday. Let me see you some time soon.

> *Crompton*

> (Oct. 31?, '05)

Dear Bertie

I enclose photo which I trust will do.

I have some more of Theo which I want to shew you. When will you come for a night?

I have failed with ———.[2] She says she thought she could have done anything for me but resolutely declines to marry me so the matter is at an end.

Harry and I are going to Grantchester next Saturday. I haven't managed a visit to Bedales yet.

I have prepared your will but think I will keep it till I see you and can go thro' it with you.

---

[1] I have worn this watch and chain ever since 1949.

[2] The woman whom Theodore loved, and whom, after Theodore's death, Crompton wished to marry.

The loss of Theodore seems still a mere phantasy and the strange mixture of dream and waking thoughts and recollection and fact leave me in bewilderment but slowly the consequences of a maimed existence remaining for me makes itself felt, as of a body that has lost its limbs and strength, and has to go on with made-up supports and medical regimen and resignation to the loss of possibilities of achievement and hopes of sunny days.

I cling to you with all my heart and bless you for loving and helping me.

Crompton

Stocks Cottage
Tring
23rd May, 1907

Dear Bertie

So now you have 'fought a contested election', which Teufelsdröck puts with the state of being in love, as being the second great experience of human life. I am the greater coward that I have never done the same, and probably never shall. I don't suppose a pair of more oddly contrasted candidates will be in the field again for another 100 years, as you and Chaplin.

What a sporting cove you are! Next time the Austrians conquer Italy you and I will go in a couple of red shirts, together, and get comfortably killed in an Alpine pass. I hardly thought you were such an adventurer, and had so much of the fine old Adam in you, till I came home (like old mother Hubbard) and found you conducting an election! !

I am very grateful to you for the article in the *Edinburgh*.[1] It did the book a lot of good, and helped to pull up the sale which began badly and is now doing well. It was, I gather from Elliot, a disappointment to you not to be able to do it at more leisure, and I want to tell you that I appreciate this sacrifice to friendship, and that it was a real service to me to have the review out in April.

I was very much interested in several things you said, especially the sentence at the top of p. 507 about the special function of the Revolutionaries. I did not guess who had written it till Alys told us, tho' I might have guessed it from your favourite story of Jowett's remark on Mazzini.

I hope you are both back in the academic pheasant preserve and that the quiet of Oxford is pleasant after such turmoil.

Yours fraternally
George Trevy

67 Belsize Park Gardens
Hampstead, N.W.
23rd October, 1907

Dear Russell

I have just read your article on Mathematics (in proof) and can't resist writing to say how much I was carried away by it. Really it's magnificent— one's carried upwards into sublime heights—perhaps the sublimest of all!

[1] A review of George Trevelyan's *Garibaldi's Defence of the Roman Republic*.

Your statement of the great thing about it seems to me absolutely clear and absolutely convincing; it gives one a new conception of the glories of the human mind. The simile of the Italian Castle struck me as particularly fine, and the simplicity of the expression added tremendously to the effect. What scoundrels the *Independent* editors were![1] And what fools!

I could go on writing for pages—such is my excitement and enthusiasm. It's terrific to reflect that I know you, and can speak to you, and even contradict you. Oh!—I shall have this engraved on my tombstone—

HE KNEW MOORE AND RUSSELL

and nothing more.

> *Yours ever*
> G. L. Strachey

> 57 Gordon Square
> London W.C.
> 3rd March, 1908

My dear Bertie

I see in the papers that you are to be made an FRS! What an honour! at your age too. Ever since I saw it I have been strutting about swelling with reflected glory. It's the first sensible thing I ever heard of philosophy doing. One can understand that if one can't your books.

Seriously though I do congratulate you most heartily. I have always looked on an FRS as superior to any position on earth, even Archbishop or Prime Minister and the feeling still survives though I know a good many personally.

> *Yours affectionately*
> Russell

> Charing Cross Hotel
> October 4, 1908

Dear Russell

I was at Oxford for three days last week, and hoped until the last day, when I found it was going to be quite impossible, to drive out and see you and Mrs Russell. It was squeezed out by other necessities. I saw Schiller and spent a night at McDougall's most pleasantly. I would fain have spent a night with you, to make up for the rather blunt way in which I declined your invitation last June. I was done-up then, and am comparatively fresh now, but a daughter and a son have come over since then and, as normal, their needs have seemed more urgent than their parent's, so the time has proved too short for many things that I should have liked to accomplish. The son remains at Oxford, in A. L. Smith's family (tutor at Balliol). The rest of us sail in the *Saxonia* on Tuesday.

One of the first things I am going to do after I get back to my own library is to re-read the Chapter on Truth in your Phil. of M., which I haven't looked at since it appeared. I want to get a better grasp of it than you have of my theory! Your remarks on Dewey (sharp as your formulation is!) in the last

[1] They had refused to print the article.

article shows that you haven't yet grasped the thing broadly enough. My dying words to you are 'Say good-by to mathematical logic if you wish to preserve your relations with concrete realities!' I have just had this morning a three-hour conversation with Bergson which possibly may account for this ejaculation! Best regards to you both, in which my wife would join were she here.

Truly yours
Wm. James

8 Grosvenor Crescent
S.W.
26th April, 1909

Dear Bertrand Russell
It is a great pleasure to know that you are elected at the Athenaeum. My own balloting—in 1877—was sufficiently anxious to make me always feel glad when any friend, however certain of success, is through the ordeal. I was not wanting on the occasion and spent a solid part of the afternoon there while your ballot was on.

Your membership will sensibly increase to me, and many others, the interest and pleasure of the Club.[1]

Remain
Yours very sincerely
George O. Trevelyan

Eleven, Cranmer Road
Cambridge
May 27/10

Dear Bertie
The College Council decided today to offer you a lectureship in Logic and the Principles of Mathematics to continue for five years, the duties being
(i) to give a course (24 lectures) of lectures in each term,
(ii) to reside in Cambridge during term time—
Also provided that you are willing to satisfy certain conditions as to the number of hours during which you will be present in College (15 hours per week during term time, I think) they offer rooms in College and dinner (i.e. *free* dinner). The stipend is £200 per year.

All this is of course entirely unofficial—I need not tell you how delighted I am about it—It will give you a splendid opportunity to 'expose' the subject —just what is wanted.

By the bye, I ought to mention that there is no implication that the lectureship will be continued after five years.—Of course the whole difficulty in this respect comes from the extremely few students who, as far as it can be *foreseen*, will be taught by you directly in lectures—I confess to a hope that there may be much more to be done—now that we know our own subject—than any of us can guarantee at present.—But the offer is for 5 years and no more, directly or indirectly.

[1] I can't think why. I never saw Sir George Trevelyan there.

The Council has been very spirited, for at the same time we elected a 'prelector' in Biochemistry.

No more news at present.

Yours affectionately
A. N. W.

Trinity Lodge
Cambridge
June 3, 1910

My dear B. Russell

We are delighted to hear that there is now more than a hope of having you among us for some time to come. Not a shred of credit can *I* claim for the step which we have so wisely taken, but I rejoice to have given the heartiest assent to the advice of your scientific friends. I can hardly hope to last out during the whole of your happy Quinquennium, but I may at least look forward to giving you an early and a hearty greeting.

With our united kindest regards to Mrs Russell.

Believe me to be most truly yours
H. Montagu Butler

There cannot be many living who, like myself, saw Lord John Russell starting from the Hotel at Callender in 1850, through a good Scotch Rain, for 'Rest and be Thankful'. I wonder if you know those delightful regions.

Merton College
Oxford
April 11/10

Dear Mr Russell

Many thanks for your letter. I have no doubt that in what I wrote I have misinterpreted you more or less. And that makes me unwilling to write at all, only no one else seemed doing it. I shall look forward to reading the off prints of the article from the Review and I will attend to what you have written in your letter.

I feel, I confess, some alarm at the prospect of you being occupied with politics, if that means that you will have no time for philosophy. Will it not be possible to combine them? If not it is not for me to venture to judge in what direction you feel the greater 'call'. The only thing I feel clear about is this that no one else will do your work in philosophy so far as human probability goes. And more than this I don't feel I have any right to say.

If you are able to write something for 'Mind' I am sure that it will be welcome to the readers thereof and not least to myself.

Yours truly
F. H. Bradley

I have no idea as to who will get this Professorship. I hear that Webb's chances are thought good on the ground that the two clerics are likely to vote for him and Warren also. But nothing is really known.

Merton College
Oxford
April 20/10

Dear Mr Russell

I am really glad to hear that you have no intention of going permanently into politics which of course are very absorbing. It is quite another thing to get a temporary change of occupation and you must have worked very hard at philosophy now for some years.

Certainly in the study of philosophy, &, I presume, in many other studies, the having to work alone so much is inhuman & trying. And I do not see any remedy for it. The amount to which one can collaborate with another is so small. My health has always been too bad for me to get a change by way of another occupation, but I am afraid that I have been driven to take a great deal of holidays instead. Another occupation might have been better.

I am too stupid now to read your article even if I had it but I shall look forward to seeing it.

I have always had a high opinion of your work from the first, & I feel no doubt whatever that philosophy would lose greatly by your permanent withdrawal. I don't see who else is going to do the work there, which you would, &, I hope, will do.

Yours truly
F. H. Bradley

CHAPTER VII

CAMBRIDGE AGAIN

'PRINCIPIA MATHEMATICA' being finished, I felt somewhat at a loose end. The feeling was delightful, but bewildering, like coming out of prison. Being at the time very much interested in the struggle between the Liberals and the Lords about the Budget and the Parliament Act, I felt an inclination to go into politics. I applied to Liberal Headquarters for a constituency, and was recommended to Bedford. I went down and gave an address to the Liberal Association, which was received with enthusiasm. Before the address, however, I had been taken into a small back room, where I was subjected to a regular catechism, as nearly as I remember in the following terms:

Q. Are you a member of the Church of England?
A. No, I was brought up as a Nonconformist.
Q. And have remained so?
A. No, I have not remained so.
Q. Are we to understand that you are an agnostic?
A. Yes, that is what you must understand.
Q. Would you be willing to attend church occasionally?
A. No, I should not.
Q. Would your wife be willing to attend church occasionally?
A. No, she would not.
Q. Would it come out that you are an agnostic?
A. Yes, it probably would come out.

In consequence of these answers, they selected as their candidate Mr Kellaway, who became Postmaster General, and held correct opinions during the War. They must have felt that they had had a lucky escape.

I also felt that I had had a lucky escape, for while Bedford was deliberating, I received an invitation from Trinity College to become a lecturer in the principles of mathematics. This was much more attractive to me than politics, but if Bedford had accepted me I should have had to reject Cambridge. I took up my residence at the beginning of the October term in 1910. Alys and I had lodgings in Bridge Street, and I had rooms in letter I, Nevile's Court. I became very fond of these rooms, which were the first place exclusively my own that I possessed since leaving Cambridge in 1894. We sold our house at Bagley Wood, and it seemed as if life were going to be settled in a new groove.

This, however, was not the case. In the Election of January, 1910, while I was still living at Bagley Wood, I decided that I ought to help the Liberals as much as I could, but I did not want to help the Member for the constituency in which I was living, as he had broken some pledges which I considered important. I therefore decided to help the Member for the neighbouring constituency across the river. This Member was Philip Morrell, a man who had been at Oxford with my brother-in-law, Logan, who had been passionately attached to him. Philip Morrell had married Lady Ottoline Cavendish-Bentinck, sister of the Duke of Portland. I had known her slightly since we were both children, as she had an aunt named Mrs Scott,[1] who lived at Ham Common. I had two vivid memories connected with Mrs Scott's house, but neither of them concern Ottoline. The first of these memories was of a children's party at which I first tasted ice-cream. I thought it was an ordinary pudding, and took a large spoonful. The shock caused me to burst into tears, to the dismay of the elders, who could not make out what had happened. The other experience was even more unpleasant. In getting out of a carriage at her door, I fell on the paving-stones, and hurt my penis. After this I had to sit twice a day in a hot bath and sponge it carefully. As I had always hitherto been taught to ignore it, this puzzled me. When Philip first became engaged to Ottoline, Logan was filled with jealous rage, and made unkind fun of her. Later, however, he became reconciled. I used to see her and Philip occasionally, but I had never had any high opinion of him, and she offended my Puritan prejudices by what I considered an excessive use of scent and powder. Crompton Davies first led me to revise my opinion of her, because she worked for his Land Values Organization in a way that commanded his admiration.

During the Election of January 1910, I addressed meetings in support of Philip Morrell most nights, and spent most days in canvassing. I remember canvassing a retired Colonel at Iffley, who came rushing out into the hall exclaiming: 'Do you think I'd vote for a scoundrel like that? Get out of the house, or I'll put the dogs on you!' I spoke in almost every village between Oxford and Caversham. In the course of this campaign I had many opportunities of getting to know Ottoline. I discovered that she was extraordinarily kind to all sorts of people, and that she was very much in earnest about public life. But Philip, in

[1] Grandmother of the Queen-Mother, Elizabeth.

common with all the other Liberal Members in the neighbourhood, lost his seat, and was offered a new constituency at Burnley, for which he was Member from December 1910 until the 'Hang-the-Kaiser' Election. The result was that for some time I did not see much of the Morrells. However, in March 1911 I received an invitation to give three lectures in Paris, one at the Sorbonne and two elsewhere. It was convenient to spend the night in London on the way, and I asked the Morrells to put me up at their house, 44 Bedford Square. Ottoline had very exquisite though rather startling taste, and her house was very beautiful. In Alys there was a conflict between Quaker asceticism and her brother's aestheticism. She considered it right to follow the best artistic canons in the more public part of one's life, such as drawing-rooms and dresses for the platform. But in her instincts, and where she alone was concerned, Quaker plainness held sway; for example, she always wore flannel night-gowns. I have always liked beautiful things, but been incapable of providing them for myself. The atmosphere of Ottoline's house fed something in me that had been starved throughout the years of my first marriage. As soon as I entered it, I felt rested from the rasping difficulties of the outer world. When I arrived there on March 19th, on my way to Paris, I found that Philip had unexpectedly had to go to Burnley, so that I was left *tête-à-tête* with Ottoline. During dinner we made conversation about Burnley, and politics, and the sins of the Government. After dinner the conversation gradually became more intimate. Making timid approaches, I found them to my surprise not repulsed. It had not, until this moment, occurred to me that Ottoline was a woman who would allow me to make love to her, but gradually, as the evening progressed, the desire to make love to her became more and more insistent. At last it conquered, and I found to my amazement that I loved her deeply, and that she returned my feeling. Until this moment I had never had complete relations with any woman except Alys. For external and accidental reasons, I did not have full relations with Ottoline that evening, but we agreed to become lovers as soon as possible. My feeling was overwhelmingly strong, and I did not care what might be involved. I wanted to leave Alys, and to have her leave Philip. What Philip might think or feel was a matter of indifference to me. If I had known that he would murder us both (as Mrs Whitehead assured me he would) I should have been willing to pay that price for one night. The nine years of tense self-denial had come to an end, and for the time being I was done with self-denial. However, there was not time to settle future plans during that one evening. It was already late when we first kissed, and after that, though we stayed up till four in the morning, the conversation was intermittent. Early the next day I had to go to Paris, where I had to lecture in French to highly critical audiences. It was difficult to bring my mind to bear upon what I had to do, and I suspect that I must have lectured very badly. I was living in a dream, and my surroundings appeared quite unreal. Ottoline was going to Studland (in those days quite a tiny place), and we arranged that I should join her there for three days. Before going, I spent the weekend with Alys at Fernhurst. I began the weekend by a visit to the dentist, who told me that he thought I had cancer, and recommended a specialist, whom, however, I could not see for three weeks, as he had gone away for his Easter holiday. I then told Alys about Ottoline. She flew into a rage, and said that she would insist upon a divorce, bringing in Ottoline's name. Ottoline, on account of her child, and also on account of a very genuine affection for Philip, did not wish for a divorce from him. I therefore had to keep her name out of it. I told Alys that she could have the divorce whenever she liked, but that she must not bring Ottoline's name into it. She nevertheless persisted that she would bring Ottoline's name in. Thereupon I told her quietly but firmly that she would find that impossible, since if she ever took steps to that end, I should commit suicide in order to circumvent her. I meant this, and she saw that I did. Thereupon her rage became unbearable. After she had stormed for some hours, I gave a lesson in Locke's philosophy to her niece, Karin Costelloe, who was about to take her Tripos. I then rode away on my bicycle, and with that my first marriage came to an end. I did not see Alys again till 1950, when we met as friendly acquaintances.[1]

From this scene I went straight to Studland, still believing that I had cancer. At Swanage, I obtained an old-fashioned fly with an incredibly slow horse. During his leisurely progress up and down the hills, my impatience became almost unendurable. At last, however, I saw Ottoline sitting in a pine-wood beside the road, so I got out, and let the fly go on with my luggage. The three days and nights that I spent at Studland remain in my memory as among the few moments when life seemed all that it might be, but hardly ever is. I did not, of course, tell Ottoline that I had reason to fear that I had cancer, but the thought of this possibility heightened my happiness by giving it greater intensity, and by the sense that it had been wrenched from the jaws of destruction. When the dentist told me, my first reaction was to congratulate the Deity on having got me after all just as happiness seemed in sight. I suppose that in some underground part of me I believed in a Deity whose pleasure consists of ingenious torture. But throughout the three days at Studland, I felt that this malignant Deity had after all been not wholly successful When finally I did see the specialist, it turned out that there was nothing the matter.

[1] Alys died on January 21, 1951.

Ottoline was very tall, with a long thin face something like a horse, and very beautiful hair of an unusual colour, more or less like that of marmalade, but rather darker. Kind ladies supposed it to be dyed, but in this they were mistaken. She had a very beautiful, gentle, vibrant voice, indomitable courage, and a will of iron. She was very shy, and, at first, we were both timid of each other, but we loved profoundly, and the gradual disappearance of the timidity was an added delight. We were both earnest and unconventional, both aristocratic by tradition but deliberately not so in our present environment, both hating the cruelty, the caste insolence, and the narrow-mindedness of aristocrats, and yet both a little alien in the world in which we chose to live, which regarded us with suspicion and lack of understanding because we were alien. All the complicated feelings resulting from this situation we shared. There was a deep sympathy between us which never ceased as long as she lived. Although we ceased to be lovers in 1916, we remained always close friends.

Ottoline had a great influence upon me, which was almost wholly beneficial. She laughed at me when I behaved like a don or a prig, and when I was dictatorial in conversation. She gradually cured me of the belief that I was seething with appalling wickedness which could only be kept under by an iron self-control. She made me less self-centred, and less self-righteous. Her sense of humour was very great, and I became aware of the danger of rousing it unintentionally. She made me much less of a Puritan, and much less censorious than I had been. And of course the mere fact of happy love after the empty years made everything easier. Many men are afraid of being influenced by women, but as far as my experience goes, this is a foolish fear. It seems to me that men need women, and women need men, mentally as much as physically. For my part, I owe a great deal to women whom I have loved, and without them I should have been far more narrow-minded.

After Studland various difficulties began to cause trouble. Alys was still raging, and Logan was quite as furious as she was. The White-heads, who showed great kindness at this time, finally persuaded them to abandon the idea of a divorce involving Ottoline, and Alys decided that in that case a divorce was not worth having. I had wished Ottoline to leave Philip, but I soon saw that this was out of the question. Meanwhile, Logan went to Philip, and imposed conditions, which Philip in turn had to impose upon Ottoline. These conditions were onerous, and interfered seriously with the happiness of our love. The worst of them was that we should never spend a night together. I raged and stormed, along with Philip and Logan and Alys. Ottoline found all this very trying, and it produced an atmosphere in which it was difficult to recapture the first ecstasy. I became aware of the solidity of Ottoline's life, of the fact that her husband and her child and her possessions were important to her. To me nothing was important in comparison with her, and this inequality led me to become jealous and exacting. At first, however, the mere strength of our mutual passion overcame all these obstacles. She had a small house at Peppard in the Chilterns, where she spent the month of July. I stayed at Ipsden, six miles from Peppard, and bicycled over every day, arriving about noon, and leaving about midnight. The summer was extraordinarily hot, reaching on one occasion 97° in the shade. We used to take our lunch out into the beech-woods, and come home to late tea. That month was one of great happiness, though Ottoline's health was bad. Finally, she had to go to Marienbad, where I joined her after a while, staying, however, at a different hotel. With the autumn she returned to London, and I took a flat in Bury Street, near the Museum, so that she could come and see me. I was lecturing at Cambridge all the time, but used to come up in the morning, and get back in time for my lecture, which was at 5.30. She used to suffer from terrible headaches, which often made our meetings disappointing, and on these occasions I was less considerate than I ought to have been. Nevertheless, we got through the winter with only one serious disagreement, arising out of the fact that I denounced her for being religious. Gradually, however, I became increasingly turbulent, because I felt that she did not care for me as much as I cared for her. There were moments when this feeling disappeared entirely, and I think that often what was really ill-health appeared to me as indifference, but this was certainly not always the case. I was suffering from pyorrhoea although I did not know it, and this caused my breath to be offensive, which also I did not know. She could not bring herself to mention it, and it was only after I had discovered the trouble and had it cured, that she let me know how much it had affected her.

At the end of 1913 I went to Rome to see her, but Philip was there, and the visit was very unsatisfactory. I made friends with a German lady whom I had met in the summer on the Lake of Garda. Sanger and I had spent a month walking from Innsbruck over the Alps, and had arrived at Punto San Vigilio, where we joined a party of friends, consisting of Miss Silcox, the mistress of St Felix School, Melian Stawell, and the latter's protegée, whose name I have forgotten. We observed a young woman sitting at a table by herself, and discussed whether she was married or single. I suggested that she was divorced. In order to settle the point, I made her acquaintance, and found that I was right. Her husband was a psychoanalyst, and apparently professional etiquette required that he should not get on with his wife. Consequently, at the time when I knew her, she was divorced. But as soon as honour was satisfied, they remarried, and lived happily ever after. She was young and charming, and had two small children. At that time my dominant passion was desire for children, and I could not see even a child playing in the street without an almost unbearable ache. I made friends with the lady and we made an expedition into the country. I wished to make love to her, but thought that I ought first to explain about Ottoline. Until I spoke about Ottoline, she was acquiescent, but afterwards she ceased to be so. She decided, however, that for that one day her objections could be ignored. I have never seen her since, though I still heard from her at intervals for some years.

An event of importance to me in 1913 was the beginning of my friendship with Joseph Conrad, which I owed to our common friendship with Ottoline. I had been for many years an admirer of his books, but should not have ventured to seek acquaintance without an introduction. I travelled down to his house near Ashford in Kent in a state of somewhat anxious expectation. My first impression was one of surprise. He spoke English with a very strong foreign accent, and nothing in his demeanour in any way suggested the sea. He was an aristocratic Polish gentleman to his fingertips. His feeling for the sea, and for England, was one of romantic love—love from a certain distance, sufficient to leave the romance untarnished. His love for the sea began at a very early age. When he told his parents that he wished for a career as a sailor, they urged him to go into the Austrian navy, but he wanted adventure and tropical seas and strange rivers surrounded by dark forests; and the Austrian navy offered him no scope for these desires. His family were horrified at his seeking a career in the English merchant marine, but his determination was inflexible.

He was, as anyone may see from his books, a very rigid moralist and by no means politically sympathetic with revolutionaries. He and I were in most of our opinions by no means in agreement, but in something very fundamental we were extraordinarily at one.

My relation to Joseph Conrad was unlike any other that I have ever had. I saw him seldom, and not over a long period of years. In the out-works of our lives, we were almost strangers, but we shared a certain outlook on human life and human destiny, which, from the very first, made a bond of extreme strength. I may perhaps be pardoned for quoting a sentence from a letter that he wrote to me very soon after we had become acquainted. I should feel that modesty forbids the quotation except for the fact that it expresses so exactly what I felt about him. What he expressed and I equally felt was, in his words, 'A deep admiring affection which, if you were never to see me again and forgot my existence tomorrow, would be unalterably yours *usque ad finem*'.

Of all that he had written I admired most the terrible story called

The Heart of Darkness, in which a rather weak idealist is driven mad by horror of the tropical forest and loneliness among savages. This story expresses, I think, most completely his philosophy of life. I felt, though I do not know whether he would have accepted such an image, that he thought of civilized and morally tolerable human life as a dangerous walk on a thin crust of barely cooled lava which at any moment might break and let the unwary sink into fiery depths. He was very conscious of the various forms of passionate madness to which men are prone, and it was this that gave him such a profound belief in the importance of discipline. His point of view, one might perhaps say, was the antithesis of Rousseau's: 'Man is born in chains, but he can become free.' He becomes free, so I believe Conrad would have said, not by letting loose his impulses, not by being casual and uncontrolled, but by subduing wayward impulse to a dominant purpose.

He was not much interested in political systems, though he had some strong political feelings. The strongest of these were love of England and hatred of Russia, of which both are expressed in *The Secret Agent*; and the hatred of Russia, both Czarist and revolutionary, is set forth with great power in *Under Western Eyes*. His dislike of Russia was that which was traditional in Poland. It went so far that he would not allow merit to either Tolstoy or Dostoievsky. Turgeniev, he told me once, was the only Russian novelist whom he admired.

Except for love of England and hatred of Russia, politics did not much concern him. What interested him was the individual human soul faced with the indifference of nature, and often with the hostility of man, and subject to inner struggles with passions both good and bad that led towards destruction. Tragedies of loneliness occupied a great part of his thought and feeling. One of his most typical stories is *Typhoon*. In this story the Captain, who is a simple soul, pulls his ship through by unshakeable courage and grim determination. When the storm is over, he writes a long letter to his wife, telling about it. In his account his own part is, to him, perfectly simple. He has merely performed his Captain's duty as, of course, anyone would expect. But the reader, through his narrative, becomes aware of all that he has done and dared and endured. The letter, before he sends it off, is read surreptitiously by his steward, but is never read by anyone else at all because his wife finds it boring and throws it away unread.

The two things that seem most to occupy Conrad's imagination are loneliness and fear of what is strange. *An Outcast of the Islands* like *The Heart of Darkness* is concerned with fear of what is strange. Both come together in the extraordinarily moving story called *Amy Foster*. In this story a South-Slav peasant, on his way to America, is the sole survivor of the wreck of his ship, and is cast away in a Kentish village. All the village fears and ill-treats him, except Amy Foster, a dull, plain girl who brings him bread when he is starving and finally marries him. But she, too, when, in fever, he reverts to his native language, is seized with a fear of his strangeness, snatches up their child and abandons him. He dies alone and hopeless. I have wondered at times how much of this man's loneliness Conrad had felt among the English and had suppressed by a stern effort of will.

Conrad's point of view was far from modern. In the modern world there are two philosophies: the one which stems from Rousseau, and sweeps aside discipline as unnecessary, the other, which finds its fullest expression in totalitarianism, which thinks of discipline as essentially imposed from without. Conrad adhered to the older tradition, that discipline should come from within. He despised indiscipline, and hated discipline that was merely external.

In all this I found myself closely in agreement with him. At our very first meeting, we talked with continually increasing intimacy. We seemed to sink through layer after layer of what was superficial, till gradually both reached the central fire. It was an experience unlike any other that I have known. We looked into each other's eyes, half appalled and half intoxicated to find ourselves together in such a region. The emotion was as intense as passionate love, and at the same time all-embracing. I came away bewildered, and hardly able to find my way among ordinary affairs.

I saw nothing of Conrad during the war or after it until my return from China in 1921. When my first son was born in that year I wished Conrad to be as nearly his godfather as was possible without a formal ceremony. I wrote to Conrad saying: 'I wish, with your permission, to call my son John Conrad. My father was called John, my grand-father was called John, and my great grandfather was called John; and Conrad is a name in which I see merits.' He accepted the position and duly presented my son with the cup which is usual on such occasions.

I did not see much of him, as I lived most of the year in Cornwall, and his health was failing. But I had some charming letters from him, especially one about my book on China. He wrote: 'I have always liked the Chinese, even those that tried to kill me (and some other people) in the yard of a private house in Chantabun, even (but not so much) the fellow who stole all my money one night in Bankok, but brushed and folded my clothes neatly for me to dress in the morning, before vanishing into the depths of Siam. I also received many kind-nesses at the hands of various Chinese. This with the addition of an evening's conversation with the secretary of His Excellency Tseng on the verandah of an hotel and a perfunctory study of a poem, "The

Heathen Chinee'', is all I know about the Chinese. But after reading your extremely interesting view of the Chinese Problem I take a gloomy view of the future of their country.' He went on to say that my views of the future of China 'strike a chill into one's soul', the more so, he said, as I pinned my hopes on international socialism—'The sort of thing', he commented, 'to which I cannot attach any sort of definite meaning. I have never been able to find in any man's book or any man's talk anything convincing enough to stand up for a moment against my deep-seated sense of fatality governing this man-inhabited world.' He went on to say that although man has taken to flying, 'he doesn't fly like an eagle, he flies like a beetle. And you must have noticed how ugly, ridiculous and fatuous is the flight of a beetle.' In these pessimistic remarks, I felt that he was showing a deeper wisdom than I had shown in my somewhat artificial hopes for a happy issue in China. It must be said that so far events have proved him right.

This letter was my last contact with him. I never again saw him to speak to. Once I saw him across the street, in earnest conversation with a man I did not know, standing outside the door of what had been my grandmother's house, but after her death had become the Arts Club. I did not like to interrupt what seemed a serious conversation, and I went away. When he died, shortly afterwards, I was sorry I had not been bolder. The house is gone, demolished by Hitler. Conrad, I suppose, is in process of being forgotten, but his intense and passionate nobility shines in my memory like a star seen from the bottom of a well. I wish I could make his light shine for others as it shone for me.

I was invited to give the Lowell lectures in Boston during the spring of 1914, and concurrently to act as temporary professor of philosophy at Harvard. I announced the subject of my Lowell lectures, but could not think of anything to say. I used to sit in the parlour of 'The Beetle and Wedge' at Moulsford, wondering what there was to say about our knowledge of the external world, on which before long I had to deliver a course of lectures. I got back to Cambridge from Rome on New Year's Day 1914, and, thinking that the time had come when I really must get my lectures prepared, I arranged for a shorthand typist to come next day, though I had not the vaguest idea what I should say to her when she came. As she entered the room, my ideas fell into place, and I dictated in a completely orderly sequence from that moment until the work was finished. What I dictated to her was subsequently published as a book with the title *Our Knowledge of the External World as a Field for Scientific Method in Philosophy*.

I sailed on the *Mauretania* on March 7th. Sir Hugh Bell was on the ship. His wife spent the whole voyage looking for him, or finding him with a pretty girl. Whenever I met him after the sinking of the *Lusitania*, I found him asserting that it was on the *Lusitania* he had sailed.

I travelled straight from New York to Boston, and was made to feel at home in the train by the fact that my two neighbours were talking to each other about George Trevelyan. At Harvard I met all the professors. I am proud to say that I took a violent dislike to Professor Lowell, who subsequently assisted in the murder of Sacco and Vanzetti. I had at that time no reason to dislike him, but the feeling was just as strong as it was in later years, when his qualities as a saviour of society had been manifested. Every professor to whom I was introduced in Harvard made me the following speech: 'Our philosophical faculty, Dr Russell, as doubtless you are aware, has lately suffered three great losses. We have lost our esteemed colleague, Professor William James, through his lamented death; Professor Santayana, for reasons which doubtless appear to him to be sufficient, has taken up his residence in Europe; last, *but* not least, Professor Royce, who, I am happy to say, is still with us, has had a stroke.' This speech was delivered slowly, seriously, and pompously. The time came when I felt that I must do something about it. So the next time that I was introduced to a professor, I rattled off the speech myself at top speed. This device, however, proved worthless. 'Yes, Dr Russell,' the professor replied: 'As you very justly observe, our philosophical faculty. . . .' and so the speech went on to its inexorable conclusion. I do not know whether this is a fact about professors or a fact about Americans. I think, however, that it is the former. I noticed another fact about Harvard professors: that when I dined with them, they would always tell me the way home, although I had had to find their house without this assistance. There were limitations to Harvard culture. Schofield, the professor of Fine Arts, considered Alfred Noyes a very good poet.

On the other hand, the students, especially the post-graduates, made a great impression upon me. The Harvard school of philosophy, until the three great losses mentioned above, had been the best in the world. I had stayed with William James at Harvard in 1896, and I had admired Royce's determination to introduce mathematical logic into the philosophical curriculum. Santayana, who had a great friendship for my brother, had been known to me since 1893, and I admired him as much as I disagreed with him. The tradition of these men was still strong. Ralph Barton Perry was doing his best to take their place, and was inspired with the full vigour of what was called 'the new realism'. He had married Berenson's sister. He already displayed, however, something of that New England moralism which caused him to be intellectually ruined by the first War. On one occasion he met, in my rooms,

Rupert Brooke, of whom he had not then heard. Rupert was on his way back from the South Sea Islands, and discoursed at length about the decay of manhood in these regions produced by the cessation of cannibalism. Professor Perry was pained, for is not cannibalism a sin? I have no doubt that when Rupert died, Professor Perry joined in his apotheosis, and I do not suppose he ever realized that the flippant young man he had met in my rooms was identical with the golden-haired god who had given his life for his country.

The students, however, as I said before, were admirable. I had a post-graduate class of twelve, who used to come to tea with me once a week. One of them was T. S. Eliot, who subsequently wrote a poem about it, called 'Mr Apollinax'. I did not know at the time that Eliot wrote poetry. He had, I think, already written 'A Portrait of a Lady', and 'Prufrock', but he did not see fit to mention the fact. He was extraordinarily silent, and only once made a remark which struck me. I was praising Heraclitus, and he observed: 'Yes, he always reminds me of Villon.' I thought this remark so good that I always wished he would make another. Another pupil who interested me was a man called Demos. He was a Greek whose father, having been converted by the missionaries, was an evangelical minister. Demos had been brought up in Asia Minor, and had risen to be librarian of some small library there, but when he had read all the books in that library he felt that Asia Minor had nothing further to offer him. He therefore saved up until he could afford a passage, steerage, to Boston. Having arrived there, he first got a job as a waiter in a restaurant, and then entered Harvard. He worked hard, and had considerable ability. In the course of nature he ultimately became a professor. His intellect was not free from the usual limitations. He explained to me in 1917 that while he could see through the case made by the other belligerents for their participation in the war, and perceived clearly that their arguments were humbug, the matter was quite different in the case of Greece, which was coming in on a genuine moral issue.

When the Harvard term came to an end, I gave single lectures in a few other universities. Among others I went to Ann Arbor, where the president showed me all the new buildings, more especially the library, of which he was very proud. It appeared that the library had the most scientific card-index in the world, and that its method of central heating was extraordinarily up-to-date. While he was explaining all this, we were standing in the middle of a large room with admirable desks. 'And does anybody ever read the books?' I asked. He seemed surprised, but answered: 'Why yes, there is a man over there now reading.' We went to look, and found that he was reading a novel.

From Ann Arbor I went to Chicago, where I stayed with an eminent gynaecologist and his family. This gynaecologist had written a book on the diseases of women containing a coloured frontispiece of the uterus. He presented this book to me, but I found it somewhat embarrassing, and ultimately gave it to a medical friend. In theology he was a free-thinker, but in morals a frigid Puritan. He was obviously a man of very strong sexual passions, and his face was ravaged by the effort of self-control. His wife was a charming old lady, rather shrewd within her limitations, but something of a trial to the younger generation. They had four daughters and a son, but the son, who died shortly after the war, I never met. One of their daughters came to Oxford to work at Greek under Gilbert Murray, while I was living at Bagley Wood, and brought an introduction to Alys and me from her teacher of English literature at Bryn Mawr. I only saw the girl a few times at Oxford, but I found her very interesting, and wished to know her better. When I was coming to Chicago, she wrote and invited me to stay at her parents' house. She met me at the station, and I at once felt more at home with her than I had with anybody else that I had met in America. I found that she wrote rather good poetry, and that her feeling for literature was remarkable and unusual. I spent two nights under her parents' roof, and the second I spent with her. Her three sisters mounted guard to give warning if either of the parents approached. She was very delightful, not beautiful in the conventional sense, but passionate, poetic, and strange. Her youth had been lonely and unhappy, and it seemed that I could give her what she wanted. We agreed that she should come to England as soon as possible and that we would live together openly, perhaps marrying later on if a divorce could be obtained. Immediately after this I returned to England. On the boat I wrote to Ottoline telling her what had occurred. My letter crossed one from her, saying that she wished our relations henceforth to be platonic. My news and the fact that in America I had been cured of pyorrhoea caused her to change her mind. Ottoline could still, when she chose, be a lover so delightful that to leave her seemed impossible, but for a long time past she had seldom been at her best with me. I returned to England in June, and found her in London. We took to going to Burnham Beeches every Tuesday for the day. The last of these expeditions was on the day on which Austria declared war on Serbia. Ottoline was at her best. Meanwhile, the girl in Chicago had induced her father, who remained in ignorance, to take her to Europe. They sailed on August 3rd. When she arrived I could think of nothing but the war, and as I had determined to come out publicly against it, I did not wish to complicate my position with a private scandal, which would have made anything that I might say of no account. I felt it therefore impossible to carry out what we had planned. She stayed in England and I had relations with

213

her from time to time, but the shock of the war killed my passion for her, and I broke her heart. Ultimately she fell a victim to a rare disease, which first paralysed her, and then made her insane. In her insanity she told her father all that had happened. The last time I saw her was in 1924. At that time paralysis made her incapable of walking, but she was enjoying a lucid interval. When I talked with her, however, I could feel dark, insane thoughts lurking in the background. I understand that since then she had no lucid intervals. Before insanity attacked her, she had a rare and remarkable mind, and a disposition as lovable as it was unusual. If the war had not intervened, the plan which we formed in Chicago might have brought great happiness to us both. I feel still the sorrow of this tragedy.

LETTERS

Jan. 15, 1911
Colonial Club
Cambridge, Mass.

Dear Russell

It is rather late to thank you for your *Philosophical Essays*, but you may soon see unmistakable evidence of the great interest I have taken in them, as I am writing an elaborate review—in three articles—for the Whited Sepulchre —which is what we call the Columbia *Journal of Philosophy, etc.* You will not expect me to agree with you in everything, but, whatever you may think of my ideas, I always feel that yours, and Moore's too, make for the sort of reconstruction in philosophy which I should welcome. It is a great bond to dislike the same things, and dislike is perhaps a deeper indication of our real nature than explicit affections, since the latter may be effects of circumstances, while dislike is a reaction against them.

I had hoped to go to Cambridge in June, but now it is arranged that I shall go instead to California, where I have never been. I am both glad and sorry for this, but it seemed as well to see the Far West once in one's life, especially as I hope soon to turn my face resolutely in the opposite direction.

Thank you again very much for sending me the book.

Yours sincerely
G. Santayana

(June 1911)
Newnham College
Cambridge

Dear Bertie

I have heard from Alys. I cannot help saying how sad I am for you as well as her—you have been thro' hell I know—that is written in your face.

May I say just this? You have always stood by me for goodness and asceticism—I shall always think of you—till you tell me not—as doing the straight hard thing.

Yours always
Jane E. Harrison

This needs no answer, forgive my writing it. You have been thro' too much these last days to want to see people, but I am always glad when you come.

Telegraph House
Chichester
6 June, 1911

My dear Bertie

Mollie and I have both received your news with much regret. We had as you say an idea, but only an idea, that the original devotion had rather passed away, and that you found each other trying, but we hoped nothing so definite as a separation would result. People of good manners can often manage to get on in the same house, once they have agreed to differ, and I hope for the comfort of both of you, and your friends, that this may still be the case. But of that of course you are the only possible judges.

In the meantime we can only regret the annoyance any such re-arrangement causes, and the break up of a union which seemed to promise well at the beginning. A broken marriage is always a tragedy.

Yours affectionately
Russell

Trinity College
Cambridge
June 11th, 1911

My dear Gilbert

Thank you very much indeed for your kind letter. The decision[1] as you know, is not sudden or hasty; and though the present is painful, I feel no doubt that *both* will in the long run be happier.

It is true that I have seen less of you than formerly—I wish it were not. But business and work seem to overwhelm one more and more. During the time I lived at Oxford I never could shake off work except by going away. I suppose that is the essence of middle age. But I do not find, on that account, that my affections grow less—it is only the outward show that suffers.

Please give my love to Mary.

Yours ever
Bertrand Russell

[1] To leave Alys.

215

June 17, 1911
I Tatti
Settignano (Florence)

My dear Bertie

I have just received a telegram, telling me of Karin's success in her Tripos, and I cannot help writing to express my gratitude to you for your overwhelming share in bringing this about. I feel most sincerely grateful. I cannot but hope further work of the same nature may be temptingly put in her way, for she seems to have a capacity to do it well, and it might 'make a man of her', so to speak. So I beg of you to continue to bear the child in mind, and suggest her doing any work that you may think it worth while for her to do.

I won't say anything about the decision you and Alys have come to, except to send you my love and sympathy in all you have certainly suffered over it, and to assure you of B. B.'s and my continued friendliness and good wishes.

Yours always affectionately
Mary Berenson

(From Gilbert Murray, on
Problems of Philosophy)

The Home University Library
14 Henrietta Street
Covent Garden, W.C.
August 10, 1911

Messrs Williams and Norgate[1] will be glad to meet Mr Russell's wishes as far as practicable, but have some difficulty in understanding his point of view. About the earwig, for instance, they are ready, if Mr Russell is inconvenienced by his suspicions of its presence in his room, to pay a rat-catcher (who is also accustomed to earwigs) two-shillings an hour to look for it and make sure, provided the total payment does not exceed Ten Shillings. (10s.) The animal, if caught, shall be regarded as Mr Russell's property, but in no case shall its capture, or the failure to capture it, be held as exonerating Mr Russell from his contract with Messrs W & N. Mr Russell's further complaint that he has not the acquaintance of the Emperor of China cannot be regarded by Messrs W & N as due in any way to any oversight or neglect of theirs. Mr R should have stipulated for an introduction before signing his contract. As to Mr Russell's memory of his breakfast and his constantly returning alarm lest his next meal should poison him, Messrs W & N express their fullest sympathy with Mr R in his trying situation, but would point out that remonstrances should be addressed not to them but to the Head Cook at Trinity College. In the meantime they trust that they do not exceed their duty in reminding Mr Russell that, in his own words, a philosopher should not always have his mind centred upon such subjects. They would observe further that their senior editor is much gratified by Mr Russell's frank admission that a bald man is, nevertheless, a man, while his next sentence has caused some little trouble among the staff. All three editors have rather good figures; at least there is no one among them who could be called conspicuously 'plain'

[1] Publishers of The Home University Library of which Gilbert Murray was one of the editors.

in that respect. Perhaps Mr Russell referred to Mr Perris?[1] If so, however, we do not quite understand who is meant by the poet. We would almost venture to suggest the omission of all these personalities. When gratifying to one individual, they nearly always give pain to others.

> The Mischief Inn,
> Madingley Road
> 26. VIII. 11

Dear Russell

I send you all I can find of the notes Frege sent me on my account of his work.

Hardy told me of your translation into symbolism of the Deceased Wife's Sister Bill. If you have time would you send it to me to include in the 'Philosophy of Mr B— R—'.[2] Also Hardy told me of your proof of the existence of God by an infinite complex of false propositions.[3] May I have this too?

> *Yrs. ever*
> *Philip Jourdain*

Georg Cantor, the subject of the following letter, was, in my opinion, one of the greatest intellects of the nineteenth century. The controversy with Poincaré which he mentions is still (1949) raging, though the original protagonists are long since dead. After reading the following letter, no one will be surprised to learn that he spent a large part of his life in a lunatic asylum, but his lucid intervals were devoted to creating the theory of infinite numbers.

He gave me a book on the Bacon–Shakespeare question, and wrote on the cover: 'I see your motto is "Kant or Cantor" and described Kant as "yonder sophistical Philistine who knew so little mathematics."' Unfortunately I never met him.

> 75 Victoria Street
> S.W.
> 16. 9. 11

Dear Mr Russell

By accident I met to-day Professor Georg Cantor, professor of Mathematics at Halle University, and his chief wish during his stay in England is to meet you and talk about your books. He was overcome with pleasure when he learnt on talking of Cambridge that I knew you a little—you must forgive my boasting of my acquaintance with an English 'Mathematiker' and I had to promise I would try to find out if he could see you. He proposes to visit Cambridge on Tuesday and Oxford on Thursday, and meanwhile is staying for a week at 62 Nevern Square, South Kensington.

It was a great pleasure to meet him though if you are kind enough to see him you will sympathize with my feeling worn out with nearly four hours conversation. He was like a fog horn discoursing on Mathematics—to me!— and the Bacon theory.[4]

---

[1] Assistant Editor.   [2] A humorous résumé of my conversations with Jourdain.

[3] Most unfortunately I have forgotten this proof, and have no note of it, so this rather important matter must remain in doubt.

[4] He thought that Bacon wrote Shakespeare and that Christ was the natural son of Joseph of Arimathea.

Could you send a line to him or to me at Woodgate, Danehill, Sussex. He is a Geheimrath & so forth. I could relate his whole family history to you!

Yours sincerely and with many apologies
Margery I. Corbett Ashby

To the Hon. Bertrand Russell
Trinity College, Cambridge

19 Sept. 1911
62 Nevern Square
South Kensington
London

Sir and dear Colleague!

From Mrs Margaret Corbett Ashby I have to present you with the ensuing letter. I am now staying here for a week about, with my daughter Mary, probably unto Sunday 24 Sept. on which day I will depart perhaps to Paris also for a week about, or to go at home. It would give me much pleasure if you could accompany us to Paris. There we could meet perhaps Monsieur Poincaré together, which would be a fine jolly 'Trio'.

As for myself you do know perhaps, that I am a great heretic upon many scientific, but also in many literary matters, as, to pronounce but two of them: I am Baconian in the Bacon–Shakespeare question and I am *quite an adversary* of *Old Kant*, who, in my eyes has done much harm and mischief to philosophy, even to mankind; as you easily see by the most perverted development of metaphysics in Germany in all that followed him, as in Fichte, Schelling, Hegel, Herbart, Schopenhauer, Hartmann, Nietzsche, etc. etc. on to this very day. I never could understand that and why such reasonable and enobled peoples as the Italiens, the English and the French are, could follow yonder *sophistical philistine*, who was *so bad a mathematician*.

And now it is that in just this abominable mummy, as Kant is, Monsieur Poincaré felt quite enamoured, if he is not bewitched by him. So I understand quite well the opposition of Mons. Poincaré, by which I felt myself honoured, though he never had in his mind to honour me, as I am sure. If he perhaps expect, that I will answer him for defending myself, he is certainly in great a mistake.

I think he is about ten years younger than I, but I have learned to wait in all things and I foresee now clearly, that in this quarrel *I will not be the succumbent*. I let him do at his pleasure.

But I feel no forcing to enter myself into the battle; others will him precipitate and I allowed to do with greater and more important things. As for the little differences between you and me, I am sure, that they will disappear soon after an oral discourse.

I intend to pay a visit today to Major Macmahon.

I hope to see you in these days in Cambridge or in London, and so I am, Sir,

Your very faithfull
Georg Cantor

On Thursday to Friday we are to follow an invitation of Mrs Constance Pott, an old friend and correspondent of mine, of London, staying now in Folkestone, 15 Clifton Crescent.

As to Kant and his successors I see, and will show you the real cause of his standing upon so *seeming*-fermly ground of success, honour, veneration, idolatry. *This cause is*, that the German Protestantism in his development to 'Liberalism' *needs* himself a *fundament* on which to build his *seeming*-Christianity, so Kant or one of his successors are picked out, by the protestant Theologians of divers scools, to be their *Atlas*. One hand washes the other, one depends on the other and *one has to fall with the other!*

I never did harm to Monsieur Poincaré; au contraire, je l'honorait fortement dans mes 'grundlagen einer allgemeinen-M. lehre'.

To the Hon. Bertrand Russell   London
 Trinity College, Cambridge   19 Sept. 1911
Dear Sir

My first letter to you was just finished as I received your despatch. If I would be free and would not depend upon the freewill of two young German Ladies, my daughter Mary and my niece Fräulein Alice Guttmann of Berlin, I would come *this just* day to meet you in Ipsden Wallingford. So probably I can generally not come to you!

       Yours faithfully
       Georg Cantor

This second letter being finished, just I receive the following despatch from my dear wife at home.

'Erich erkrankt—sofort Halle kommen.'

You see, dear Sir, destiny playing upon me. The two young ladies I spoke of, are just departed to see Westminster.

It is my *only* son Erich, *quite healthy* when I left him; he is the Doctor of one division of a large Hospital of alienates in Bunzlau (Silesia). He is 32 years old.

I will hope that the worst has not happened.

He had been married three months ago and we assisted at his wedding with a very amiabel good and clever young girl, daughter of a tanner in the little Saxonia town Nossen in the Kingdom of Saxony.

My address in Halle a.d. Saale is: Handelstr. 13. We depart this evening. I hope to be here in the last half of August 1912 to the international Congress.

I had been also just writing a short description of my journey to and sojourning at Saint Andrews, and I intented to offer it to the editor of 'Review of Reviews'.

I could not go to Major Macmahon as had been my intention to do; you will see it in my first letter.

In Saint Andrews I have seen with great pleasure my very good friend Mr Hobson of Cambridge, who was going to Mailand to a congress of Mr Felix Klein, the great field-marshall of all german Mathematicians. Neither my father nor my mother were of german blood, the first being a Dane, borne in Kopenhagen, my mother of Austrian Hungar descension. You must know, Sir, that I am not a *regular just Germain*, for I am born 3 March 1845 at Saint Peterborough, Capital of Russia, but I went with my father and mother and brothers and sister, eleven years old in the year 1856, into Germany, first sojourning at Wiesbaden, then at Frankfort a/Main, then at Darmstadt, four years, then at Zürich, Berlin and Göttingen, coming then as 'Privat Dozent' Easter of the year 1869 to Halle a.d. Saale where I stay now *forty two* years and more.

Dear Sir

The last word of mine to you is *a good one*, just I receive from my wife the second telegram: 'Erich besser.' But you will understand that we must return this evening at home.

41 Grosvenor Road
Westminster Embankment
October 11th (1912)

My dear Bertrand

I am so sorry not to see you when you called the other day, and I feel that I cannot let your visit pass in silence.

Now don't be angry with me, if I ask you to put yourself in our place. Supposing you and Alys were living in absolute happiness in complete comradship [*sic*], and you became aware that Sidney had repudiated me, and that I was 'living on in a state of dark despair'. Would you not, both of you, feel rather sore with Sidney?

I know nothing of the cause of your estrangement—all I know is that Alys wants us to be friends with you. And that is also my own instinct. I have always admired your very great intelligence, and tho' I have sometimes had my doubts about the strength of your character, I have always felt its peculiar charm.

So don't think that I have withdrawn my friendship; and if, at any time, I can be of use to you, with or without your complete confidence let me know and come and see me. And now that I have expressed quite frankly what is in my mind come and see us, if you feel inclined, and talk about the world's affairs without reference to your and Alys' troubles.

We had a delightful time in the Far East and India—there are wonderful new outlooks in Human Purpose and Human Destiny, both in Japan and among the Hindus in India. We were wholly unable to appreciate China and found ourselves unsympathetic to Mohamedan India.

Now we are again immersed in British problems: but the memory of our travels is a constant refreshment. Why don't you go for a long holiday and complete change of thought?

Ever your friend
Beatrice Webb

37 Alfred Place W
South Kensington, S.W.
13 October 1912

Dear Mr Russell

Thanks for your kind letter. I will ask Dr Seal to pay you a visit at Cambridge, when you will have an opportunity to know him.

I read your article on the Essence of Religion in the last issue of the *Hibbert Journal* with very great interest. It reminded me of a verse in the Upanishad which runs thus—

'Yato vácho nivartanté aprápya manasá saha
Ánandam Brahmano Vidván na vibhéti Kutushchana.'

'From him words, as well as mind, come back baffled. Yet he who knows the joy of Brahman (the Infinite) is free from all fear.'

Through knowledge you cannot apprehend him; yet when you live the life of the Infinite and are not bound within the limits of the finite self you realize that great joy which is above all the pleasures and pains of our selfish life and so you are free from all fear.

This joy itself is the positive perception of Brahman. It is not a creed which authority imposes on us but an absolute realization of the Infinite which we can only attain by breaking through the bonds of the narrow self and setting our will and love free.

Yours sincerely
Rabindranath Tagore

Trinity College
13th Feb. 1913

My dear Goldie

It was very nice to see your handwriting, and such parts of your letter as I could decipher interested me very much! (In fact, there was very little I didn't make out in the end.) I am interested to see that India is *too* religious for you. Religion and daily bread—superstition and the belly—it doesn't sound attractive. I expect you will find China much more interesting—much more civilized, and more aware of the subtler values—at least if you could get in touch with the educated people.

I haven't much news. I suppose you have become aware that the Tories have dropped food taxes, and are on the move about protection in general; also that the Germans are accepting a 16 to 10 naval proportion, so that the public world is rather cheerful. Here in Cambridge things go on as usual. There is another agitation against Little-Go Greek being got up, and everybody is saying what they have always said. It all seems rather remote from anything of real importance. My friend Wittgenstein was elected to the Society, but thought it a waste of time, so he imitated henry john roby[1] and was cursed.

[1] Henry John Roby was elected a member of the Society, but wrote to say that he was far too busy to attend the meetings and was therefore ritualistically cursed and his name was spelt thenceforth without capitals. Ever after when a new member was elected the curse was solemnly read out.

I think he did quite right, though I tried to dissuade him. He is much the most apostolic and the ablest person I have come across since Moore.

I have done nothing to my Discourse. All the later summer I tried in vain to recapture the mood in which I had written it, but winter in England being in any case hopeless for that sort of writing I gave up for the present, and have been working at the philosophy of matter, in which I seem to see an opening for something important. The whole question of our knowledge of the external world is involved. In the spring of next year, I am going to Harvard for three months to lecture. I doubt if the people there are much good, but it will be interesting. Santayana has brought out a new book, *Winds of Doctrine*, mostly on Bergson and me. I have only looked it through so far—it has his usual qualities. Karin read a paper in praise of Bergson to the Aristotelian the other day—Moore and I attacked her with all imaginable ferocity, but she displayed undaunted courage.—Frank Darwin is going to marry Mrs Maitland, as I suppose you have heard.—There—that is all the news I can think of—it all seems curiously trivial. We here in Cambridge all keep each other going by the unquestioned assumption that what we do is important, but I often wonder if it really is. What is important I wonder? Scott and his companions dying in the blizzard seem to me impervious to doubt—and his record of it has a really great simplicity. But intellect, except at white heat, is very apt to be trivial.

I feel as if one would only discover on one's death-bed what one ought to have lived for, and realize too late that one's life had been wasted. Any passionate and courageous life seems good in itself, yet one feels that some element of delusion is involved in giving so much passion to any humanly attainable object. And so irony creeps into the very springs of one's being. Are you finding the Great Secret in the East? I doubt it. There is none—there is not even an enigma. There is science and sober daylight and the business of the day—the rest is mere phantoms of the dusk. Yet I know that when the summer comes I shall think differently.

I wish I were with you, or you with me. Give my love to Bob.[1]

> *Yours ever*
> B. Russell

The Doves Press
April 1913

My dear Bertie

At last, at last the Miltons are bound and I am sending them to your address at Trinity. I also was at Trinity this year just half a century ago and this same year just the same long time ago first saw your mother then Kate Stanley. I am not sorry then to have so long delayed as to make my little offering in this same year of grace.

In a little while this will be closed and I shall be printing no more books—did I send you my swan-song? I forget. But before I close I shall have printed

---

[1] Trevelyan.

the letters in their year of anniversary, 1914, and that will make a fitting end. Let me hear of you and see you when next you come to Town.

Affectionately always
T. J. Cobden-Sanderson

Hon. B. A. W. Russell   29 Sparks Street
Trinity College   Cambridge, Mass.
Cambridge, Eng.   June 15, 1913
Esteemed Colleague

My son, Norbert Wiener, will this week receive his degree of Ph.D. at Harvard University, his thesis being 'A comparative Study of the Algebra of Relatives of Schroeder and that of Whitehead and Russell'. He had expected to be here next year and have the privilege of being your student in the second semester, but as he has received a travelling fellowship, he is obliged to pass the whole of the year in Europe, and so he wishes to enjoy the advantage of studying under you at Trinity during the first half of the academic year. He intended to write to you about this matter, but his great youth,—he is only eighteen years old and his consequent inexperience with what might be essential for him to know in his European sojourn, leads me to do this service for him and ask your advice.

Norbert graduated from College, receiving his A.B., at the age of fourteen, not as the result of premature development or of unusual precocity, but chiefly as the result of careful home training, free from useless waste, which I am applying to all of my children. He is physically strong (weighing 170 lbs.), perfectly balanced morally and mentally, and shows no traits generally associated with early precocity. I mention all this to you that you may not assume that you are to deal with an exceptional or freakish boy, but with a normal student whose energies have not been mis-directed. Outside of a broad and liberal classical education, which includes Greek, Latin, and the modern languages, he has had a thorough course in the sciences, and in Mathematics has studied the Differential and integral Calculus, Differential Equations, the Galois Theory of Equations, and some branches of Modern Algebra (under Prof. Huntington). In philosophy he has pursued studies under Professors Royce, Perry, Palmer, Münsterberg, Schmidt, Holt, etc., at Harvard and Cornell Universities.[1] His predilection is entirely for Modern Logic, and he wishes during his one or two years' stay in Europe to be benefited from those who have done distinguished work in that direction.

Will he be able to study under you, or be directed by you, if he comes to Cambridge in September or early October? What should he do in order to enjoy that privilege? I have before me The Student's Handbook to Cambridge for 1908, but I am unable to ascertain from it that any provisions are made for graduate students wishing to obtain such special instruction or advice. Nor am I able to find out anything about his residence there, whether he would have to matriculate in Trinity College or could take rooms in the city. This

---

[1] Nevertheless he turned out well.

is rather an important point to him as he is anxious, as far as possible, to get along on his rather small stipend. For any such information, which would smooth his first appearance in a rather strange world to him I shall be extremely obliged to you.

I shall take great pleasure to thank you in person for any kindness that thus may be shown to my son, when, next year, you come to our American Cambridge to deliver lectures in the Department of Philosophy.

Sincerely Yours
Leo Wiener
Professor of Slavic Languages and
Literatures at Harvard University

Capel House
Orlestone
Nr. Ashford, Kent
4 Sept. 1913

Dear Sir

Why bring a bicycle in this windy, uncertain weather? The true solution is to take a ticket (by the 11 a.m. train from Charing Cross I presume) to Hamstreet (*change* in Ashford after a few minutes' wait) where my boy will meet you with our ancient puffer and bring you to the door before half past one. Then there is a decent train at 5.48 from Ashford to get back to town a few minutes after seven.

Whether there's anything in me to make up for you the grind of the journey I don't know. What's certain is that you will give me the very greatest pleasure by coming. So you may look upon the expedition as something in the nature of 'good works'. I would suggest Wednesday, since, as far as I know, there is no Act of Parliament as yet to stop the running of trains on that day of the week—our new secular Sunday.

Believe me very faithfully yours
Joseph Conrad

Capel House
Orlestone, Nr. Ashford
13 Sept. 1913

My dear Russell

Your letter has comforted me greatly. It seems to me that I talked all the time with fatuous egotism. Yet somewhere at the back of my brain I had the conviction that you would understand my unusual talkativeness. Generally I don't know what to say to people. But your personality drew me out. My instinct told me I would not be misread.

Let me thank you most heartily for the pleasure of your visit and for the letter you had the friendly thought to write.

Believe me sincerely yours
Joseph Conrad

Capel House
Orlestone, Nr. Ashford
22 Dec. 1913

My dear Russell

Just a word of warmest good wishes from us all.

I am glad I read the little book before coming to your essays. If in reading the first I felt moving step by step, with delight, on the firmest ground, the other gave me the sense of an enlarged vision in the clearest, the purest atmosphere. Your significant words so significantly assembled, seemed to wake a new faculty within me. A wonderful experience for which one cannot even express one's thanks—one can only accept it silently like a gift from the Gods. You have reduced to order the inchoate thoughts of a life-time and given a direction to those obscure *mouvements d'ame* which, unguided, bring only trouble to one's weary days on this earth. For the marvellous pages on the Worship of a free man the only return one can make is that of a deep admiring affection, which, if you were never to see me again and forgot my existence tomorrow, will be unalterably yours *usque ad finem*.

Yours ever
J. Conrad

P.S.—I have been reading you yesterday and today and I have received too many different kinds of delight (I am speaking soberly) to be able to write more today.

3 Claremont Crescent
Weston-super-Mare
Jan. 31, '14

Dear Mr Russell

Many thanks for your letter which has come on here where I am, I hope, getting over a short period of illness and incapacity. I am sure that I need not tell you that my expressions of admiration for your work were not mere words. I am not able to agree with your views in some points (at least as I understand them) but I don't feel the smallest doubt about their great value. And I am full of hope and expectation that you will go on to do still better and better, though I am afraid that I can't hope for much longer to be able to appreciate and enjoy any speculation.

I think I understand what you say as to the way in which you philosophize. I imagine that it is the right way and that its promises are never illusions, though they may not be kept to the letter. There is something perhaps in the whole of things that one feels is wanting when one considers the doctrines before one, and (as happens elsewhere) one feels that one knows what one wants and that what one wants is there—if only one could find it. And for my part I believe that one does find it more or less. And yet still I must believe that one never does or can find the whole in all its aspects, and that there never after all will be a philosopher who did not reach his truth, after all, except by some partiality and one-sidedness—and that, far from mattering, this is the right and the only way. This is however only faith and I could not offer to prove it.

I am sure that in my own work, such as it is, I have illustrated the partiality —if nothing else. I am afraid that I always write too confidently—perhaps because otherwise I might not write at all. Still I don't see that in doing so one can do much harm, or run the risk of imposing on anyone whose judgment is of any value.

If I have helped you in any way by my objections, that I feel will justify their existence more or less—even where they are quite mistaken—and it will be a very great satisfaction to me always to have had your good opinion of my work.

Perhaps I may add that I am getting the impression that I have been tending more and more to take refuge in the unknown and unknowable—in a way which I maintain is right, but which still is not what I quite like.

Wishing you all success with your work and venturing to express the hope that you will not allow yourself to be hurried.

I am
Yours truly
F. H. Bradley

[END OF VOL. I]

The letters from Joseph Conrad are included by permission of J. M. Dent Ltd, and the Trustees of the Joseph Conrad Estate.

INDEX

GEORGE ALLEN & UNWIN LTD

London: 40 Museum Street, W.C.1

Auckland: P.O. Box 36013, Northcote Central, Auckland, N.4
Bombay: 15 Graham Road, Ballard Estate, Bombay 1
Barbados: P.O. Box 222, Bridgetown
Buenos Aires: Escritorio 454–459, Florida 165
Calcutta: 17 Chittaranjan Avenue, Calcutta 13
Cape Town: 68 Shortmarket Street
Hong Kong: 105 Wing On Mansion, 26 Hancow Road, Kowloon
Ibadan: P.O. Box 62
Karachi: Karachi Chambers, McLeod Road
Madras: Mohan Mansions, 38c Mount Road, Madras 6
Mexico: Villalongin 32–10, Piso, Mexico 5, D.F.
Nairobi: P.O. Box 4536
New Delhi: 13–14 Asaf Ali Road, New Delhi 1
Ontario: 81 Curlew Drive, Don Mills
Rio de Janeiro: Caixa Postal 2537–Zc–00
São Paulo: Caixa Postal 8675
Singapore: 36c Prinsep Street, Singapore 7
Sydney: N.S.W.: Bradbury House, 55 York Street
Tokyo: P.O. Box 26, Kamata

BERTRAND RUSSELL: A LIFE

HERBERT GOTTSCHALK   *Unwin Book. Crown 8vo*

Bertrand Russell's eminence of intellect and person has long been
unassailable. Besides his distinction as mathematician and philosopher,
and a vast output of books, articles, lectures and talks on most aspects
of the human condition, there is his continuing concern for day-to-day
political issues, his championing of individual freedom and his readiness
to stand for a cause to the point of imprisonment. To have distilled the
essence of his ninety-odd years into this little book is itself quite an
achievement. It has been called 'a pocket guide to greatness' and forms
a useful complement to the longer and slightly earlier study by Alan
Wood, also in this series, *The Passionate Sceptic*.

THE PASSIONATE SCEPTIC

ALAN WOOD   *Unwin Book. Crown 8vo*

'Fascinating', 'brilliant', 'oddly moving', 'a warm human picture'—
this biography was enthusiastically received when it came out in
1957. And no wonder. It is not only the lively story of a distinguished man but a lucid account of his work and its significance.
The author, who was himself a philosopher and journalist, has
followed the bright thread of Russell's personality with affectionate
insight, from the three-day-old baby who looked about him 'in a
very vigorous way', and the boy who jibbed at taking Euclid on
trust, through the many turns of his life, to the undimmed octo-
genarian, still questioning and still deeply concerned. The subject is
a great one and the biographer has matched it.

The following titles by Bertrand Russell are available in paper-back
editions: ON EDUCATION, SCEPTICAL ESSAYS, POWER, IN PRAISE OF
IDLENESS, MARRIAGE AND MORALS, CONQUEST OF HAPPINESS, THE
PRACTICE AND THEORY OF BOLSHEVISM, MYSTICISM AND LOGIC,
POLITICAL IDEALS, LEGITIMACY VERSUS INDUSTRIALISM, FREEDOM
VERSUS ORGANIZATION, WHY I AM NOT A CHRISTIAN

GEORGE ALLEN AND UNWIN LTD